"This deeply reflective volume is a timely, thoughtful, and holistic snapshot of contemporary music therapy practice from the perspective of a new generation of practitioners and is essential reading for aspiring music therapists and experienced practitioners alike. The editors' transparency and compassion exemplify their commitment to humanistic, trauma-informed, and anti-oppressive discourse, and centering the voices of students and early-career practitioners and their internal processes spotlights new perspectives that significantly enrich the knowledge base. The accessible yet profound narratives provide intimate and poignant insight into everyday practices, and nurture and facilitate reader engagement with often-challenging ideas."

Dr. Beth Pickard, Senior Lecturer, Researcher and Music Therapist, University of South Wales, UK

"Much of my music therapy training was filled with extraordinary stories of clients' transformation through the power of music and the therapeutic relationships that developed through it. This book offers different narratives that are grossly missing in music therapy literature that are no less important – the everyday practice of music therapy. Drs. Potvin and Myers-Coffman have purposefully curated narratives from authors who have carefully considered their sociocultural identities, theoretical orientations, and current socio-political-cultural goings-on in the world, and how these elements have informed their everyday practice. These case studies beautifully detail examinations of clinical interactions and decisions, honor the music and lives of the everyday music therapy client(s), and invite the readers to do the same."

Dr. Ming Yuan Low, PhD, MT-BC, Assistant Professor, Music Therapy, Berklee College of Music, USA

Portraits of Everyday Practice in Music Therapy

Portraits of Everyday Practice in Music Therapy is an edited volume of case studies providing music therapy students and new professionals with critical reflections on everyday clinical practice across a variety of treatment settings, theories, approaches, and cultural contexts.

These case studies articulate the important foundational work occurring around clinical breakthroughs to illustrate less of what music therapy *could be* given extraordinary circumstances and more of what music therapy frequently *is* given realistic circumstances. Additionally, each author explores the impacts of cultural values, expectations, and roles on clinical contexts through examinations of their sociocultural identities and how they intersected with those with whom they worked. Discussion prompts at the end of chapters help readers engage in similar reflective practices and sustain engagement with introduced concepts and ideas.

By providing ecological real-world contexts for practice and culturally reflexive lenses through which to understand how therapeutic processes evolved, music therapy students and professionals can be better prepared for the authenticity and complexity of everyday clinical work.

Noah Potvin, PhD, LPC, MT-BC is an assistant professor at Duquesne University. His practice and scholarship focus on developing culturally reflexive, resource-oriented approaches in hospice music therapy that facilitate healthy end-of-life processes in response to individuals' cultural traditions and social identities.

Kate Myers-Coffman, PhD, MT-BC is an assistant professor at Molloy University whose work focuses on trauma-informed, resource-oriented music therapy for youth and families who have experienced trauma and loss as well as culturally humble approaches to music therapy practice, pedagogy, and research.

Portraits of Everyday Practice in Music Therapy

Edited by
Noah Potvin, PhD, LPC, MT-BC
Kate Myers-Coffman, PhD, MT-BC

Routledge
Taylor & Francis Group

NEW YORK AND LONDON

Designed cover image by Anna Oborotova

First published 2023
by Routledge
605 Third Avenue, New York, NY 10158

and by Routledge
4 Park Square, Milton Park, Abingdon, Oxon, OX14 4RN

*Routledge is an imprint of the Taylor & Francis Group, an informa
business*

Library of Congress Cataloging-in-Publication Data
Names: Potvin, Noah, editor. | Myers-Coffman, Kate, editor.
Title: Portraits of everyday practice in music therapy/edited
    by Noah Potvin, Kate Myers-Coffman.
Description: [1.] | New York: Routledge, 2023. | Includes
    bibliographical references and index.
Identifiers: LCCN 2022056516 (print) | LCCN 2022056517 (ebook) |
    ISBN 9780367642877 (hardback) | ISBN 9780367642860 (paperback) |
    ISBN 9781003123798 (ebook)
Subjects: LCSH: Music therapy—Case studies.
Classification: LCC ML3920. P846 2023 (print) | LCC ML3920
    (ebook) | DDC 615.8/5154-dc23/eng/20221202
LC record available at https://lccn.loc.gov/2022056516
LC ebook record available at https://lccn.loc.gov/2022056517

ISBN: 978-0-367-64287-7 (hbk)
ISBN: 978-0-367-64286-0 (pbk)
ISBN: 978-1-003-12379-8 (ebk)

DOI: 10.4324/9781003123798

Typeset in Garamond
by Apex CoVantage, LLC

Noah: This book was inspired by over a decade's worth of sharing in music and other vulnerable spaces with so many individuals and caregivers in end-of-life care settings. The collective narrative these stories tell is tribute to their generosity in allowing me to walk some of their journey with them and learn from their struggles and triumphs, their joys and sorrows, their shadows and light. My life has been enriched and inspired by their wit and wisdom, and my hope is that this book helps pay forward their legacies by ultimately improving the quality of care future people will receive in music therapy.

Kate: This book is dedicated to all the individuals I've shared space with over the years of my music therapy practice – those I've collaborated with; learned from; shared emotion, meaning, community, courage, and vulnerability with; and been in musical relationship with. I also dedicate it to the colleagues and learners I've crossed paths with who inspire me to work on projects such as this to help showcase beautiful examples of thoughtful, authentic, and culturally humble music therapy practice.

Contents

List of Contributors   xiii
Foreword: To Students From a Student   xviii
Foreword: To Clinicians From a Clinician   xxi
Foreword: To Supervisors From a Supervisor   xxiii
Foreword: To Educators From an Educator   xxvi
Acknowledgments   xxix

Introduction   1

UNIT 1
Developing Clinical Readiness as a Music Therapist
in Training   9

1 Navigating Countertransference With Clinical
   Supervision   11
   KIMBERLY WOODMAN AND KATIE LAHUE

2 From Culture Shock to Integrating Preferred Music by
   Youth: An International Music Therapist in Training's
   Journey Towards Cultural Reflexivity   24
   YIQING XIANG

3 Cases From the Heart: A Journey of Vulnerability,
   Trust, and Growth for Intern and Supervisor   34
   SARA LANGENBERGER AND SPENCER HARDY

4 Developing Adaptability and Bridging Authentic
   Relationships in Entry-Level Music Therapy Training   47
   GABRIELA ESPINAL-SANTIAGO AND KATHRYN MACGOWN

UNIT 2
Aligning Personal Values and Emerging Clinical Identities as a New Professional   57

5 Discovering Self Through Reflexivity and Shared
   Social Identities With Clients   59
   ALEX PEUSER

6 Finding Intimacy Through Supervision   69
   JOY KAMINSKI

7 Expanding Practice by Exploring Clinical
   Limitations   78
   CATHLEEN FLYNN

8 How Much Giving Is Enough?   89
   YU-CHING RUBY CHEN

UNIT 3
Attuning, Adapting, and Maturing in Practice   99

9 Connecting, Disconnecting, and Reconnecting
   Through Changes in Therapeutic Context   101
   CRYSTAL LUK-WORRALL
   ILLUSTRATED BY ANNA OBORATOVA

10 Regaining Trust in the Music: Music Therapy
   with Emily   114
   CONIO LORETTO

11 The Ever-Changing NICU: A Journey Through Crisis   125
   ELISABETH BOMBELL

12 Discovering Artistic Truth in Music Therapy   136
   CASSANDRA BYERS

13 The Ebb and Flow of the Therapeutic Journey:
   Adjusting Theoretical Orientations in Clinical
   Practice   146
   KATE MYERS-COFFMAN

UNIT 4
Embracing Complexity and Ambiguity
in Practice   157

14 The Extended Discharge: Relationship
Building, Meaning-Making, and Advocacy
in Long-term Treatment   159
JESSE ASCH-ORTIZ

15 I Can Be With What She Brings   170
STEPHENIE SOFIELD

16 Sound, Silence, and Spoken Word: Music as
a Holistic Aesthetic of Experience   182
NOAH POTVIN

17 Reconnecting Musicians With Music at the
End of Life: Developing Musical Identity Beyond
Performance   194
DALITA GETZOYAN

18 "Luchando tu Estas": Interdisciplinary Collaboration
in the Pediatric Intensive Care Unit   203
GABRIELA ASCH-ORTIZ, SUZANNE MILLER, AND ABBY PATCH

UNIT 5
Embracing Loss in Therapeutic Closure   215

19 How It Feels to Be Free: Reflections on the
Relationship Between Music and Spirituality at the
End of Life   217
JASMINE EDWARDS

20 Clinical Termination and Emotional Closure: Two
Sides of the Same Coin   229
ANTHONY BORZI

21 It's Time to Say Goodbye: Stories of Music Therapy
Endings in Private Practice   240
LINDSAY MARKWORTH

**22 Integrating Loss Into Life: Termination in
    Bereavement Counseling and Music Therapy**   251
MOLLY G. HICKS

Index   262

Contributors

Gabriela Asch-Ortiz (she/her), MS, LCAT, MT-BC – Gabriela is a music therapist and licensed creative arts therapist at New York-Presbyterian Hospital and PhD candidate in music therapy at Temple University. Gabriela is trained in Nordoff-Robbins Music Therapy and Austin Vocal Psychotherapy, working within a cultural-relational and anti-oppressive lens of music therapy practice, research, and pedagogy.

Jesse Asch-Ortiz (he/they), MS, LCAT, MT-BC – Jesse is a licensed creative arts therapist and music therapy supervisor and clinician working within mental health care in the Bronx, NY. Jesse is also trained in Nordoff-Robbins Music Therapy and oriented to psychodynamic, resource-oriented, and community-centered approaches to care.

Elisabeth Bombell (she/her), MMT, MT-BC – Elisabeth is a music therapist at Advocate Children's Hospital in Oak Lawn, IL. Elisabeth completed her undergraduate degree at the University of Evansville in 2014, and her graduate degree at Augsburg University in 2022. Much of Elisabeth's work centers around medically fragile infants, focusing on parent-infant relationships and parental role attainment.

Anthony Borzi (he/him), MA, MT-BC – Anthony is a music therapist at Cincinnati Children's in the neonatal intensive care unit and transitional care center. He has additional experience working with hospitalized youth facing mental health challenges. His research interests are where neurodevelopment, mental health, and family systems intersect in the pediatric medical setting.

Cassandra Byers (she/her), MMT, MT-BC – Cassie holds a master's degree in music therapy from Shenandoah University and a bachelor's degree in music therapy from Eastern Michigan University. She has worked in a variety of settings, including psychiatric hospitals, pediatric hospitals, early childhood development centers, memory care units, and hospice.

Yu-Ching Ruby Chen (she/her), MM, MT-BC – Ruby is Manager, Creative Arts Therapies, at The MetroHealth System in Cleveland, Ohio. She serves patients of all ages in acute and intensive care and leads the team of Art and Music Therapists in MetroHealth's Center for Arts in Health in the Institute for H.O.P.E.™

Jasmine Edwards (she/her), MA, LCAT, MT-BC – Jasmine is an adjunct faculty member at Howard University, New York University, Montclair State University, and Duquesne University. Jasmine is also a Doctoral Fellow within NYU's music education program with a focus in music therapy. Jasmine is trained in NICU-MT, First Sounds: Rhythm, Breath, Lullaby, and Austin Vocal Psychotherapy.

Gabriela Espinal-Santiago (she/her) – Gaby is a recent music therapy graduate of Molloy University and in the process of becoming a board-certified music therapist. She is continuing in the Graduate Music Therapy Program at Molloy and is starting her new position as the Graduate Research Assistant at the Rebecca Center for Music Therapy at Molloy University.

Cathleen Flynn (she/her), MA, MT-BC – Cathleen is a board-certified music therapist pursuing a doctorate in clinical psychology at Duquesne University in Pittsburgh, PA. Her professional background includes clinical work with adults and children impacted by trauma, grief, psychiatric conditions, and life-limiting illness.

Dalita Getzoyan (she/her), MA, MT-BC, LCAT – Dalita holds a master of arts degree in clinical mental health counseling with a specialization in music therapy from Lesley University. Her clinical interests include cultural considerations in treatment and trauma-informed care. She works as a music therapist for Hospice of New York.

Spencer Hardy (he/him), MA, MT-BC – Spencer is the Director of Family Support Services at Primary Children's Hospital and works part-time as a music therapist for the Utah Pride Center. Spencer received his bachelors and masters in music therapy from Berklee College of Music. Spencer is passionate about anti-oppressive practices within music therapy.

Molly G. Hicks (she/her), MMT, MT-BC, FT – Molly is a bereavement coordinator and music therapist with Penn Medicine Hospice in the Philadelphia, PA area, where she works with adults in individual counseling and support groups. She received her Fellow in Thanatology (FT) credential from the Association of Death Education and Counseling in 2021.

Joy Kaminski (she/her), MT-BC – Joy earned a bachelor's degree in music therapy from Nazareth College in Rochester, NY. For more than a decade, she has been working in mental health care settings in upstate New York. She is exploring master's degree programs to continue to deepen her understanding of humanistic work within clinical relationships.

Katie Lahue (she/her), MA, SCMT, MT-BC, ACMHC – Katie received her bachelor's degree in music therapy/music education from Wartburg College in 2014, her master's degree in music therapy at Saint Mary-of-the-Woods College in 2018, and her counseling license in 2021. Katie is Expressive Therapies Manager at Primary Children's Hospital in Salt Lake City and serves as the music therapy internship director.

Sara Langenberger (she/her), MT-BC – Sara received her BS in music therapy from Saint Mary-of-the-Woods College, where she is also pursuing her MA in music therapy. Sara is a pediatric music therapist at Primary Children's Hospital in Salt Lake City. Sara is passionate about trauma-informed care in pediatrics, pediatric oncology, and pediatric cardiology.

Conio Loretto (he/him), MS, LCAT, MT-BC – Conio serves as the head of the music therapy program at The Center for Discovery, where he has spearheaded the development of a variety of innovative programs, including a musical theatre program for young adults with autism. He is also an adjunct professor at SUNY New Paltz.

Crystal Luk-Worrall (she/her), MA music therapy, HCPC registered Music Therapist – Crystal runs a private practice, Clap and Toot, in the UK. She works with children facing emotional challenges. Her work is informed by humanistic and psychodynamic approaches. Crystal is passionate about making information about therapy more accessible for children so they are empowered in the therapeutic process.

Kathryn MacGown (she/her), MT-BC – Kate is a newly board-certified music therapist working at St. Mary's Healthcare System for Children. She earned a BS degree in music therapy from Molloy University, and is continuing her graduate studies there, pursuing a MS degree in music therapy. She has experience working with a variety of individuals, from children with developmental disabilities to medical patients in hospital settings.

Lindsay Markworth (she/her), MMT, MT-BC – Lindsay is a Nordoff-Robbins music therapist and founder of Twin Cities Music Therapy Services, LLC in Minneapolis, MN. She believes in a collaborative, relationship-based approach to music therapy work, centering the clients' identity and empowering them to connect and build upon existing inner resources and strengths.

Suzanne Miller (she/her), LCSW – Suzanne is a licensed clinical social Worker with seven years of experience at Mount Sinai Hospital. Her bachelor's degree is from NYU and her master's of social work from Columbia University. She is additionally trained in the field of trauma, palliative and end-of-life care, and psychoanalysis.

Kate Myers-Coffman (she/they), PhD, MT-BC – Dr. Myers-Coffman is an assistant professor at Molloy University whose work focuses on trauma-informed, resource-oriented music therapy for youth and families who have experienced trauma and loss, as well as culturally, critically reflexive approaches to practice, pedagogy, and research.

Abby Patch (she/her), MS, CCLS – Abby is a certified child life specialist at Mount Sinai Kravis Children's Hospital. Her master's degree in child life is from Bank Street College of Education. Her clinical experience has been in the Pediatric Intensive Care Unit and Pediatric Cardiac Intensive Care Unit for nearly eight years.

Alex Peuser (he/they), MM, MT-BC – Alex is a doctoral student in clinical psychology at Adler University in Chicago. Alex earned his degrees in music therapy from the University of Missouri – Kansas City and Colorado State University. Alex works for the Center for Diversity and Inclusion at Adler University and is a clinical psychology practicum student.

Noah Potvin (he/him), PhD, LPC, MT-BC – Dr. Potvin is an assistant professor and program director of the Master of Music Therapy program at Duquesne University. His practice and scholarship focus on developing culturally reflexive resource-oriented approaches in hospice music therapy that draw from individuals' cultural traditions and social identities to facilitate healthy end-of-life processes.

Stephenie Sofield (she/her), MM, MT-BC – Stephenie is a music therapist at Avanzar, a social justice agency in New Jersey, where she provides music therapy to child witnesses of intimate partner violence. She is currently a PhD candidate at Drexel University. Stephenie's clinical and research interest include child liberation, examinations and disruptions of harmful power dynamics, and feminist approaches to music therapy.

Kimberly Woodman (she/her), MT-BC – Kimberly is a board-certified music therapist currently working to complete her master's in music therapy at Colorado State University. She recently started a private practice, Encircled Community-Centered Music Therapy, Ltd, with a focus on providing services to infants, children, and adolescents within a family and community-centered framework.

Yiqing Xiang (she/her), MMT, MT-BC, NMT – Yiqing is a board-certified music therapist currently working at a private practice in Ontario, Canada. Yiqing earned her master's in music therapy from Temple University and practiced in the US for one year. She has worked in a variety of clinical areas, including inpatient psychiatry, autism, and developmental disability.

Foreword: To Students From a Student

During my senior year of undergraduate music therapy studies, I enrolled in a new class, Community Engaged Practicum. This course brought student-led music therapy services to Pittsburgh communities that otherwise had no music therapy programming. In teams of two, it was our responsibility to develop and implement treatment plans under the guidance of our supervisor. After our first few visits, we would independently run sessions without our supervisor present. Since my academic training was predominantly focused on a clinical approach up until this point, shifting gears to a community-oriented approach was challenging. More broadly, I found it difficult to practice flexibility and adaptability. I fiercely clung to the session plan as if it were a security blanket protecting me from uncertainty, loss of control, and failure. At this stage of my journey, I was unsure what it meant to be a professional and, more importantly, how to balance that professionalism with authenticity. Throughout my time in Community Engaged Practicum, I felt a range of emotions oscillating between excitement and sheer terror.

Being a white woman of Western European descent studying in an academic setting that greatly mirrors my own identity, certain values were impressed upon me from an early age. I had grown accustomed to having my thoughts and words graded on a numerical scale, allowing that number to define my worth. As my musical studies progressed, the highly competitive nature of Western music training chipped away at my self-esteem and confidence. The nagging need to always be perfect followed me through Community Engaged Practicum well into my first two years of board certification. The uncertain student music therapist can find great comfort in the words of clinicians such as Stephenie Sofield and Cathleen Flynn, who candidly share in their chapters relatable internal experiences as they navigate their clinical encounters. *Portraits of Everyday Practice in Music Therapy* eloquently illustrates a realization that took me years to discover: music therapy in everyday practice is more nuanced than a checklist of skills to master. It turns out my clients did not need me to be perfect. They needed me to be authentic and present.

Towards the end of my undergraduate studies, I accepted a music therapy internship with a hospice agency in upstate New York. The transition from clinical practicum placements two hours per week to a full-time music therapy internship was a monumental change. Of course, I had clinical and musical skills to strengthen, medical jargon to become familiar with, and the newfound independence of creating a daily schedule. My car became my workspace, and anywhere I could safely park and document served as my office. The introduction to Molly G. Hicks' chapter on extended grief services closely parallels my experience as an internship student. I would suggest this chapter to anyone working as a traveling music therapist navigating a large caseload. However, surprising me even more than this new pace of work were my reactions and emotions that surfaced throughout my work, often catching me off-guard. I struggled to navigate boundaries and took on others' pain, believing I had to join in their experience to be an empathetic music therapist. This book echoes similar experiences in cases representing diverse settings, theories, and approaches, all deepened by the reflexivity of each clinician.

Unexpected reactions surfaced not only when interacting with clients but also when working with the interdisciplinary team. At long-term care facilities, I was uncomfortable communicating with nurses, certified nursing assistants, or health aides, making it challenging to advocate effectively for clients in need. If interdisciplinary team members were irritable or short-tempered, I took it personally instead of considering other possible factors unrelated to me, such as the stressors of the healthcare system at large. Again, my fear of how others perceived me got in the way of what I was truly there to do. I had heard about burnout but I was naive to its implications for healthcare workers and clinicians. As I continue to collaborate with an interdisciplinary team deeply burned out from working through the COVID-19 pandemic, Jesse Asch-Ortiz's chapter reminds me of the importance of stepping out of the traditional clinical role to become the advocate working alongside instead of in opposition to the treatment team. Gabriela Asch-Ortiz, Suzanne Miller, and Abby Patch provide students with a ground-level perspective on what intensive interdisciplinary collaboration can look like. Jasmine Edwards demonstrates how a music therapist's scope of practice can align with the chaplain's in response to client needs.

Looking back, I remember frantically getting into the music. I felt an urgent need always to be musicing, or else what I was doing wasn't "real" music therapy. As I settled into the flow of internship, there were instances my supervisor insisted were crucial to the music therapy process but didn't seem to fit into the strict music therapy methods and interventions that I had diligently memorized. For example, what about the family members who followed me out to the car, expressing their anticipatory grief out of earshot from their dying loved one after a bedside music therapy visit?

What about the poet transitioning to long-term, no longer able to read small print, and asking if I could read his favorite Rilke poems aloud as he lay in bed? Despite not fitting into the original session plan, I grew to understand how impactful these moments were. In retrospect, my desire to implement the perfect music therapy treatment plan often overshadowed the present needs of the clients sitting in front of me, a struggle that multiple authors explore in their practice. Conio Loretto's chapter on developing new treatment planning approaches touches on this pitfall of getting caught up in the outcomes at the expense of our client's individual needs. Joy Kaminski and Cassandra Byers share experiences of rejecting original session plan ideas to be more emergent and community-oriented to better support those they worked with. Herein lies one of the many strengths of this book: it is an excellent supplement to didactic instruction as it introduces lived aspects of everyday music therapy practice not readily captured in the classroom.

Of course, understanding music therapy competencies is necessary for solid clinical work. However, I found a disconnect between knowing the competencies on paper and visualizing them in everyday practice. What resonates with me most is the vulnerability of each author in re-telling case examples that shaped their clinical practice and identity. *Portraits of Everyday Practice in Music Therapy* bridges the gap from clinical training to professional practice by exemplifying real-life scenarios the student music therapist may encounter as they transition into professional practice and begin cultivating their clinical self.

Sarah Mayr (she/her), MT-BC
Graduate Student, Molloy University

Foreword: To Clinicians From a Clinician

When I was a new music therapist, I walked into the doors of agencies, homes, and healthcare centers bright-eyed and ready to deliver the interventions I spent years learning and practicing. After internship I felt the weight of many "shoulds": I should know, I should be, I should do. Many times, however, my expectations of music therapy work were very different when applied in the real-world context. Until I began my career, I couldn't anticipate that being a music therapist would bring so many moments of beauty and equally as many moments of awkwardness and unreadiness. I hadn't yet imagined my perspective of a successful session could be a room filled with silence, or that achieving goals could look like being immersed in a world of dinosaurs flying on drums that turned into spaceships.

Now, after more than a decade of experience as a clinician, I continue to learn that clinical realities are far more complex than I was prepared for. Experience has not been my only teacher. Listening to the stories of others and knowing they had walked similar paths provided me with perspective for facing new challenges and embracing reflexivity in my work. *Portraits of Everyday Practice in Music Therapy* offers clinicians accessible, vulnerable, and evocative stories that can validate their experience and support them in their growth.

Reading through the chapters transported me to a music therapy conference, having coffee with a colleague, sharing stories, and offering guidance to each other. As a queer woman living with a hidden disability, I am a clinician with multiple intersecting identities and share in many of the experiences of the authors. They gave voice to some of the barriers I too had encountered early in my career, and I related to the experience of questioning how those identities impact decision-making at work. Dr. Potvin and Dr. Myers-Coffman have woven a clinically relevant book by centering the voices of a diverse array of student and clinician authors who have told their stories with vivid imagery and transparency.

Definitions learned in school from textbooks are often aspirational gold standards. *Portraits of Everyday Practice in Music Therapy* offers the reader a chance to learn from the clinical decision-making process of their peers and uses the case stories to highlight lessons learned from the field. Reading these chapters feels like a clinical experience; the authors provide readers a front-row seat to the treatment space, and I was struck by the honesty of each case study. I did not feel as though the authors were telling me what I wanted to hear or what "should" be done. Instead, they shared the reality of their experience from their lens, guiding us through their process step-by-step. I especially appreciated when authors shared how they navigated systems involved in patient care such as intersecting identities, multidisciplinary care, and funding. Early in my music therapy career, it was difficult to traverse those intersections of advocacy, team, and my own identities. Students and clinicians at all stages can learn from these relatable stories of feeling lost but also finding your way back.

As I continue to practice and research best practice in music therapy, I find the clinician experience is often left out of the conversation. Textbooks, randomized controlled trials, and case studies alike often neglect the many variables that interplay in the clinical space: the worldview of the music therapist, the identities of patient and therapist, funding streams, daily life, and so much more. Storytelling is a powerful form of evidence, and the strength of this text is the focus on diverse clinician perspectives through case examples. Opportunities for reflexivity with thoughtful prompts at the end of each chapter aid in processing the information and integrating the stories into practice. All music therapists, no matter how long they have been in the field, can learn something from the cases presented in this book and immediately integrate them into their work.

Intentional and comprehensive, *Portraits of Everyday Practice in Music Therapy* provides an in-depth view of clinical decision-making processes within real-life intersecting contexts. Authors illustrate the thought process behind their work and offer reflections on how it felt to make those choices. It is exciting to see the voice of the clinician take center stage with Drs. Potvin and Myers-Coffman harnessing the power of peer learning. As a reader you will learn, but equally as important, you will feel.

Caitlin Krater (she/her), MS, MT-BC
Music Therapist, Riley Hospital for Children
Adjunct Professor,
Indiana University – Purdue University Indianapolis

Foreword: To Supervisors From a Supervisor

Clinical supervision is vital to the practice of ethical and reflexive music therapy. For students moving through each phase of their training from practicum through internship to professional practice, clinical supervision is invaluable. Supervision, whether within a supervisor/supervisee relationship or in peer supervision, continues to be important throughout a music therapist's career. Perhaps the greatest challenge for supervisors is supporting supervisees in arriving to sessions authentically, opening to the client experiences, and remaining responsive to their needs. As much as students and professionals alike crave to be taught "the right way" to do things, there is no one right way when navigating people and therapy. There is no right intervention, song, or thing to say. Ultimately music therapists need to be humans, connecting with the clients as humans. Throughout these chapters, readers will find the authors doing just that. These human journeys can support the journeys that emerge in supervision. The explorations of authenticity, humility, sociocultural reflexivity, sensitivity to oppression, and therapeutic relationships woven throughout these chapters detail the types of growth that can emerge through supervision.

This volume explores and validates the importance of embracing the humility of not knowing and not being an expert. Celebrating the parallel processes that occur in supervision (i.e., client-therapist-supervisor) and in clinical work (i.e., client-therapist), the authors in this volume acknowledge how these parallel processes cultivate collaborative growth. Most importantly, readers will engage with clients' and music therapists' emotions, life histories, communities, dreams, and journeys, and witness how they come out of their comfort zones to embrace growth, experience healing, and find closure. These chapters allow and encourage music therapists throughout their careers to always be curious about what music therapy means for them and how it is experienced by others without having to master one way of knowing.

Of great importance is the attention to the social locations of the music therapists, clients, and communities. As a supervisor and clinician, it is refreshing to experience chapter after chapter exploring how the intersecting social locations of the clients and therapists hindered, helped, and simply existed in the therapeutic relationship. Being privy to so many relationships with varying social identities welcomes the readers to stretch their conceptions. For example, while Kimberly Woodman and Dalita Getzoyan describe how shared social identities and personal historicities with clients opened the path to relationship, Noah Potvin describes how sharing in his case increased challenging countertransference. Yiqing Xiang details working through countertransferences arising from tensions with client-preferred lyrical content when coming from a different cultural background, while Alex Peuser shares intimate explorations of how holding similar identities as his clients was at times confusing as an intern and made boundary-setting challenging.

Supervisors can share these chapters with music therapists they work with to guide explorations of self-awareness as well as reflections of the potential impacts one's social identities can have within therapy. Further, the chapters can provide an important reminder and model for how to explore the impact of social locations within the supervisory relationship itself.

Reckoning with how systemic oppression impacts both the client's health and access to treatment is another important consideration found throughout the book. Reading about how music therapists struggle with and navigate oppressive systems can provide insight, validation, and an opening to discuss these systems and their effects during supervision. For instance, Lindsay Markworth battles with reimbursement to be able to see clients and contemplates the dissonance between her values and the system she is beholden to, while Yu-Ching Ruby Chen details finding the balance between her personal values, client expectations, and hospital system demands.

Many authors also describe with care different ways that oppressive systems, both in the health care settings and beyond, harm clients, families, and communities, robbing them of safety. Confronting oppression in music therapy, in music therapy education, and in supervision is crucial, yet it can be daunting. Despite holding immense privilege as a white, cishet woman with a master's degree and years of clinical experience, engaging in these confrontations often brings up feelings of inadequacy as an advocate, fear of causing harm, and isolation. However, such confrontations are an ethical obligation and are important in avoiding burnout from conflating failures of oppressive systems as failures as a music therapist. Again, the openness and honesty in this volume create a space and an impetus for readers to engage and consider their respective roles in these types of systems.

Closure is a definite component of an internship and practicum. Early on and often, I tell the clients I work with when to expect student supervisees to complete their work with them. During internships wherein clients are seen long-term, we start working on closure at least 6 weeks out, first with reminders, then reintegrating me into sessions as a co-leader, and finally with termination rituals for the entire last week. Multiple chapters in this volume frame discharge, death, or ending of treatment in reflexive ways that can guide readers to reflect on and confront endings in their own clinical work during supervision.

Through their openness, the authors in this volume allow readers to connect with the struggles, emotional processes, and growth present in their journeys. Being fortunate enough to consider several of the authors as colleagues, friends, peer supervisees, collaborators, classmates, and individuals whom I admire, I found myself intrigued by learning more about the detail in which they ultimately grew with the clients through their work. I was often moved to tears while reading and found myself needing to stop to text "Your chapter is so powerful" and "I loved everything you wrote." Both the humility and the deep connectivity to the clients displayed by the authors allowed me to feel connected as well.

As supervisors share this work with supervisees, they might point out how the music therapists, even those with multiple years of experience, didn't always know what to do. They shared about shedding tears, doubting themselves, and doubting music therapy. They presented themselves as humans and the clients and their families as partners and collaborators. They opened themselves up to each other, and figured it out together, or with the support from supervisors and peers. As a resource for supervisors, *Portraits of Everyday Practice in Music Therapy* can provide an impetus for the exploration of authenticity, humility, cultural reflexivity, the effects of oppression in treatment and in supervision, and how all these factors show up in the therapeutic relationship. When supervisors share this volume with their supervisees, they are sharing models of how to be human as music therapists.

Audrey Hausig (she/her), MMT, MT-BC
Owner, Philadelphia Music Therapy
www.philadelphiamusictherapy.com

Foreword: To Educators From an Educator

What an honor to read *Portraits of Everyday Practice in Music Therapy* and provide a forward from the perspective of an educator to other educators. What a beautifully written book by a group of wonderful clinicians and first-time authors, many of whom I recognize from their scholarly work from presentations and service work to the music therapy field. In the past, there have been unspoken rules about who gets to be an author based on the number of their degrees, their length of practice in the field, and with whom they collaborated for their ideas to be taken seriously. This book sets the tone for the new generations of music therapists and demonstrates that with reflective practice and an intention to bring new authors to the "writing table," music therapy scholarship and writing is for everyone, and there are no rules about how long you must practice before you can successfully contribute to the field. That being said, I would like to say congratulations to the editors in selecting a variety of authors and developing a unit and chapter structure that matches the title. I also congratulate the authors for providing reflective and often vulnerable accounts of their work as therapists; the tone they set makes this book accessible to many students, interns, and entry-level clinicians and will truly help to train many current and future generations of therapists.

Portraits of Everyday Practice in Music Therapy is divided into 5 units, with each unit containing 4–5 chapters. Each chapter is a case study from a student or clinician that embeds a location of self, explanation of the case, and insight into the author's clinical decisions into the narrative, and ends with reflective questions for the readers. This textbook is everything I have wanted a music therapy textbook to have, yet in my experience I usually have to go to other resources in related therapeutic fields, resulting in high textbook costs for students and, usually, something missing because those other fields are not music therapy. So many of our music therapy textbooks focus on populations, specific parts of the treatment process, interventions, methods, and theoretical foundations. This text takes topics that are briefly covered in music therapy textbooks and provides an in-depth exploration of the topic in a music therapy setting. This book fills a gap in the literature by outlining many spaces that the new music therapist will encounter that only come from engaging in daily practice through internship and first jobs, rather than attending weekly practicum sessions. The pacing of this book is great. I can see myself using it in introduction classes, upper-level classes, practicum classes, and as assignments during internship. This book could be read in the order that is provided, or individual chapters could be revisited due to a student's need during practicum or internship or for an entry-level clinician's needs in new settings.

The book starts in internship settings. As an educator, I believe this is such as an interesting and exciting place to start. Internship is a part of education that is often imagined but not observed. I can share with my students that there is a difference between attending practicum 1–2 times a week versus being immersed in a clinical setting for 40 hours a week as a music therapy intern. However, this level of understanding is often not achieved until the student enters the internship and experiences it for themselves. Having the authors of the first few chapters talk about countertransference and culture shock in the internship setting is so important because some of these experiences may not occur in practicum settings due to the length of time spent with clients each week. There are so many takeaways from each unit that will spark discussion for the reader. The authors of chapters in the first unit remind readers why supervision is so important, and that countertransference can happen to anyone. The authors also challenge us to continue to unpack our cultural bias and assumptions and how those implicit biases may show up in our clinical thought and decision-making.

Each unit continues in a similar manner, with authors sharing cases related to the theme of the unit, such as how to process and move through spaces of frustration in treatment, how to expand one's theoretical framework to best meet client needs, how to still show up as a music therapist when music isn't used in each session, how to set boundaries in terminal settings, and how to embrace and process loss in termination. These concepts are often read about in textbooks but not necessarily experienced in practicum settings or internships.

Being able to read about, for example, a music therapist's experience with termination of a client and observing the emotions and rituals they use to process the loss, serves two purposes. First, it allows a reader to explore their own emotions and process what they may or may not do in a similar situation. Second, it provides permission to the reader to set boundaries, to feel emotions that arise during a therapeutic relationship, and to process all of those things with themselves and potentially a supervisor, which in the end keeps our field growing and elevates one's music therapy practice. Each author shares their case and clinical experience with such clarity that a reader can easily transport themselves to the clinical setting with the author. Since the authors are so reflective and vulnerable, readers are challenged to become just as reflective in their own clinical practice, as well as imagining themselves as the clinician in the case study.

It was an honor to read the cases provided in this volume, and I highly recommend it as an addition to everyone's music therapy library. I cannot wait to use this book in my classes.

Melita Belgrave (she/her), PhD, MT-BC
Associate Professor of Music Therapy, School of Music,
Dance, and Theatre
Associate Dean for Culture and Access, Herberger
Institute for Design and the Arts
Arizona State University

Acknowledgments

We send our greatest appreciation and thanks to the authors who put forth such incredible time, effort, and dedication to these chapters; our families who supported this venture, especially when it meant logging evening and weekend hours; our colleagues who provided guidance when called upon; Gianna DeRusso, Teressa Sambolin, Morgan Maxwell, and Charlotte Pegg for proofreading the chapters; and Teressa Sambolin for helping with the indexing.

Introduction

Case studies hold an important role in the training and education of entry-level music therapists, providing learners the opportunities to gain proximity to clinical scenarios they have yet to experience. For students, case studies help demystify the experience of music therapy, taking the abstract idea of "using music to help people" and grounding it in evidence, rigor, and process to provide music therapy both form and function. For new professionals, they expand the seeming boundaries of practice, helping readers to engage with settings and philosophical lenses that they do not have access to or that they never even imagined.

Oftentimes, however, case studies eschew the elements of everyday practice that can inform entry-level professionals, instead spotlighting once-in-a-career clinical situations that reflect extraordinary circumstances deep into the author's career. Without question, the extraordinary has a role in entry-level training, for it helps to dream of what could be, to aspire to reach new heights in the construction of new dimensions of practice. But for students and new professionals who are still experiencing vulnerability and perhaps even fragility in their professional identities and practice, the extraordinary can be intimidating, even oppressive.

When a new learner's introduction to music therapy is the extraordinary, it threatens to set up unrealistic and unattainable standards. For students moving into internship, they can begin to wonder why their songwriting projects are not yielding the triumphant odes that are spotlighted at a conference. For new professionals moving into their initial years of practice, they might question their competency as their practice does not reach the epiphanal and cathartic climaxes they read about in Session 25.

Consequently, it is common for students and new professionals to read a case study and feel as if they are unable to engage in a similar type of work as described by the author. In some instances, this is appropriate; for instance, if the author was trained in a specific type of advanced practice beyond the scope of the entry-level clinician, or if the author framed the story through a specific cultural lens distinct from readers' cultural traditions. Many times, however, readers' feelings of inadequacy are due to

DOI: 10.4324/9781003123798-1

missing details in the case study that are necessary for understanding how the process informed the product, or because the product is not accurately contextualized as an outlier.

Portraits of Everyday Practice in Music Therapy was conceptualized as a direct response to this gap in the literature. The guiding vision for this project was to provide students and new professionals a comprehensive, depth-oriented perspective of everyday practice that both captures and honors the inherent messiness of ethical, culturally humble, and reflexive work. Each of these chapters are divorced from spotlighting fully realized clinical products, replaced with authors critically examining their internal process in context of their external work, and vice-versa.

Conceptualization and Development

As with any journey of growth and learning, this volume has experienced an evolution since our initial proposal to our publisher. We began with the idea of six broad chapter units: (1) Therapeutic Relationships, (2) Therapeutic Closure, (3) Clinical Supervision, (4) Treatment Planning, (5) Professional Development, and (6) Telehealth. Dimensions of ethics, social justice, and cultural reflexivity were to be embedded in each chapter. Our aim was to connect students and new professionals with clearly identified topic areas reflected in other music therapy textbooks.

To aid in our book proposal submission, we invited five colleagues to write chapters; all five were full-time clinicians with little to no publishing record at the time who we trusted to bring forth compelling stories with cultural reflexivity. Upon learning of the book proposal's acceptance, a call was placed through multiple professional channels for chapter abstract submissions to be anonymously reviewed. We prioritized music therapy clinicians and students so that we could platform new voices who might not have had traditional, well-established pipelines for publications. We presented an evaluation rubric that focused less on writing skill and more on telling a story from which students and early career professionals might draw a great deal of meaning and learning.

Upon completing this review and inviting accepted authors to write a full chapter, we embarked on a dialogic relationship through the writing and editing process that included meetings, mentorship, deep questions, and multiple drafts. We have great gratitude to these authors for their willingness and readiness to really dig into personal processes on stories that touched them and, in some cases, left everlasting marks. Given the emotional and spiritual intimacy of these stories, the writing journey for authors was no small feat.

For many, the clinical experience they spotlighted was still unfolding all the way through the writing process. This presented a unique challenge as the case study became a medium, not only to tell a story, but through which to process the clinical experience. As editors, our feedback in meetings and in response to drafts often bordered on clinical supervision to help authors further unpack the meaning of the clinical experience and its personal and professional impact on them. Of particular note, the call for chapters went out in Fall 2020, barely 6 months following the global shutdown in response to the COVID-19 pandemic. For those authors whose stories were still evolving, the similarly evolving pandemic played an indelible role that colored every facet of the clinical experience and how they ultimately told the story.

Similarly, we experienced incredible shifts and learning by witnessing and engaging in the authors' stories. Our meetings were often filled with organic discussions on how these chapters were shifting understanding of our music therapy education and training experiences; our views on pedagogy and andragogy; our values and worldviews in therapy; our conceptualization of what it meant to be a culturally reflexive music therapist; our navigation of multiple roles and systems; our philosophy on anti-oppressive discourse when languages surrounding social concepts and identities are so fluid, and so much more. Also, at various times throughout the process, life presented challenges to one of us that required the other to assume a disproportionate amount of responsibility and load so that the project could move forward. While we had a friendship and collegial relationship prior to this project, we needed to learn each other's strengths and how to parlay them into a compassionate and complementary partnership that could navigate the ebbs and flows of such an intensive developmental process. Integral to this partnership was developing a well of reciprocal trust that tasks would be completed, that we could navigate difficult situations in sensitive and healthy ways, and that we could be jointly vulnerable in this shared learning process.

As these transformations took place, we became less connected to the initial chapter units, which had already begun shifting by removing the telehealth heading and embedding that content throughout the other units. The authors' stories were so rich, complex, and encompassing multiple facets of clinical practice that they could not simply be compartmentalized in any single unit category. We decided to adopt the old headings (supervision, treatment planning, closure, relationship, and professional development) as tags for each chapter to help readers be targeted in their chapter selections, and develop thematic units that could more fully capture the depth and breadth of the chapters: (1) Developing Clinical Readiness as a Music Therapist in Training; (2) Aligning Personal Values and Emerging Clinical Identities as a New Professional; (3) Attuning, Adapting, and Maturing in Practice; (4) Embracing Complexity and Ambiguity in Practice; and (5) Embracing Loss in Therapeutic Closure.

Structure and Content

Central to our process was critical consideration of how to embrace the light and shadow in the authors' work while threading a trauma-informed and anti-oppressive discourse throughout the chapters. We believe such lenses are necessary dimensions of all contemporary music therapy practice regardless of philosophical positioning or theoretical orientation. Consequently, this volume frames a dynamically emergent and non-prescriptive approach to culturally reflexive practice that honors the positionality of both the music therapist and other individuals in their shared musicking.

To that end, content warnings have been provided for chapters to help guide readers and prepare them for stories that might be activating and requiring self-care. We also conversed for hours over whether to allow authors to call the individuals they work with by a given label based on their personal preference and/or work norms (e.g., client, patient, service user, etc.), or to select a single label for all chapters given how many traditional labels hold oppressive roots. We ultimately decided on the former to give authors autonomy in telling their story the way it lives in their memory.

Authors were asked to share the sociocultural locations of those they worked with in relation to how they self-identified. If they were unsure of any cultural or social identity, we asked them not to assume and only to present the information they were made aware of so as to not risk perpetuating locating someone by external perception. For example, individuals were referenced through they/them pronouns if gender identification was not explicitly shared. Similarly, because individuals across the lifespan may differ on their preference of identity-first versus person-first language, authors took care to present how the individuals identified themselves in relation to diagnoses, conditions, or life experiences. If authors were unsure (e.g., they worked with a person unable, due to age or communication preferences, to clarify this), we used identity-first language. These few instances arose when describing music therapy with autistic and disabled individuals; therefore, we drew from the input of self-advocates preferring identity-first language.[1,2,3] When diagnoses were used, we took care to consult with relevant stakeholders to determine contemporary usages most aligned with anti-oppressive practices.

We challenged authors to write as much about their clinical and internal processes as the person or people they worked with. This was to help them better capture those everyday moments – the humility they navigated, their struggles and challenges, and the ways they accessed resources as learners and clinicians – so readers could be brought into the authors' worlds as much as the specific cases. As part of this process, we made sure that one level of cultural reflexivity was explored in each case, whether it was related to race, ethnicity, nationality, age, gender, sexual orientation, disability, musical background, family context, or another sociocultural identification.

We also gave authors agency in how they described themselves in their sociocultural situatedness. For example, some authors preferred to use terms like cis, cisgender, or hetero-cisgender to describe themselves, and we did not edit this language. Other authors chose to capitalize White in relation to racial identification while others maintained it in lowercase. Because we are aware of justice-oriented and anti-oppressive arguments for capitalizing[4] and using lowercase[5] in relation to whiteness, we felt it appropriate to honor each person's decision as long as the awareness surrounding the discourse remained present. Ultimately, how these overlapping cultural ecologies impacted the work is different from one author to the next, presenting a dynamic mosaic of reflexive practice.

Each case ends with a set of summarizing statements and questions for reflection. We intend for these questions to serve as discussion points for educators or supervisors, peer supervision groups, or music therapy book clubs. Authors crafted questions inspired by the processes they experienced and the questions they had to navigate as they moved through their cases. By organizing chapters in themed units and providing tags, readers can explore a range of questions for discussion on a given theme to reflect in deeper, more nuanced ways.

To introduce the content of the various units in this volume, we'll start with **Developing Clinical Readiness as a Music Therapist in Training**, where we learn stories from authors who were students at the time of writing their chapter, as well as students and professionals reflecting on past internship experiences. Kimberly Woodman and Katie Lahue write about the supervisee and supervisor experience of processing countertransference experienced during internship when working with a family sharing similar life and medical experiences in pediatric medical care. Yiqing Xiang shares her story of overcoming culture shock when engaging preferred music by youth having trauma histories, and developing a culturally reflexive practice through reflecting on her cultural values and the ways they manifested in countertransference. Sarah Langerberger and Spencer Hardy share perspectives of working in a supervisory relationship in pediatric medical care and the ways this relationship led to developing confidence and individuation as an intern. Gabriela Espinal-Santiago and Kathryn MacGown write about completing their undergraduate training during the COVID-19 pandemic and how they learned to bridge authentic relationships with youth and families delivering telehealth music therapy services.

In **Aligning Personal Values and Emerging Clinical Identities as a New Professional**, readers learn about the impact of cultural and critical reflexivity on emerging clinical identities, often with the support of clinical supervision. Alex Peuser shares their story of developing a LGBTQIA2+ support group for adolescents in a residential mental health facility while reflecting on their experience as a queer individual. Joy Kaminski explores finding intimacy and authenticity through the development of her clinical identity in supervision when working in inpatient psychiatric care. Cathleen Flynn details her emerging understanding of clinical limitations and the role they played in working with a woman in hospice care. Ruby Chen touches on themes of boundary setting and giving too much of oneself when connecting humanistically with a woman navigating multiple admissions in medical care support.

Attuning, Adapting, and Maturing in Practice starts with Crystal Luk-Worrall detailing an evolving relationship through telehealth and in-person music therapy offered to a child and his family, ebbing and flowing between family-centered and individual-centered care. Conio Loretto explores how to balance authentic expressions of his clinical identity with the documentation and treatment planning demands of the organization. Elisabeth Bombell shares her experiences of exploring and integrating concepts of spirituality in NICU-based family care. Cassandra Byers writes about shifting from clinical to community music approaches with a woman in hospice care. Kate Myers-Coffman shares their experience of shifting and integrating cognitive-behavioral and humanistic theoretical orientations when supporting a woman navigating grief, depression, and anxiety.

Embracing Complexity and Ambiguity in Practice begins with Jesse Asch-Ortiz navigating therapist and advocacy roles when working with a woman navigating extended care in an acute care setting. Stephenie Sofield explores developing new understandings and practices in trauma-specific care when supporting a young girl through music and play. Noah Potvin illustrates, through work with a man in hospice care who seldomly engaged in traditional music experiences, how he came to understand music as a holistic aesthetic comprising multiple mediums of experience. Dalita Getzoyan shares how moving away from an exclusively Western musical identity afforded a formerly trained musician at the end of his life meaningful opportunities for engaging in music therapeutically. Gabriela Asch-Ortiz, Suzanne Miller, and Abby Patch detail their collaborative experiences working as an interdisciplinary team of music therapist, social worker, and child life specialist with an infant and her family navigating challenging experiences, and ultimately a death, in NICU care.

Lastly, **Embracing Loss in Therapeutic Closure** details the parallel processes music therapists experience in navigating types of loss in therapeutic closure. Jasmine Edwards shares her experience of developing nuanced understandings of death and dying through the way a teenage girl with cancer drew on her spirituality. Anthoni Borzi writes about his evolving role within the family unit when caring for a medically fragile infant and how he processed the loss of this infant. Lindsay Markworth explores ethical practices of closures experienced as a private practice business owner. And finally, Molly G. Hicks details her process of navigating loss experiences while supporting a man adapting to bereavement following the death of his partner.

The Evolving Narrative

Case studies are snapshots of certain periods taken at certain vantage points, and there are limitations to such a concrete product representing such a fluid period in history. From the time that this book was first conceptualized in 2018 through its completed writing in 2022, the United States has weathered a great deal of (necessary) upheaval to society's norms and standards regarding how we conceptualize and engage with humanness. The language used by authors in these chapters is different, both in tone and taxonomy, from what would have been expected from a similar volume 5 years ago, and we expect that in another 5 years language will have continued to transform.

With that in mind, we offer these portraits of everyday practice as representative, not timeless, stories. Even so, our hope is that these portraits capture essential aspects of practice that will continue to resonate with future generations of music therapists even as the contexts around ethical and reflexive practice (again, necessarily) evolve.

Notes

1 Organization for Autism Research (2020, September 30). *1,000 people surveyed, survey says . . .* Organization for Autism Research. https://researchautism.org/1000-people-surveyed-survey-says/

2 Sharif, A., McCall, A. L., & Bolante, K. (2022). *Should I say "disabled people" or "people with disabilities"? Language preferences of disabled people between identity- and person-first language.* The 24th International ACM SIGACCESS Conference on Computers and Accessibility (ASSETS 22). Association for Computing Machinery. https://athersharif.me/documents/assets-2022-identity-first-vs-person-first.pdf

3 Levy, L., Li, Q., Sharif, A., & Reinecke, K. (2021). *Respectful language as perceived by people with disabilities* (pp. 1–4). The 23rd International ACM SIGACCESS Conference on Computers and Accessibility (ASSETS 21). Association for Computing Machinery, Article 83. https://athersharif.me/documents/assets-2021-respectful-language-as-perceived-by-people-with-disabilities.pdf

4 Nguyễn, A. T., & Pendleton, M. (2020). *Recognizing race in language: Why we capitalize "Black" and "White".* Center for the Study of Social Policy. https://cssp.org/2020/03/recognizing-race-in-language-why-we-capitalize-black-and-white/

5 Daniszewski, J. (2020). *Why we will lowercase White.* The Associated Press. https://blog.ap.org/announcements/why-we-will-lowercase-white

Unit 1

Developing Clinical Readiness as a Music Therapist in Training

Chapter 1

Navigating Countertransference With Clinical Supervision

Kimberly Woodman and Katie Lahue

Abstract

Countertransference can impact professional development in ways both expected and unexpected for students and supervisors. Clinical supervision coupled with personal processes of growth can help the new professional to become aware of the countertransferences emerging from past experiences and trauma, and subsequently learn how to ethically and effectively utilize countertransference in therapeutic processes.

Tags: Clinical Supervision; Therapeutic Relationship

Kim

Countertransference is an inevitable part of music therapy practice. Supervision can help students experiencing countertransference develop the necessary skills, intuition, and confidence to successfully navigate that experience. I received this type of skillful care from my internship supervisor, Katie, when working with an infant diagnosed with a terminal brain tumor, Darby, and her family.

I am a white, middle-class, cisgender woman in my late 30s who is heterosexually married with three children. My second was diagnosed with a rare, aggressive brain tumor when he was 4 months old and died 13 months later after treatment, remission, and relapse. His treatment took place at a large pediatric hospital where, nine years later, I completed my music therapy internship.

Before beginning my internship, I anticipated significant countertransference because of my experiences with my child in that same setting. Additionally, I was diagnosed with PTSD a year into my graduate program, for which I received several years of therapy before starting my internship. My primary goal in therapy was to develop self-awareness about parts of my traumatic experiences being activated through different academic content and clinical situations. I was simultaneously learning and practicing

DOI: 10.4324/9781003123798-3

self-regulation and self-care skills needed to manage triggers as they would arise over the course of my education and career. While at the beginning of my degree program I believed that self-care would mean avoiding work with pediatric populations, I came to realize that returning to the site of my trauma had the potential for personal growth and for bridging the divide between parental experience and professional training. I felt powerfully drawn to this work, which I later learned is referred to as "trauma mastery."[1] Throughout my internship, I disclosed relevant information about my life experience, trauma, and countertransference to members of my supervisory team so they could provide supervision in support of these goals.

Katie

I join the story of Darby as Kim's clinical supervisor. I met Darby during her music therapy assessment but did not interact with her family in-person. I was at Kim's side throughout the planning and processing of this case that came with heavy countertransference. I am a female in my late 20s, younger than Kim and Darby's parents, and do not have children. Similar to Kim and Darby's parents, I am white and heterosexually married.

This case took place at the end of Kim's internship, making it appropriate to approach supervision from a humanistic perspective versus a competency-based model that is more successful at the beginning of the internship experience.[2] Throughout, I applied unconditional positive regard, genuineness, and empathy to help Kim build her confidence and self-esteem as a clinician. As part of that process, I supported Kim in building strong therapeutic relationships and experiencing countertransference. Central to my philosophy of supervision is learning how to process countertransference in order to use it to strengthen the therapeutic alliance.

Developing Rapport with Darby Through Countertransference

Kim

I met Darby when she was 6 months old and receiving care in the pediatric intensive care unit after diagnosis. She was the second child of Alex and Brenda, and little sister to Caitlyn. Darby was referred to music therapy for developmental support, which was typical for infants hospitalized for extended periods of time.

My early work with Darby brought up feelings that I experienced during my own child's hospitalization and treatment. I worked with her one-on-one twice a week, which allowed me to fully immerse myself in Darby's world. She was often distressed when I arrived, which called up my own feelings of distress and helplessness from when my son was in treatment and experiencing pain and sleeplessness. In this situation, though, I had the skills to use music in ways that helped Darby relax and fall asleep, which allowed me to begin to gain a sense of mastery around those aspects of my own traumatic experience. I established a close, responsive connection with Darby; she held my gaze during our sessions and, as I musically reflected her emotions and experiences, she appeared to feel heard and comforted.

There was something about having sessions without her parents that viscerally connected me to guilt I experienced about not being with my son every minute of his hospitalization. It was as if I was viewing the parts of my son's life that took place while I wasn't there. I remembered walking into my son's room and finding him cuddled up on someone's lap, rocking in the chair by his bed. I recalled the mix of gratitude and jealousy that I felt towards that person, a stranger who was loving my son in my absence. I had wanted to know that stranger, and I wanted Darby's parents to know about my relationship with their child.

Katie

Kim was almost entirely independent at this point in her internship; I was primarily an observer and chose to let her take this case on her own. I was not present for sessions after assessment but provided ongoing and (as needed) supervision throughout. However, during the assessment, I noticed a connection between Kim and Darby. Kim seemed to have a heightened sense of awareness of Darby's needs and brought patience and attentiveness while playing music at her bedside.

I believe that countertransference is present in all music therapy sessions and, although I wasn't consciously aware of Kim's countertransference during the assessment, I was attuned to the therapeutic alliance that was forming. Kim had previously disclosed her personal trauma surrounding her son's death to me and I quickly recognized some similarities between Darby and Kim's son. I attributed the strong relationship between Kim and Darby to these similarities, which clued me in that supervision for this case would be important in order to help her navigate any countertransference that arose. For that reason, I was glad to not be working directly with the patient and family. It allowed me to bring a more objective perspective informed by experience and practice. Taking a supporter role also allowed me to acknowledge and communicate my belief in Kim's abilities as a clinician.[2]

Kim

Those early reminders of my own experience led me to consider ways that I might offer direct support to her parents in a way that centered them and their needs and wants. Given Darby's poor prognosis, I believed a legacy-making songwriting intervention could provide an opportunity for her family to participate in a flexible process that incorporated their thoughts and feelings about this experience.

My countertransference informed this decision-making. When my son was dying, the nursing staff offered to create hand molds for us. We were initially excited, but the process of creating the molds was rushed and the staff appeared frustrated and impatient with my husband and I throughout the process. I did not believe the nurses related to our son as a full human being, nor did they view this activity as being part of our larger family narrative.

From the moment we met, I understood Darby to be fully her own person. I wanted my involvement in her life to reflect that recognition. I wasn't there to create a product, but rather to be in relationship with her and her family. While I was developing a strong therapeutic connection with Darby, my work schedule did not align with her parents' schedule, and I had yet to meet them. To help initiate that connection, I developed a songwriting journal with a series of prompts in lieu of in-person discussions and interviews. I planned to write a letter to the family to introduce the project, but Katie suggested a phone call would be more personal and appropriate.

Katie

When Kim initially brought the idea of a legacy song for Darby to me, I was hesitant. It seemed early in the therapeutic process, especially as she had no relationship with the parents. I suggested calling the parents to establish rapport and explore their needs before presenting them with the legacy song, which could potentially be triggering. When this communication wasn't possible and we were hearing more about Darby's prognosis, I felt it was appropriate to attempt the journal that Kim put together.

Kim

I wanted the journal to be perfect before presenting it to the family. I purchased a journal myself, approached Katie multiple times to discuss questions and prompts, and aimed to draft evocative questions conveying respect for the sensitivity of this process. I wanted to ensure my offer of support was not perceived as a voyeuristic desire to increase my sense of importance through proximity to their child and family's difficult experience, which was something I had navigated within my community when my son was sick. I recognized the inherent difficulty of communicating true motivations without the context of a personal relationship, but it wasn't until I wrote this chapter that I realized those feelings of discomfort were a signal that the legacy journal project was not appropriate.

Katie

I became aware of the countertransference happening between Kim and Darby's family when I observed the detail and time she put into the project. I knew the project could have some potential therapeutic benefit, but I did not feel as connected to the idea as Kim. She had briefly mentioned her experience with legacy projects for her son, and therefore I assumed the countertransference was coming from her personal feelings around that experience or, perhaps, with the legacy project itself. I proceeded with caution and took Kim's experience into account in assessing the appropriateness for Darby and her family.

Kim

Katie's thoughtful questions about the journal and my intended mode of delivery provided space to examine my feelings and motivations. This allowed my experience to guide my process as opposed to relying on someone with more clinical experience and authority. I felt my confidence and clinical judgment grow as a result. I became aware of my resentment about the few options I had for individualizing my son's legacy project and the shame I felt when his nurses rejected this desire. This led me to present a project that centered on options for Darby's family in ways I wished for my family. The biggest challenge was working with two irreconcilable impulses: providing a meaningful legacy project and honoring that I wasn't a part of their immediate support network.

Developing Rapport With Darby's Parents Through Self-Disclosure

Katie

I anticipated self-disclosure coming up for Kim at some point during her internship because of her trauma history and experience in the pediatric medical setting. I remember her prompting me to discuss this with her prior to it coming up in any of her cases.

Kim

Self-disclosure was a topic of concern for me coming into my internship. I finished my coursework with the impression that it was largely a negative force, but this did not align with my personal experiences as a client in therapy. Katie appeared to have spent a lot of time considering how self-disclosure could be beneficial to the therapeutic process, and I sought her supervision to help me reconcile these two different perspectives.

Katie

I advised Kim to utilize self-disclosure as a tool with clinical intent, and to be aware of the potential for a desire to use it for personal processing or connection. I knew her education had taught her extreme caution in this area, which helped me trust that she would act judiciously in utilizing self-disclosure. Additionally, she had disclosed to me that she had participated in personal therapy, and I suspected she had productive experiences with her therapist self-disclosing to her. I, too, had participated in several years of therapy and came to realize that the experience of being the client significantly informs my practice. Given all these factors, I had confidence in Kim's ability to use this clinical skill appropriately and effectively.

Kim

Before I had a chance to call the family, I met Alex in person one afternoon when he left work early to spend time with Darby. I was immediately struck by his sense of humor and openness. Alex interacted in ways familiar to me as a caregiver, using humor to ease moments of intense emotion, displaying no discomfort with my presence, and expressing negative feelings about the situation and aspects of care being received. He even once commented on my conservative appearance, as though to test my response. I was immediately comfortable recognizing this interaction style and felt capable of holding space for him.

One challenge he expressed was concern about being simultaneously present for both Darby and her sister, Caitlyn. This called up feelings from the final weeks of my son's life. I was spending long stretches of time away from my older child and felt guilt and shame about being what felt like a poor mother to her. I reasoned that I would be able to make it up to her later, whereas these were the last moments that I would ever have with my son. I expressed some of these feelings to a friend who, instead of validating my conflict, emphasized how much my daughter needed me. Her response was crushing and contributed to years of difficulty processing my feelings about being a bad mother to my older daughter.

I attempted to reassure Alex that he was not a bad parent. He waved a hand dismissively, stating that it was my job to say that but that I didn't really understand. I knew that self-disclosure always posed some risk and that it was possible I was projecting my feelings of guilt onto him, but I assessed the higher risk being Alex leaving our encounter believing himself to be a bad parent. I decided to self-disclose to offer the support I was uniquely positioned to provide.

Katie

I was grateful to hear that Kim was able to meet Alex. When she came to me and shared that she utilized self-disclosure, I became concerned for her, worried that she might have rushed into it in an attempt to create a personal connection around a shared experience or prove herself in some way.

Kim

It wasn't as much about proving myself as it was establishing credibility in some way. My disclosure was brief, and I did not share specific details of my situation; however, I stated I had experienced similar feelings and concerns through a similar situation nine years earlier and told him I knew he was doing the best he could in an impossible situation. Alex made eye contact with me and visibly calmed, saying: "Oh! You don't just empathize; you actually get it!"

Katie

When Kim repeated this dialogue to me between her and Alex, I was at ease. It seemed that she shared only the minimum in an attempt to build rapport and trust with Alex, and that self-disclosing made this possible. I was proud of her for recognizing this as an opportunity for self-disclosure while being thoughtful about how to present it and brave enough to be vulnerable with a stranger. At the same time, I became hyper-aware of her countertransference and how it might impact the therapeutic process moving forward. I recognized that for the first time in her internship, she had willingly opened up the door to her trauma in the clinical setting. I wanted to offer her the space to navigate that extreme vulnerability in the clinical setting with as much support as she needed, an experience I knew she might not get as a new professional, while also being mindful of the needs of the patient and family.

Kim

The dynamic had shifted between Alex and me. I believe he may have felt safer being vulnerable with me after my disclosure because of a level of shared understanding. I asked Alex if he and Brenda might like to write a song for Darby with me. He expressed interest and agreed to the journal approach due to mismatched schedules with Brenda. Later, when leaving the songwriting journal at Darby's bedside, I had the opportunity to meet Brenda and Caitlyn. Brenda was quite a bit more reserved than her husband, and I was mindful about matching her energy in the conversation.

Transitioning to End-of-Life Care

Kim

When Darby's next MRI revealed significant disease progression, the family elected to transition to end-of-life care and began spending more time at Darby's bedside. When my son was dying, my first priority was to spend as much time as possible with him, and I deprioritized burdensome tasks not absolutely vital to the immediate situation. I believed the songwriting journal was one of these deprioritized tasks for Alex and Brenda because they had not engaged with it, but I still wanted to offer them an opportunity to talk about their experiences with trusted people outside their immediate family circle, to have witnesses to their experiences.

During the first session after Darby's transition to end-of-life care, as I was providing musical support for relaxation and bonding between Alex and Darby, Alex became tearful and began to share his feelings about her prognosis and preferences for her end-of-life care. I quietly listened with a few verbal validations. I asked Alex if they would like to continue with the songwriting process with in-person discussions instead of the songwriting journal. Alex responded positively and, after a brief correspondence with Brenda, requested that I come first thing the next morning.

Katie

In my clinical work, when I want a treatment plan to move in a certain direction but the client appears uninterested or resistant, I recognize this may be resulting from countertransference. I sensed this could be occurring for Kim with the songwriting journal; however, I felt that she was not causing harm by presenting it and that she was being thoughtful in her preparation and presentation. I wanted to honor her instincts and trust her clinical decision-making, so I allowed her to learn by doing versus learning by being told, which was appropriate for where she was in her internship. When I learned that they arranged an in-person interview for a legacy song, I felt relief. I knew that at this time, it was clinically indicated and appropriate because Alex was asking for it.

Experiencing Countertransference in the Supervisory Relationship

Katie

At some point, I noticed my countertransference with Kim arising. I faced feelings of inadequacy and insecurity as her supervisor because I did not have the experience of losing a child. I questioned my instincts and resorted to a more passive role in the supervisory relationship, saying less than I might have with another student but reassuring myself that I would more actively intervene if someone was at risk of harm. Looking back on this now, I recognize these same feelings and thoughts were also in play when I initially stepped away from the case and when I chose to not intervene in the song-writing journal despite my feelings of hesitation. I was balancing trusting my experience, skills, and training as a therapist and supervisor with trusting her instincts as a person with a similar lived experience to this family.

Our age difference also contributed to my feelings of insecurity. I suspect these feelings were a result of my own unresolved lifelong struggle with judgment from older women in my life. This is something I was working on in my personal therapy at the time and have been doing since. I did not disclose any of this to Kim, but following each time we processed the case, I reflected on my feelings and validated myself as an experienced clinician while leaving room to continue learning from Kim and her experience.

At the time I was receiving supervision, but it focused more on my clinical work. I wish I would have brought this case up in my supervision – perhaps I was too insecure to admit I was not sure what I was doing. Since this case, one of my goals in supervision is to discuss students. Additionally, I have learned to speak directly to my students about my intentions and choices as a supervisor. This helps me self-check any personal feelings or struggles that may be impinging on the supervisory process or relationship and provides supervisees an opportunity to trust I am making decisions for their growth and not to protect my feelings. It is common for me to now say to a student, "I am going to step away from this case so you can build confidence and independence."

Kim

I was unaware of Katie's process of growth and exploration behind the scenes, most likely because of the professional boundaries we maintained. These boundaries increased my trust in her judgment. She consistently provided me with honest, reasonable feedback throughout my internship, and I had confidence in her ability to provide an external check on me if she was worried that I would cause harm. She seemed to know when to give me space to process my feelings, and I believed that she trusted me to make sound and sensitive clinical decisions. Her steadiness helped to ground me and allowed me to ultimately have greater confidence.

Experiencing Countertransference in the Legacy Songwriting Process

Kim

During our pre-arranged session, one of the questions I asked Alex and Brenda was about what they had learned from being Darby's parents. Alex immediately responded: "That life is miserable." Brenda expressed surprise at his bluntness and appeared uncomfortable, possibly even embarrassed at his willingness to speak this out loud.

My first reaction was to back away from Alex's response out of a fear that, in pursuing that line of thought further, I might create an unsafe situation for Brenda. After that impulse, however, I realized that it was possible Brenda's response was more about a fear of my judgment. I chose to lean in, to convey that it was safe and appropriate for them to share the full range of their experience. I asked Alex if he would like to say more about his response, and he talked about learning to be present for both Darby and Caitlyn when recognizing he could not fix the situation. Brenda, who had been fairly quiet up until that point, suddenly appeared to resonate with what Alex said, emoting that they had not even been able to take Darby swimming.

In those few words, she somehow expressed the lonely ocean of grief that I felt about every milestone and achievement I would never see my son experience. I immediately recognized the significance of what she said and wanted to incorporate it into their song, knowing that it would memorialize and validate a profoundly painful sentiment. I provided support about the value of including their complicated thoughts and feelings in the song, emphasizing how this project was meant to be a space for expressing what was most important to them. After a few moments, Brenda and Alex agreed to include the difficult aspects of their experience.

Katie

I remember Kim writing Darby's legacy song vividly. I could see her wrestling with herself. This signaled to me a vulnerability in Kim that I had not seen before, which happens throughout internship when feelings arise unexpectedly.[3] I supported Kim throughout the songwriting by remaining present while being careful not to intrude in a way that would disrupt her process. Again, I wanted her to learn from doing and not by being told, and I remained available as a resource to ensure no harm was occurring through that learning process. She was also seeking support from her co-intern related to music skills and songwriting, something he had more experience with. I was proud of them for working together effectively. This also allowed me to observe from a distance and support by not directly intervening, instead giving reassurance through my silence and willingness to engage when Kim asked.

Kim

When I sat down to write Darby's song, I felt alone with the weight of holding pieces of another family's story. When my child was dying, there were times when I felt I had to lie about our horrible reality to get vital support for my family and myself. Other times I spoke my truth and people responded with anger and rejection. When crafting the lyrics, I was scared that I would emphasize the wrong aspects and cause them the same type of trauma I had experienced. I recognized this as an opportunity to affirm their feelings and preserve the "realness" of their full experience and hoped that it might be protective against future invalidations.

I felt vulnerable, and seeking supervision from Katie throughout this process felt like an act of bravery. I did not want to cause harm to Darby or her family, and I recognized the importance of having external feedback because of my internal state. Katie received the song with equanimity, and while I got the impression that she was concerned in ways that she didn't verbalize, she also didn't reject my approach.

Katie

Kim presented the song to me using Brenda's words, "We never got to take you swimming," as the main hook. While I agreed with Kim's desire to include the difficult parts of Darby's life in the song, I was initially resistant to that being the climax for several reasons. First, it felt heavy and dark, different from many legacy songs I had written before. Second, I had a fear that, even though this sentiment was true for Alex and Brenda in the present moment in the midst of acute grief, it might not hold true or be how they wanted to remember the experience in the distant future. Third, I was worried that Kim was writing about her own experience in the song. However, when she sang the lyrics "so we learned to be here with you," I knew that was not her personal experience. I was reassured that, although her experience was influencing the songwriting process, she was not projecting her legacy song for her child onto Darby's family.

This was a big area of growth for me, as I now understand my initial hesitance more clearly. My discomfort with lyrics I perceived as darkness was likely my discomfort around difficult emotions and death, something I've spent a lot of time processing while working in this setting. I also now recognize my instinct to remove the family's expression of pain from the song could have invalidated their experience of a pain they will likely always remember and feel. I came to these conclusions after listening to and learning from Kim's personal experience.

Reflections

Kim

I began my internship knowing I would need to be vigilant about managing my countertransference; however, I did not understand how that countertransference could enhance the therapeutic process. Katie's curiosity about the dimensions of my experiences, trust in my ability to manage my emotions, and sensitivity in guiding and supporting my growth helped me understand the ethical clinical applications of countertransference. I saw the value that my lived experience brought to my clinical practice, and I gained a greater sense of self-efficacy. This growth allowed me to enter the profession with increased self-awareness and confidence to navigate future experiences of countertransference. I also learned what to look for when I seek out professional supervision as needed in my future career.

Katie

In reflecting on this experience, I see how I served as a steady, consistent presence throughout the therapeutic process. It was my role to be grounded during a time when Kim might not feel grounded due to countertransference. I was careful never to immediately react or disagree – even in the moments that I internally experienced discomfort – and to sit with the feelings that came up for both of us, to be curious and cautious using my own clinical experience and judgment to guide Kim, and to remain open to learning from her thoughts, ideas, and experience. More than anything, I learned to constantly evaluate my own feelings in regard to students and their processes, and to remain steady and calm through times of constant change and learning.

Summarizing Ideas and Questions for Discussion

1. Countertransference may be a positive force within the therapeutic relationship. It can be used with intention to increase sensitivity and understanding.

   a. How have you used countertransference to increase your understanding of your patients' experiences or perspectives?

b. What is a circumstance under which you could foresee potential problems arising from countertransference, and how can you prepare yourself to skillfully navigate that situation?

2. With skilled supervision, navigating countertransference can be an opportunity for students and professionals to further refine their clinical intuition. Skilled supervisors bring self-awareness to their supervisory relationships while centering the needs of the patient.

a. Think of a situation in which you were either the supervisor offering guidance or the supervisee receiving guidance about navigating countertransference. What type of guidance was most helpful?

b. Have you ever experienced transference or countertransference within a supervisory relationship and, if so, how did you approach that situation?

Notes

1 van Dernoot Lipsky, L., & Burk, C. (2009). *Trauma stewardship: An everyday guide to caring for self while caring for others.* Berrett-Koehler Publishers, Inc.

2 Eyre, L. (2019). Theoretical approaches to supervision. In M. Forinash (Ed.), *Music therapy supervision* (2nd ed., pp. 9–25). Barcelona Publishers.

3 Feiner, S. (2019). A Journey through internship supervision revisited: Roles, dynamics, and phases of the supervisory relationship. In M. Forinash (Ed.), *Music therapy supervision* (2nd ed., pp. 157–156). Barcelona Publishers.

Chapter 2

From Culture Shock to Integrating Preferred Music by Youth

An International Music Therapist in Training's Journey Towards Cultural Reflexivity

Yiqing Xiang

Abstract

Integrating client-preferred music in sessions may invite a range of lyrical content, including explicit language and topics such as sex, violence, misogyny, and drugs. This can trigger responses from the music therapist that could negatively impact the therapeutic space, especially when such lyrics are contradictory to the music therapist's cultural values. Engaging in a reflexive, culturally humble practice and thoughtfully processing countertransference can benefit future therapeutic encounters.

Tags: Professional Development

As an intern, I worked with youth (8- to 17-year-olds) with adverse experiences in an inpatient unit of a psychiatric hospital. The youth were predominantly Black, though I also served some White and Hispanic/Latinx youth. Some stayed in the hospital for several months up to a year waiting for foster care or rehabilitation placement, but most clients were receiving short-term stabilization treatment due to behavioral and emotional needs. Their diagnoses included attention deficit disorder, oppositional defiant disorder, disruptive mood dysregulation disorder, depression, and post-traumatic stress disorder.

Soon after starting my internship, I was shadowing a music therapist facilitating a group. The session was focused on communication and socialization using musical games and free dancing. At the end of the session, the lead music therapist let the group freely pick dancing songs. A 10-year-old Black girl picked Cardi B's "W.A.P.", a song with explicit sexual references (e.g., "W.A.P." is an acronym for "wet ass pussy"). The lead music therapist knew the content of the song and still chose to play the unedited version, allowing the children to express themselves creatively. The girls in the

DOI: 10.4324/9781003123798-4

group began singing the lyrics loudly and twerking along with the beat, while a few younger boys in the session seemed to have no idea what the song was about. Maybe the girls did not understand the meaning of the lyrics, but they were still attracted to the rhythm of the song.

A few seconds later, the lead music therapist decided to cut off the song because it was considered inappropriate in the hospital to play a song with explicit lyrics for children's groups. I felt shocked and awkward coming out of this experience. I couldn't believe such a sexually explicit song was being sung by such young children. This phenomenon does not usually happen in my culture. Growing up in a southern city in mainland China, I lived and was educated in a more conservative cultural environment, where we usually avoided talking or singing about sex in public.

I did not walk into this situation completely unprepared. As an international student completing music therapy clinical training in the United States (US), I applied a lot of effort to adapt and acculturate to a new culture. To deliver mental health treatments in the US, international students must gain a high level of English proficiency, cross-cultural understanding, and good communication skills.[1] I became aware of the significance of culture in clinical practice when I took a required class in my program on multiculturalism in music therapy. In addition, I had opportunities to train for three semesters in varied settings, meeting clients from diverse cultural backgrounds. I came to accept and adapt to the cultural differences between the US and my culture.

Even so, witnessing youth singing sexually explicit music was jarring. Growing up in China, I did not think much about cultural competence or cultural identity. Before I came to the US, I thought cultural differences were simply differences of ethnicity or language, but I overlooked how cultural values could cause personal bias, including "race, gender, sexual orientation, socioeconomic class, age, ability, size."[2] While my entry-level training helped expand my awareness, I nevertheless experienced culture shock coming out of that experience. Culture shock refers to when people enter into a new culture and "encounter different value systems, communication patterns, signs and symbols of social contact, and interpersonal relationship patterns."[3]

In this case, I will unpack and reflect on how my internship experiences helped me better understand cultural differences, including how my cultural values led to personal biases and intense, but productive, counter-transferences in response to my culture shock. My internship was essential for informing me about the importance of cultural reflexivity, specifically in music experiences, and helping me understand how it could influence my professional and personal growth as a music therapist.

Developing Cultural Reflexivity and Experiencing Culture Shock

English is my second language, so music became a significant bridge for me to connect with clients. When I started my internship, cultural barriers in music were the first challenge I faced, which caused a series of culture shocks. While living in China, I had access to a wide range of trending English language music, but I found that the available music was limited and narrow, with limited access to Spanish-language, jazz, country, soul, and blues songs. In addition, I had no experience working with teenagers in the US. So, while I spent time becoming familiar with general teenagers' preferred music from YouTube with titles such as "Best Hip-Hop and Rap Songs Playlists 2020," I soon learned that while rap and hip-hop were the dominant genres, the youth often preferred different artists.

This cultural difference, coupled with my formal training in classical music, led me to feel significantly limited in my musical skills for clinical practice. Thankfully, experiential classes in my music therapy training exposed me to different genres of music. I had opportunities to exchange music with students from different cultural backgrounds, learn about others' music (e.g., language, lyrics, cultural characteristics, history, etc.), and replicate different genres of music. Still, I found there were dimensions to cultural differences I was unable to prepare for until working with clients in person. As I became familiar with the popular artists the youth at my internship listened to, I was shocked by the openness of the artists singing and rapping about violence, sex, and drug use. The session I described earlier left the biggest impression on me. It was the first time I had heard a group of youths singing a sexually explicit song. I heard this song on the internet when it was first released and felt astonished by the way Cardi B described the experience of sex in a song.

I returned to the office after the session, and the shock of the young girls singing and dancing along with "W.A.P." had my head spinning with confusion. *Did they understand the meaning of the sexually suggestive song? Why did they feel attracted to this song?* The children seemed to benefit from the song: they were highly engaged in the music through singing and dancing, and it enhanced the group's cohesion. And yet, it felt incorrect to play the song.

My cultural identity was shaken because music containing explicit content about violence, sex, and drug use is prohibited in Chinese culture. In that moment, I was not sure how to reconcile my unsafe feelings while still practicing a client-centered approach. I struggled to honor my culturally transmitted values in the context of the youths' cultural values and expectations while maintaining my personal sense of safety. With the musical bridge connecting me and the clients broken, the culture shock of the clients' preferred popular music became an obstacle in my own sessions that could not be ignored.

Navigating Struggles With the Clients' Music Selections

To increase engagement and develop relationships, I largely utilized the youths' preferred music to plan music experiences, such as musical games, emotion identification, songwriting, and lyric discussions. However, I felt challenged at the start by the clients' music selections, especially when there was a lot of explicit content in rap music. There was one embarrassing occasion in a female teenager group when I played the explicit version of a youth-chosen song before listening to it. In China, there are no explicit versions, so I did not know to play the edited versions of songs in session. A technician eventually walked in to interrupt the session and clarify that the girls in this group could not listen to that kind of music.

After that, I started to use the word "inappropriate" to describe music with explicit content for several reasons. First, I learned it was a common, yet unspoken, rule for all staff to play edited versions of popular music for youth in hospitals or schools. I felt uncomfortable pushing back against that expectation because I already felt vulnerable as an intern and an international student. Second, these songs were not consistent with my values or worldview. For instance, the description of female genitalia and women being the dominant partner in sex reflected a society becoming more open about discussing human sexuality, a progressiveness for which I was not initially prepared. There are many Chinese-language songs that depict intimacy, but few with direct sexual descriptions. Third, calling it "inappropriate" allowed me to project my cultural values onto the youth so that I could feel more comfortable. I found listening to "W.A.P." unpleasant because, as a privileged adult who could make choices in my life, I was not sure that youth with adverse experiences would acquire healthy sex education from this song. Similarly, I was worried they would develop unhealthy coping strategies – such as drinking alcohol – if they resonated with the seeming message from "WRLD On Drugs" by Future & Juice WRLD that sobriety was equivalent to being dead.

However, I never got the chance to understand how or why those young girls connected with "W.A.P." because the music therapist shut off the song. With neither of us following up, I took time afterwards to consider what drew them to the song. It is possible Cardi B's powerful voice and the song's strong beats engaged them even if they did not fully understand the lyrics. I also researched other perspectives about this song from content creators on YouTube and discussion boards on popular music forums, learning the song could be viewed as feminist and empowering. I saw this in lyrics that broke stereotypical images of women by forcibly pushing back against the notion that they're most desirable when they're cooking and cleaning. When considering these alternative takes on the importance of "W.A.P.", I had to confront my culturally informed internal biases and assumptions and their conflict with women being empowered by singing about a private body part in the public domain.

Identifying and Working Through Countertransference

As I processed my internship in supervision, I started recognizing my countertransferences with the music I had begun calling "inappropriate." When I first heard explicit music in the youth group session, I quickly developed a sense of discomfort and worry, as if I were doing something that was not allowed. This may be because I went to traditional schools in China all the way through my undergraduate degree, where students usually regarded the teacher as an authority and did not question a teacher's words. Hence, when I faced underage clients playing music that clashed with my cultural values, it felt wrong to produce or listen to music that would have been banned by the authorities in my culture, and I projected myself as an authoritarian teacher in the therapy space.

As a defense mechanism, I initially refused to accept that this music made me uncomfortable and similarly refused to learn why clients related to the explicit music. I even avoided building relationships with the youth. Once, when a young girl chose a song that explicitly mentioned sexuality, I told her: "We need to set boundaries for not playing this song in a group session and in a hospital. I'm not going to play songs about sexuality." My rationale was that since I did not agree with what these songs expressed, I would not know how to help clients process the lyrics and did not want the youth to develop maladaptive coping strategies or behaviors that reflected the values in these songs.

This way of setting boundaries through direct rejection was not going to improve our therapeutic relationship. More importantly, it unbalanced the power between me and the clients by depriving them of their right to listen to their preferred music. It could have been potentially harmful, because it might trigger someone who had, in the past, experienced a lack of choice and agency from a traumatic event. When I refused to play the song, the girl looked very disappointed and asked me questioningly: "Not playing sexuality song?" I remained silent and did not know what to say. I had put my feelings first and ignored her need to listen to this song, depriving her of the opportunity to engage with music she identified with and the therapeutic benefits it may have had for her.

I also resisted understanding their music because it did not meet my ideals. At that time, I had hoped to be a "good" music therapist and have youth only listen to music that reflected what I believed to be healthy cultural norms and values[3] (i.e., music that made them "happy"). However, after seeing how the youths shut down when I used the "setting boundaries" excuse and refused to play their preferred explicit music, I realized how resisting their music based on my cultural values was not a long-term solution for resolving this internal conflict. I brought my concerns to my internship supervisor, who asked me: "Why don't you think about what they need instead of what you want to do for them?" This helped me recognize that something deep inside me needed to be unpacked, namely how my countertransference and resistance to explicit music turned me away from a client-centered and culturally reflexive practice.

I began considering my use of the word "inappropriate" to describe preferred client genres, and questioned whether defining "appropriateness" was really about their needs or if it was about meeting mine. As my practice shifted from framing music as "inappropriate," I experienced pressure to continue using that language because of its common usage in the hospital. I had adopted the term from other staff and used it throughout my internship to identify music that contrasted with my cultural values. Yet, as I reflected on what I defined as "inappropriate" and why, I gained a clear understanding of how my cultural values were impacting the potential therapeutic benefits of using explicit music. With this new clarity and support from my supervisor, I wanted to speak with the nurses and hospital staff to advocate for using explicit music in sessions.

Ultimately, though, I did not engage in this level of advocacy because of my status as an intern. I felt that, since I was not yet board-certified, my word would not be taken seriously. I had also barely acquired any experiences in my life to advocate for myself or for what I think is beneficial for the clients. In hindsight, this could have been an opportunity for me to think critically and discuss the clinical language that I had learned from other staff in the context of what I was learning from the clients. Nonetheless, I removed the word "inappropriate" from the ways that I spoke about this music with clients and other professionals.

Having made this shift, I focused on developing insight about how the youth connected to explicit music. It did not seem to bother the youth whether I played the edited version or not. They still enjoyed the music by singing the lyrics, dancing to the rhythm, and laughing with peers. Through verbal discussions with the youth – the kind we did not have following the use of "W.A.P." in session – I learned that sometimes their connection had nothing to do with the lyrical content, especially for the younger children who were not developmentally ready to understand the full meaning of the lyrics. Other times their connection was through the singer and their background, and the community aspect of the song, such as associated social dances (e.g., "Tootsie Slide" by Drake). Once, a teenage girl chose a rap song with a lot of profanity in the lyrics. I asked this girl why she liked this song and she responded: "I just like it. There are no reasons for liking a song."

As these insights developed, I reflected on my cultural values[4] as a precursor to understanding the client's culture. As I mentioned earlier during the post-session reflection, I grew up in a conservative cultural environment; people rarely discussed sex in public in China compared to the US. In addition, China has very strict drug laws, including marijuana. Artists who smoked marijuana would be banned from the market forever. Therefore, drugs never appear in music in China. Guns are not allowed in China either, so youth are generally less exposed to violence and trauma than in societies that have a gun culture. When these cultural values were expressed in popular music in the US, they went against what I was taught and what was reinforced in me.

After comparing my experience with the youth from the US, I became aware that my countertransference and resistance were normal. Once I put aside my bias and rooted cultural upbringings, I tried to listen and accept the explicit music with an open mind. After a long period of reflection that has continued through the writing of this case, I gained deeper insights into how youth resonated with explicit music. They tended to be exposed to an environment where drugs and violence were more present, and I wanted to be more connected to the emotions they drew from the music.

When I asked the youth to use color markers to circle lines or words of lyrics representing emotions, a lot of times I was surprised about their capabilities to elaborate on emotions from the songs. When I started to read the lyrical content of some rap music from which the youth got the most emotions, it was like reading stories. I remembered once when we were verbally processing the lyrics from the song "Empty" by Juice WRLD, where he sang about solving problems with Styrofoam, which refers to drinking a potentially lethal alcoholic beverage called lean,[5] and shared about feeling extreme emptiness (e.g., "a black hole"). A 15-year-old male commented: "This is my life." In another session, I facilitated lyric discussion to process the connection in the youth group, and one male teenager, in response to "Cold Summer" by Fabolous, stated: "It is not a happy or sad song – the song tells a life experience that I am related to." These songs I once thought of as inappropriate content accurately described their real lives and feelings.

Behind the Lyrical Content

In addition to describing adverse life experiences that resonated with youth, the lyrics in rap and hip-hop songs selected by clients often provided them opportunities to hear experiences they did not have in their real lives.[6] A lot of rappers also sing about rap taking them from poverty to riches[6], which can be a motivation for youth coming from socioeconomically disadvantaged spaces. In particular, I acquired a new understanding of the impact of rap music on Black communities, such as rappers' advocacy for social and political change.[7]

Music containing language depicting violence or gang activity may be considered by some as inappropriate for youth, out of fear it might encourage them to become involved in violence, and such content may indeed elicit traumatic events and triggered responses.[6] Also, rap and hip-hop are not only the music genres that reference violent acts. However, music therapy provided the youth I worked with a platform to identify the impact of explicit content by verbally processing potential triggers and discussing corresponding coping strategies. They also found that this content resonated with their personal lives and provided them an emotional outlet.[8] The listening experience provided an environment for self-expression that was perceived as physically and emotionally safe.[6]

For example, in one group we listened to "1-800-273-8255" by Logic, which had lyrics about wanting to die. We discussed how the lyrics did not mean to encourage audiences to hurt themselves or attempt suicide, but rather depicted an extreme hopelessness. This led to the youth speaking about what they might do if they had suicidal thoughts. Sometimes, if I identified a song as explicit and wondered how the clients related to it, especially rap music containing lots of slang I did not understand, I would authentically disclose my interpretation of the song based on what I understood from the lyrics and ask the clients if they had different interpretations of the song. My cultural humility made it easier for them to open up and verbally process.

That said, the youth were often hesitant to verbally express their feelings or experiences. To stimulate verbal dialogue after music, I prepared a series of probing questions but did not receive much response. In fact, the youth often preferred listening to music in group sessions rather than verbally expressing themselves. After continued supervision and discussion with other music therapists, I realized listening to music might be a safer space of expression in a group than verbalization. Asking too many probing questions was another way my countertransference as an authoritarian teacher emerged; I had assigned myself a power that pushed the youth to talk. To balance that power dynamic, I began respecting their silence after the music. I provided choices in the therapeutic process for them to say "yes" or "no" to what they deemed helpful, such as choice of music, choice of activity (e.g., instrumental playing and songwriting), and creative ways of self-expression (e.g., poetry, coloring, and singing).[4]

Conclusions

Though this case focuses on the development of cultural reflexivity from the experience of an international student in a new culture, I encourage new professionals from all cultural locations to reflect on their identity and values when developing a deep understanding of clients' preferred music. Even in writing this chapter, I found articles by English-speaking music therapists in the US who also navigated feelings of fear and concerns about inappropriateness when using rap with youth.[6,7,8] I felt reassured that I had these feelings, not just because English was my second language or because I came from another country. These articles influenced me to listen to explicit music with a critical ear and look deeper than the words I had previously labeled as "inappropriate." It also helped me understand that the work of cultural humility is not reserved for people of color, immigrants, or members of other marginalized communities.

When identifying and processing my countertransference toward different cultural values in music, I had to first realize that it was a natural process in a therapeutic encounter. I further learned that my countertransference had the potential to be a positive force in the therapeutic process, and that my culture shock was an opening to more deeply understanding and connecting with my clients. I am still constantly learning about my cultural values and how they interact with the cultures around me, and this process of reflection and reflexivity encourages me to embrace the differences between me and those I am working with as a resource to be accessed.

Summarizing Ideas and Questions for Discussion

1. Music therapists may experience culture shock when encountering clients' preferred music. To better understand a client's culture and enhance cultural reflexivity and practice cultural humility, music therapists can reflect on their cultural values and beliefs.

   a. What are some differences in cultural values you identify between you and your clients?
   b. When do you recognize cultural issues that may influence your therapeutic relationships with your clients?
   c. What helps you develop cultural reflexivity in your practice?

2. Music therapists may experience intense emotions towards a client's preferred music and project those emotions onto the client. A therapist's countertransference can influence the therapeutic relationship; however, identifying and working through the countertransference caused by cultural conflicts can transform countertransference into a positive tool for enhancing the therapeutic relationship.

   a. What personal reflections have you done related to a client's preferred music?
   b. How does your personal reflection on music influence your use of music?
   c. What countertransference do you identify when using music in your clinical practice?
   d. How may your countertransference influence your musical relationships with clients?

Notes

1 Nilson, J. E., & Anderson, M. Z. (2004). Supervising International students: The role of acculturation, role ambiguity, and multicultural discussions. *American Psychological Association, 35*(3), 306–312. https://doi.org/10.1037/0735-7028.35.3.306
2 Hahna, N. D. (2017). Reflecting on personal bias. In A. White-Pleaux & X. Tan (Eds.), *Cultural intersections in music therapy: Music, health, and the person* (pp. 43–56). Barcelona Publishers.

3 Wu, H. P., Garza, E., & Guzman, N. (2015). International student's challenge and adjustment to college. *Education Research International, 2015*, 1–9. https://doi.org/10.1155/2015/202753

4 Heiderscheit, A., & Murphy, K. (2021). Trauma-Informed care in music therapy: Principles, guidelines, and a clinical case illustration. *Music Therapy Perspectives, 39*(2), 142–151. https://doi.org/10.1093/mtp/miab011

5 SMF (2019, March 9). Juice WRLD's "empty" lyrics meaning. *Song Meanings and Facts*. www.songmeaningsandfacts.com/juice-wrlds-empty-lyrics-meaning/

6 Austin, A. (2021). Hip hop's influence on African American youth (prospectus). In J. Townsend (Ed.), *Understanding literacy in our lives: First year writing perspectives*. MSL Academic Endeavors. https://pressbooks.ulib.csuohio.edu/understanding-literacy-in-our-lives/chapter/5-4-2-hip-hops-influence-on-african-american-youth-prospectus/

7 Wilson, N. (2018). Rap music as a positive influence on Black youth and American politics. *Advanced Writing: Pop Culture Intersection, 21*. https://scholarcommons.scu.edu/engl_176/2

8 Fletcher, J. S. (2018). Rap in music therapy with Appalachian youth with adverse childhood experiences: Struggle, reflection, and self-work as a music therapist. *Voices: A World Forum for Music Therapy, 18*(4). https://doi.org/10.15845/voices.v18i4.2591

Chapter 3

Cases From the Heart

A Journey of Vulnerability, Trust, and Growth for Intern and Supervisor

Sara Langenberger and Spencer Hardy

Abstract

The relationship between an intern and their supervisor is complex and dynamic, constantly evolving through each phase of the internship process. When approached collaboratively, the supervisory relationship becomes a space for intern and supervisor to experience parallel or shared professional growth, requiring courage from both as they navigate being vulnerable in the supervision space in context of the trust they have cultivated in each other. In this case, the intern and supervisor relationship evolved across three specific cases from an infant-centered and family-centered approach addressing the needs of infants on ventricular assist devices.

Tags: Clinical Supervision; Therapeutic Relationship

As music therapists rooted in family-centered, infant-centered,[1] and eclectic approaches, this case will focus on an intern's (Sara's) professional development and how her supervisor (Spencer) supported her in that growth across three similar cases with widely different needs and outcomes. This process emerged through work with three infants with congenital heart defects (CHD), the most common type of birth defect and one of the leading causes of birth defect-associated infant illness and death.[2] Each of these infants had a surgically implanted ventricular assist device (VAD), a mechanical pump supporting heart function and blood flow. This surgically implanted device is placed into one or both ventricles of the heart and can help patients survive as a 'Bridge to Transplant' or for their heart to return to normal function.[3,4]

Sara

Before I began my internship, I set a personal goal to be as open to the learning process as possible, which meant saying "yes" to opportunities even

DOI: 10.4324/9781003123798-5

when apprehensive, leaning into my feelings of discomfort, being open to feedback, and asking as many questions as I could. Supervision was an area of internship that gave me a safe space to grow musically, personally, and clinically, and I found it meaningful to be vulnerable in supervision and not stifle feelings that came up throughout the process. Amazing things happened for me in supervision when we started to view it as a journey of mutual growth rather than that of the assessor and the assessed.

Spencer

As a supervisor, I strive to meet interns where they are in their personal growth and clinical skill development to help them develop self-awareness and trust in their therapeutic skills alongside a sense of autonomy and readiness. This requires both structure and support to find the nuance between setting expectations on a fixed timeline and allowing growth at their own pace. To accomplish this, I provide opportunities for explorations of personal growth, readiness and confidence, clinical instincts, countertransference, and therapeutic relationships. It is a process requiring trust and vulnerability on both sides, with the end goal being the intern developing self-awareness, autonomy, and readiness.

Chadwick

Chadwick was a 2-month-old Pacific Islander male with cardiomyopathy. Due to the unique nature of his CHD, a BiVAD (one VAD for each ventricle of his heart) was surgically implanted. After being on the device for over three months, he received a heart transplant.

Spencer

In our initial session with Chadwick, I asked Sara to lead. I could tell she did not feel confident assessing such a small infant, but I felt sure that with guidance, she would be ready. She had observed several sessions like this one, and I could talk her through in the moment how to shift the music and respond to his cues. Her observation skills and awareness were highly developed, and she just needed that little push to start applying those skills.

Chadwick was orally intubated and currently weaning off sedation and pain medications. As we approached the crib side, he was awake and alert. When Sara gently introduced her voice and guitar, Chadwick oriented towards her and the music. His eyes widened and locked on her from the moment she began to play. Sara was very aware of his subtle responses and adjusted her volume and tempo throughout to avoid overstimulation. Chadwick and Sara began to entrain with Sara's tempo aligning with Chadwick's heartbeat, and vice-versa.

Sara

Even years later, I can picture this first session with Chadwick so clearly. At this point in my internship, I had observed several assessments with young infants but had not conducted one independently. When Spencer told me that I would be leading this session on my own, I was immediately filled with anxiety. *Would I know what to do? What if something went wrong?*

As we opened the door, the large crib made Chadwick seem so small. I quietly began to sing and play a "hello" song while visually monitoring for any signs of overstimulation. When Chadwick turned his gaze toward me, we made eye contact, and my anxiety went away. Suddenly, we were just two human beings sharing the same moment in time. I adjusted my playing to any signs Chadwick gave me (e.g., entraining my tempo to his heart rate and changing accompaniment patterns depending on his responses), and as he began to fall asleep, he smiled at me over his endotracheal tube.

After this initial assessment, we determined that Chadwick's primary treatment goals would be increasing relaxation, reducing pain/anxiety/agitation, and providing positive environmental stimulation. His family was not available to participate in the treatment planning, but these goals aligned with the referral from the medical team. Chadwick was frequently agitated due to pain and discomfort, and we focused on helping to calm him while he received routine medical care (e.g., taking temperature, blood pressure, changing diapers), which for infants can disrupt sleep and be uncomfortable. Music therapy can provide support similar to four-handed care, where positive touch/stimulation is provided simultaneously with medical care.[5]

After working with Chadwick for about a month, his needs shifted as he began to better tolerate being awake and adjust to life with the VAD. The treatment goal changed from increasing relaxation to providing developmental play/stimulation. To support this new type of engagement, we incorporated recreative music therapy into the sessions.

Spencer

Developmental play with such a small infant was still new to Sara, and in our first session of this type we introduced small percussion instruments for Chadwick to explore. I could see Sara's hesitance to engage Chadwick. I encouraged her to put down the guitar in order to provide more hand under hand support for Chadwick, and just play! As a supervisor, these types of sessions are simple and yet so powerful, often resulting in an intern's "a-ha" moment when they begin to notice all the subtle cues and responses that elicit a dynamic interplay between patient and therapist. When talking Sara through things in the moment, I offered adjustments and pointed out the way Chadwick was responding to her cues. I love these moments when I can support an intern's growth at a critical developmental period. I saw Sara's base of understanding grow exponentially with this first experience supporting such a young, fragile infant. Additionally, we had now opened the door for a new level of engagement with Chadwick, addressing important developmental milestones.

Sara

One of the most unique parts I have found about working with infants is the feeling that I was growing with them. As Chadwick became more medically stable, he was able to engage in more age-appropriate activities. And as I became more comfortable with my clinical skills and decision-making, I was able to take more risks in my development. Being asked to put down the guitar and take a hands-on approach was a terrifying request. I felt vulnerable and exposed. The guitar often acted as a barrier or shield between myself and the patient and, without it, I felt defenseless with no clinical tool to help me. However, pushing me to put down the guitar helped me to see the therapeutic tools that I had besides the guitar. I no longer required my shield because I had other skill sets at my disposal. I was so afraid of hurting Chadwick by accident, but Spencer helped me understand that infants are tougher than we think and will let you know if they don't want to do something.

Hudson

Hudson was a 12-day-old white male with hypoplastic left heart syndrome. He was placed on a single ventricle VAD at 24 days old and waited over five months before receiving his heart transplant. Our initial assessment with Hudson took place before the placement of his VAD. He was intubated but not on any pain medication or recovering from surgery. When we arrived for our initial assessment, our visit coincided with his nurse and respiratory therapist performing routine care. Due to the strain that COVID-19 placed on the family, no parents were present at the bedside, and Hudson appeared to be very agitated with a high heart rate and visible facial grimaces.

Sara

Pulling from my previous experience with Chadwick, I began with slow, arpeggiated guitar and soft humming. Hudson became increasingly agitated, demonstrating signs of high auditory sensitivity such as increased movement, grimacing, and increased fussing. I decided to stop humming, leaving only slow arpeggiated guitar, and Hudson quickly began to calm to the music. Despite my growth in working with Chadwick, there was still quite a bit of apprehension and anxiety when it came to clinical work. Because each infant was so unique it felt like a totally new world with each patient. Spencer helped me to make the connections between patients and encouraged me to find their similarities as well as acknowledge what made them unique. Following our initial session, we determined that the primary goals would be to reduce anxiety/agitation, provide sleep support, and increase auditory tolerance.

Spencer

When Sara and I began working with Hudson, there was a level of confidence and independence in Sara that I had not seen with Chadwick. This let me step back and give Sara more freedom to step in to assess Hudson's needs in the moment and set goals after that initial session. That sense of protectiveness I have over "my patients" must shift in order for Sara to have a sense of partnership, collaboration, and shared responsibility. I felt proud of her initiative and positive risk-taking with Hudson.

Twelve days after we met him, Hudson was placed on a single ventricle VAD. Post-surgery, we focused on pain management and sleep support. Hudson began to tolerate more auditory stimulation. He would initially present as agitated or distressed but would almost immediately calm to the music. In subtle ways, Hudson responded differently to the music than Chadwick, and Sara began to see the way even very young infants may have different musical needs. Sara and I continued to work on how she could musically adjust by avoiding providing the same songs and interventions "prescriptively" for each infant and shifting in response to individual needs presented in the moment.

Sara

We had almost exclusively worked on pain management and sleep support during the first three months, so while we had some idea about what Hudson's musical preferences and personality were like, they truly emerged in the last months of his treatment. In a session during month four, I finally had a breakthrough when Hudson smiled at me. Up to that point, Hudson had been agitated or asleep during sessions, and this was the first opportunity to see him exhibit playful and joyful behaviors. This was also the first session where Hudson started in a calm state. By being free of pain and awake, we were finally able to connect interpersonally. Up until that point, we had been connecting exclusively through adjusting the music in response to his physiological changes and vital signs. I felt proud of having moved through my initial anxiety to be present and responsive to Hudson during this long period of physical distress. It was during this time that I discovered Hudson's unique musical preferences, which were incorporated into future sessions. There was a change in the therapeutic relationship when Hudson exhibited social responses, introducing a human connection we had previously been lacking. Up until this point, all of our work was primarily based on vital signs, but now we were able to connect in new ways and expand our assessment to include signs of overstimulation and expressions of happiness, discomfort, or pain.

Spencer and I worked as a team during the subsequent sessions, taking turns either playing guitar or utilizing hand under hand techniques to help Hudson work on developmental goals and build strength. Prior to each session, we would typically discuss goals, but Spencer allowed the therapeutic process to unfold naturally and without a mapped-out session plan. It could sometimes feel intimidating to be without a solid plan, but I found comfort in knowing this was a safe learning environment where I could try new things.

Spencer

Sara was very dedicated to her work with Hudson. She checked on him regularly and could clearly articulate that he was a higher-priority patient due to the acuity of his needs and goals. So it was a natural transition when, without hesitation, she began leading some sessions independently without me present. His care still felt like a partnership; however, in supervision, we continued to debrief on Hudson's progress. Sara would articulate which approaches she had used, process his present needs, and discuss how to best support him. Sara's ability to self-reflect and clearly articulate her approach had developed in a way that was exciting and refreshing. When Hudson began presenting as more alert and showing signs of readiness for stimulation and play, it was a huge milestone that opened up new opportunities for bonding and connection within the therapeutic relationship. At this time, I continued to go with Sara to her sessions intermittently, helping her transition these goals of care.

About halfway through our fifth month of treatment, Hudson received a heart transplant. He developed significant postoperative complications, but recovered and was eventually transferred to a step-down unit before being discharged.

Sara

I learned from working with Hudson that treatment can be a team effort, not only between the medical team but between intern and supervisor. During our initial sleep support and pain management sessions, Spencer and I would sing and hum together so that Hudson could hear us over the constant noise of his VAD. Those moments felt like a musical partnership. When we processed in supervision, we focused both on how the work with Hudson was developing and the emotions that come with seeing a baby in pain and connected to a medical device.

Seeing a child in pain was, and continues to be, a very visceral, human experience for me. Bearing witness to these events took a heavy toll on my emotions and self-care was important during this time. When we began working on developmental play, Spencer and I would work in tandem to provide both musical and tactile support to Hudson. In those moments, we weren't only supervisor and intern, but rather co-therapists working together as equals to provide the best support possible. As co-therapists, a natural balance of leading and following would emerge that had developed from the strong supervisory relationship we had cultivated in the preceding months. That foundational relationship helped make the transition to independently facilitating sessions much easier. Spencer challenged my clinical skill development while providing a safety net that allowed me to make mistakes. This supported the development of clinical and personal confidence that stayed with me throughout my internship.

Amy

Around the time we were seeing Hudson, we were referred to a new infant with CHD. Amy was a 22-day-old white female with severe structural abnormalities of the heart. She was almost immediately placed on a single ventricle VAD at just 7 days old. We first met Amy when she was 15 days post-VAD placement. Amy was in her mother's arms when we arrived. Our first session with Amy was a powerful opportunity to connect with Amy's mother and to hold space for her processing in response to her daughter's medical condition and hospitalization. Spencer provided musical and emotional support to Amy's mother while Amy slept quietly. For Sara, because of COVID and the strict visitor policy, this was her first infant session that was truly family-oriented.

Sara

It can be an intimidating experience to talk to parents on what is often the worst day of their life, and I appreciated seeing how Spencer engaged with Amy's mom and provided support to her. When we arrived for our next session, Amy was awake, calm, and alert, so we began to play guitar softly. Amy became quickly overstimulated and only tolerated about five minutes of gentle guitar playing before becoming agitated with an increased heart rate. Almost all of our sessions with Amy over the next two months would look very similar. Spencer and I tried everything we could think of to get her to engage with the music (e.g., humming, solo guitar, a cappella, and different musical styling), but nothing appeared to benefit her. I couldn't help but feel like a failure.

Spencer

I struggled with finding a way to soothe Amy. Something that seemed to work one day did not appear to work the next, and it began to feel futile. There were large chunks of time when we did not see Amy because of various complications she was having, and we struggled to help her develop a familiarity with the music. Navigating supervision with Sara around this time was difficult for me, as I myself was unsure of my clinical decision-making. I had to allow my uncertainty and vulnerability to be present during supervision and not be self-conscious about sharing that with Sara.

This modeling and authenticity are important to me in the supervisory relationship. My ability to model and share in that uncertainty with Sara contributes to growth in both of us as clinicians, but also allows Sara to see that uncertainty in assessment and ongoing treatment can be a normal part of the therapy process.

Sara

I remember processing these sessions with Amy during supervision with Spencer. There was a feeling of helplessness during that time, that no matter what I did during sessions, everything was overstimulating for Amy. While certain aspects of our work with Chadwick and Hudson were challenging, this period with Amy was frustrating and made me feel like a failure. *Had I learned anything from the prior two patients? Does this "failure" in Amy's sessions make me a bad therapist? Am I even cut out for this work?* I wrestled with these thoughts and brought them into supervision. Spencer encouraged me to think about the role of assessment with infants, and to think about each session, regardless of the outcome, as an opportunity to learn something new rather than an opportunity for failure. Through that lens, I began to see how Amy was informing us of her boundaries and letting us know what she could or couldn't tolerate.

Spencer

I found myself navigating Sara's genuine anxiety about causing harm to her patient. We were constantly assessing for signs of overstimulation, and then shifting and minimizing our approaches as necessary. As a student, it was completely understandable that Sara did not feel comfortable leading – mirroring my own discomfort at the time – and often questioned why we were continuing to see this patient. I focused on guiding Sara to see that what we were doing did have positive implications and reassure that we could continue to assess Amy's needs without causing harm. This situation certainly brought up much of my concern about what I could be doing to better support Amy. In supervision, I began to speak openly with Sara about my doubts and concerns, letting her know that such insecurities are not exclusive to interns. This shared vulnerability opened an authentic dialogue on how we could best support Amy and her family.

Around the end of month three of Amy's admission, following several weeks where Amy was too medically fragile to receive any therapies, we received a call to come to see her. For the first time, Amy was totally clear of any infection and was medically stable, with the exception of a CPAP machine that provided her with extra breathing support.

Sara

When we finally returned to see Amy, I remember my hands shook as I picked up the guitar and started to slowly pluck the strings. I looked down at her as I played and, to our total shock, she was sitting there comfortably looking up at her mobile. I tentatively began singing "Twinkle, Twinkle" and Amy's eyes started to move in my direction, with the rest of her head soon to follow. Amy's eyes locked with mine and she began to smile. For the first time, Amy appeared to be physically and emotionally well, and the big, gummy smile that spread across her face wouldn't stop from that moment on.

Spencer

At this time, I felt a powerful shift in Sara's role with Amy. It was clear that Sara's work in supervision to better understand her role with Amy was paying off. I was no longer the primary music therapist, and Sara quickly and confidently stepped into that role. Sara's growth and development working with Chadwick and Hudson had paved the way for a much more independent and dominant role at this point in her internship. Over the next few months, I was able to step back and guide Sara as she became more confident in her support of Amy, with Sara eventually seeing her independently.

Over months four and five, we began providing Amy with opportunities for developmental play. We worked on tracking, grasping, and encouraging her to reach. She quickly began to recognize our voices and faces. As soon as Amy saw us, that beautiful smile would appear, and she was ready.

Sara

By month six, Amy was scheduled for a heart transplant. In my final session with Amy before her transplant, I sat down on the floor next to her and began to play her our "hello" song. Just like in our session all those months ago, Amy's eyes raised to meet mine and that big grin appeared once again. She never broke eye contact with me and started to excitedly vocalize. I had never heard Amy vocalize before, and so I sang "If All the Raindrops" to support her to continue. I didn't know it at the time, but that would be my last session with Amy where she was awake and alert.

Amy's heart transplant was a success, but she soon developed severe postoperative complications. Five days post-transplant, we were called to help with agitation and pain. I began to quietly play my guitar and sing our "hello" song. Amy was breathing rapidly, and Spencer suggested we only sing to her a capella. In our work with medically fragile infants, we typically began with simple musical structures and gradually transitioned to more complex ones in a process:

1. humming grounding tones
2. humming a familiar melody
3. singing a familiar melody on an *oo* or *ah* vowel sound
4. singing a familiar song/melody with words
5. singing and playing simple guitar accompaniment (triple meter finger picking)
6. singing and strumming together

Amy began to show signs of agitation as we added complexity, and we decided to remove layers of stimulus to not add to an already overstimulating environment. The nurse encouraged us to hold her hands, and standing on either side Spencer and I began to sing as we held her hands. The goal was to cover her with a "blanket" of familiar sounds to help her feel secure, grounded, and safe. Soon after we began to sing, Amy became visibly more relaxed, closed her eyes, and fell asleep.

There was no way to prepare for a moment like this prior to experiencing it. Amy's parents were unable to be with her at this moment, and she was in pain and scared. Seeing all of the machines, tubing, wires, and drains attached to an infant who had been smiling and playing just days before was both frightening and sad. Spencer and I continued to provide her support and comfort with voices that, after months of careful and consistent work, she had become familiar with. In that moment, I could see the transformative power of music and the therapeutic relationship, even with someone so small and so fragile. This ended up being my last session with Amy due to the conclusion of my internship.

Spencer

As a supervisor, having Sara conclude her internship while Amy was still hospitalized was quite challenging. On the one hand, Sara had the opportunity to see Amy finally get her heart transplant and to celebrate that win before leaving her internship. But on the other hand, Amy was in kidney failure and continuing to decline. Soon after Sara's internship ended, I was informed that Amy did not have a lot of time left. I provided memory-making and legacy support for the family, including a heartbeat recording and live music while family members and staff said their goodbyes.

Navigating the ethical boundaries of HIPAA and whether or not it is appropriate to keep a former intern updated on their patient's progress is challenging, particularly when a patient begins to decline and ultimately passes away. After Amy passed away, I called Sara to tell her. After our call, Sara texted me and said: "That day when we held her hands and sang while she went to sleep will stay with me forever." It was painful and sad, but ultimately meaningful to support such a resilient and compassionate student through the significant loss of a patient. This process was a reminder that as a supervisor I am constantly teaching and guiding interns, not just during sessions or in supervision, but also in how we build and maintain our relationships and continue the mentoring relationship after internship.

Conclusion

These three cases were transformative for us both in varying ways and pushed us clinically and professionally. Sara matured and individuated over the course of her internship through her work with Chadwick, Hudson, and Amy. Similarly, Spencer was challenged to introspect and grow as a supervisor. These parallel processes required a level of trust and vulnerability between both intern and supervisor. Each infant developed their own musical personality and connection to the clinicians. With all three infants, the role of music and the nature of our therapeutic relationships were unique.

Sara

As an intern, these cases challenged me in every aspect of my life. Musically, because all three of them had distinct musical personalities, I had to learn a lot about adapting new repertoires in the moment. Clinically, working with medically fragile infants pushed me to develop skills responsive to each patient's changing medical status from day to day. Personally, I was challenged to remain grounded and focused while moving through the intense emotions these cases evoked. However, I knew I had a support system with my supervisor, who created a space for me to grow through trying new things. This, in turn, fostered a positive attitude for continued education that I maintain as a professional. Internship was one of the most difficult periods of my life, but it was ultimately an experience that helped me to become a better clinician and human being. I will always remember these patients and be grateful for the time Spencer and I had working with these patients and families.

Spencer

In a lot of ways, these three cases were not patients I "taught" Sara about, but rather learned from right alongside her. Navigating new experiences as a clinician while simultaneously supporting and supervising Sara challenged me to expand my awareness and responsibility, both to my patients and interns. In these moments, I learned alongside Sara by reviewing the relevant literature, consulting with the multidisciplinary team in the cardiac ICU, and engaging in supervision to ensure my learning and growth process could serve as a model for Sara.

Sara pushed and challenged me through her curiosity, tenaciousness, and genuine concern for the wellbeing of each patient. We experienced a natural shift in our relationship over these cases, as Sara assumed greater responsibility first as a co-therapist and then as the primary music therapist. Through this dynamic collaboration, we were better able to facilitate music therapy that had a meaningful impact on each infant's quality of life.

This chapter is dedicated to Chadwick, Hudson, and in memory of Amy.

Summarizing Ideas and Questions for Discussion

1. The personal, clinical, and musical growth that occurs during supervision is vital to the development of both new professionals and supervisors.

    a. Students, in what ways can you grow/foster personal, clinical, and musical skills to achieve the most growth during your practicum and internship?
    b. Supervisors, in what ways can you facilitate a space of learning where vulnerability and authenticity are encouraged?
    c. What are important qualities interns and supervisors can bring to the supervision process to ensure a successful learning environment that effectively and competently delivers music therapy services?

2. Supervisors and interns stand to learn from one another as they process and move through different clinical situations together.

    a. Students, what are ways you have, or wish you had, experienced collaborative growth with your supervisor?
    b. Supervisors, what are ways you have, or wish you had, experienced collaborative growth with a student?
    c. Aspiring supervisors, how do you envision an experience of collaborative growth with future students?

Notes

1 Shoemark, H. (2013). Full term hospitalized newborns. In J. Bradt (Ed.), *Guidelines for music therapy practice in pediatric care* (pp. 116–151). Barcelona Publishers.
2 Centers for Disease Control and Prevention (CDC) (2020, January 7). *Critical congenital heart defects*. www.cdc.gov/ncbddd/heartdefects/cchd-facts.html

3 National Heart, Lung, and Blood Institute (NHLBI) (n.d.). *Ventricular assist device.* www.nhlbi.nih.gov/health-topics/ventricular-assist-device
4 Mayo Clinic (2020, May 14). *Ventricular assist device (VAD).* www.mayoclinic.org/tests-procedures/ventricular-assist-device/about/pac-20384529
5 Monackey, H. (2012, November 29). WakeMed neonatal intensive care unit certified for providing developmentally supportive care. *WakeMed Voices.* https://wakemedvoices.com/2012/11/wakemed-neonatal-intensive-care-unit-certified-for-providing-developmentally-supportive-care/

Chapter 4

Developing Adaptability and Bridging Authentic Relationships in Entry-Level Music Therapy Training

Gabriela Espinal-Santiago and Kathryn MacGown

Abstract

Music therapists in training are tasked with addressing multiple areas of growth, including developing professional identities, becoming comfortable in a range of clinical situations, navigating communications with clients and families, and implementing interventions for the first time. While the COVID-19 pandemic became an additional barrier for many students in having to experience these tasks through online service delivery, the journey towards finding authenticity in practice still remained.

Tags: Therapeutic Relationship

We would like to begin with a brief introduction of ourselves, as it will provide further insight into our experiences shared in our cases. Our names are Kathryn and Gabriela, but we call ourselves Kate and Gaby. At the time of writing this case, we both recently graduated with our bachelor's degrees, completed our internships, and are preparing for the board-certification exam. We also intend to continue with our graduate studies. We identify as cisgender women in our early twenties living on Long Island, NY. Kate's racial identity is white with a primarily Northern and Western European ethnic identity. Gaby identifies as Hispanic and Latina and of Dominican and Puerto Rican heritage.

These cases are from Kate's experiences at a music therapy center housed on her university's campus supporting neurodivergent individuals. Gaby's experiences at a preschool focused on supporting young children with learning disabilities. Both practicums took place during the 2020–2021 academic year and were impacted by COVID-19 safety regulations. We were required to adapt to telehealth while still learning how to facilitate these sessions in-person.[1] Both of us had limited training experience in the profession up until that point. Kate had only done one semester of clinical observation in person, and Gaby had completed one semester of in-person practicum.

DOI: 10.4324/9781003123798-6

We felt like we were just starting to find our footing with in-person training when everything shifted and we had to pivot. *Were we going to have a site to do anything? Were we going to be able to continue our fieldwork?* We recognized how unique this moment was. Everything was going to be through telehealth for the foreseeable future, even though we'd only been taught how to provide services in person. Nonetheless, we were able to journey through it and learn how to build therapeutic relationships remotely, practice telehealth service delivery, and emerge into who we are today as therapists.

Kate's Experience: Working With John and His Family

John was a 3-year-old white boy diagnosed with autism spectrum disorder and attention deficit hyperactivity disorder. He lives with his mother, father, and older sister. He was referred to music therapy by his mother, Jane, who had in mind a goal of developing language skills. Over the course of his sessions, John presented as a joyful and energetic child, eager to explore his creativity and environment through music and other expressive mediums. He participated in a total of 8 individual sessions co-led by myself and my supervisor at that time. John, Jane, myself, and my supervisor each attended these sessions from our own homes. During each of John's sessions, Jane took on the role of a facilitator within their home. She ensured that the tablet she and John utilized to join sessions was functioning properly.

During John's first two music therapy sessions, he was in a highchair set up by Jane in the kitchen of his house. I observed these initial sessions while my supervisor invited John to engage in improvisational and recreative music experiences through stationary body movements, body percussion, and vocalizations. Jane provided John with support during his sessions, verbally prompting him to vocally respond to the music.

During the second session, John communicated a desire, both verbally and through hand gestures, to show a toy in his house to my supervisor and I. Jane allowed John to leave his highchair, and he remained out of the highchair for the rest of the session. This enabled him more flexibility to move his body and engage more creatively within his space.

After this session, my supervisor encouraged me to draft an email to Jane requesting that John be permitted to remain out of his highchair in future sessions so that he could bring more aspects of himself into the therapeutic space, such as getting toys, showing us things in his house, and exploring himself in a larger and more open area. We hadn't articulated to Jane a need for John to stay in the chair – we presumed it was an assumption she brought into the therapy space relating to common expectations of young children being taught to sit down and stay quiet for certain tasks. Yet we were asking John to do the opposite during our sessions, and the tasks we wanted to engage him in required space for movement and exploration.

Being one to never turn down a learning opportunity, I nervously agreed to draft the email and thought: *I hope she doesn't take this as me being demanding or telling her what to do, but more so highlighting this really great thing that happened.* My supervisor reviewed my email, approved it, and sent it with both of our names on it. Jane received it well, saying she did not realize him being out of the chair was a good thing and she was happy to accommodate.

John's music therapy sessions significantly shifted at this point. He selected which rooms he wanted to attend sessions from and moved between different rooms with Jane following along holding the tablet. In displaying increased mobility and freedom in his movements within music, John utilized different objects and musical instruments in his house to further engage with the music. John incorporated toys within the music experiences through storytelling and musical play. He modeled body movements and moved his toys, forming associations between many familiar music experiences and specific rooms of his house. Occasionally, he used a keyboard in his bedroom.

By the third session, I became more of a co-therapist than an active observer. I introduced a song, "Upside Down" by Jack Johnson, that I believed captured the energetic joy so fundamental to John's personality. Within a couple of weeks of playing the song each session, he appeared to relate to the music in nuanced ways. In ways that were so embodied, he took specific small lyrical phrases and incorporated them into his own movements, introducing new movements every time I sang the song. For example, the first time I played "Upside Down," he tried to do a handstand when I would sing about going upside down. The next time I played it, when I sang about finding things that can't be found, he would seek little objects and toys in his room to bring to me, leaving off screen and coming back to musically introduce aspects of himself through those objects. In the next session, I was dynamically building up the bridge of the song where Jack Johnson sings about spinning around, and John began spinning around on the floor. As I played faster, he spun faster.

Intersubjectively, we were so connected and reciprocal in the music that it didn't matter that there was maybe a second or two of sound lag. We were still able to take our therapeutic connection to a level where I thought: *This is what I've seen all the music therapists do. I'm finally doing this.* I hadn't been sure I would be able to, but I was doing it. I was connecting with someone so deeply in the music that it didn't matter that I was on the screen and so was he.

Because John was a very young child, I often wondered whether he recognized that my supervisor and I were actively engaging with him or if he had thought we were more similar to characters on his television due to the virtual nature of our sessions together. *Am I being perceived as a person? Or am I being perceived like a character on a TV screen, just like any other show John might watch on his iPad?* These questions replayed in my mind until I made the connection that John was still engaging in the music in the best way that he could. He was picking up on so many little nuances of the music, that he didn't necessarily need to perceive me as a live person if he was engaging in the experience and socially developing.

In supervision, I was validated for my feelings around these thoughts and questions, and realized I was wondering if I was being a "good enough" therapist through these virtual sessions. My supervisor reminded me that John was perceiving me the way he was receiving me, that he was trying to interact with me in whatever capacity he could, and that if I wasn't being perceived as a live person it didn't mean I wasn't doing anything "good enough." Whether I was real or not to John didn't make me any less of an effective or good therapist. Once I could sit in the discomfort, explore these thoughts and feelings, and work my way through it, I found the beauty in our music making.

The more I worked with John and Jane, the more I understood her world, which also better positioned me to support John. After each session, Jane often remained on the video call to provide us with any relevant updates about John's life, such as him starting piano lessons. My academic supervisor noticed my self-criticism and self-doubt in the way I spoke about my work and helped me recognize how, in focusing on myself, I wasn't processing what Jane was sharing in those moments. I was missing her sentiment of wanting John to enjoy himself in music therapy.

I don't know what it is like to be a parent at all, but I could see a lot of overwhelm in her general state. She was taking John to different types of therapy and not fully understanding the nuances of how each one functioned, all while balancing caring for another child, living through a pandemic, and remaining at home with both kids. By learning how to pay less attention to my music therapy training concerns, I was better positioned to center her needs and focus on providing a musical space for John and Jane to be together.

Shortly before the start of John's seventh session, my supervisor informed me that John would not be able to continue music therapy sessions over telehealth. John was present for his session on that day and was only able to attend one more session after that. His mother needed to be available to take care of John's other family members, and John would not be able to use the tablet to join his sessions on his own.

Although my academic semester was beginning to close, I did not initially expect my time with John to end so suddenly. I composed my own song to be played at the very end of John's final music therapy session, compiling all of his favorite music experiences into one last song and thanking him for his music. Compiling highlights of John's sessions into one final song was helpful for my closure with John's termination of services. It allowed me an opportunity to reflect on all of the ways in which John's creativity grew in our time together, and I felt proud of the role that I played in that space. The end of John's final session was bittersweet, but also served as a celebration of everything that he achieved over the previous eight weeks.

Gaby's Experience: Working With Sofia's Class

I had the pleasure of working with a group session from Sofia's class every Monday morning for five months of my fieldwork placement: Noel, Osheen, Patrick, Quinn, Ruby, and Sy. They ranged from 3–5 years of age and were accompanied by at least one caregiver for each 30-minute session. Their racial, ethnic, and religious backgrounds were not specifically disclosed to me. Each class focused on students developing their interpersonal relationships with their caregivers. This was encouraged through interactive experiences involving their caregivers that centered in working towards the students' communication and social skills. These goals were addressed through recreative approaches within a structured session plan consisting of a greeting experience, three singing/vocal interventions, one movement intervention, and a goodbye experience. The students were each provided with tablets from the New York City Department of Education during the pandemic, and these were used for joining music therapy sessions using video chat software. The students usually stayed within the same area of their homes when they attended sessions; however, the tablets allowed caregivers to change the placement and angle of their camera during movement interventions. The socioeconomic backgrounds of each family were taken into consideration to ensure that no student faced barriers to continuing their education during the pandemic. While some students utilized their family's own smart devices, the tablet's availability was another form of support for students.[2]

My work with Sofia's class was such a new experience for me. As a student, it was a bit intimidating to take on a therapy setting that was just being introduced within our curriculum. I found myself eager to learn, but anxious about what was expected of me. Reflecting on it now as a recent graduate, this practicum experience most directly shaped my clinical training for telehealth.

I began by observing sessions for a couple of weeks, participating in music making and documenting different musical and verbal techniques my supervisor implemented. I also considered where each student was in their own home during sessions and noticed that they were all joining from their living rooms. I admired how seamless these sessions were, and how personable and expressive each interaction was. I had this assumption that such a structured session format would be very rigid in implementation, yet my supervisor facilitated sessions with enough fluidity for the students to express themselves within each experience. There was a sense of comfort and support in my supervisor's guidance that I was looking forward to implementing in my future sessions. This was also a great opportunity to observe the students and their interactions with their caregivers.

A key component during this observation period was noticing the diversity amongst the students, as both individuals and as dyads with their caregivers. Noel and Osheen presented bright facial affects with physical support from their parents and verbal support from my supervisor; their parents usually joined in, providing verbal support and often implementing a hand-over-hand technique to support them during movement experiences. Ruby and Sy eagerly joined sessions with a lot of singing and movement; Ruby danced frequently with a huge smile on her face, accompanied by her mother in their living room, and Sy was accompanied by both of his parents, who verbally encouraged him to sing and move while joining him in the movement. Quinn and Patrick attended sessions intermittently during my time with this class; when present, their caregivers turned their cameras and microphones off. Patrick first attended sessions with his camera on, but his video and audio were off completely for future sessions. Quinn's video and audio were off as well. At times, both joined the sessions late.

With such a diverse group of students and caregivers present in each session, I wondered what our therapeutic relationship would look like individually and collectively. I had never done a group session prior to this placement, let alone telehealth, so it was very intimidating and overwhelming. Especially as a student feeling like I didn't know what I was doing, leading a session directing parents and caregivers with their children was challenging. I wanted to focus and consider all of the students and what they were offering the group individually, while balancing the caregivers offering different forms of parenting and engagement. There was such individuality and I thought: *Ok, who are these people? Who are these students? These caregivers? Who are we together?* It was a complex dynamic that shaped my understanding of how to be a part of a group, especially a pre-existing one already established by my supervisor. I was adding another layer as a new person in the group.

The main component in our therapeutic relationship was how the caregivers utilized the video chat to support their children when they would experience distress or discomfort during sessions. In Sofia's class, this encounter happened occasionally with Osheen. He was one student who expressed tiredness and discomfort by crying and moving towards his father for support. At the beginning of facilitating sessions, I would provide verbal support within music by saying in the music: "It's all right, Osheen. We hear you and we are here for you." I then provided additional verbal support after the intervention was finished. My intent was to acknowledge Osheen's feelings while providing a continued foundation of support within the music for him and the rest of his classmates. Osheen's father, however, would at times turn off the camera and mute their audio during these moments. At first, I was confused about how I could support Osheen with his camera and audio off, and I worried about his processing. *How can I support him? How can Osheen feel supported in the music? Are there any other ways I can support Osheen at this moment? Is this a boundary that is being established by his father?* These questions arose during the beginning of facilitating sessions because I knew even though I could not hear or see them, they were still there in the music with all of us in the telehealth session.

Through supervision, I expressed these and other concerns. Not only did I seem to think that the student was experiencing a specific feeling or emotion, but there were also other students and their caregivers present in the same session. Already finding the group dynamic via telehealth to be challenging within itself, I was consistently overwhelmed by how much I had to consider in each moment in the group and often thought: *I didn't do that right. That was the wrong thing to do.*

My supervisor discussed the importance of supporting the student while also modeling and teaching the caregiver how they, too, can support their child. We acknowledged how that process might look different in each session. I realized that developing that clinical knowledge and skill would come with time, as would knowing how to respect the boundary of the caregiver in supporting their child via telehealth. It was unrealistic to have expected to know how to support each student in any moment right from the start of our therapeutic relationship. I soon understood that trust was at the root of the therapeutic relationship and that it is developed between the music therapist, the student, and the caregiver in exploring these feelings together within music.[3]

To start supporting the student and caregiver, my supervisor introduced a breathing exercise for grounding during moments of distress. This exercise would have the whole class and their caregivers joining me and my supervisor in breathing through the nose ("smell the flowers") and breathing out through the mouth ("blow out the candles"). This imagery component provided a creative outlet for the students to mimic the specific breathing movements. I modeled sensory support by verbally prompting students and their caregivers to gently squeeze their arms, shoulders, and even hug their child gently. Through these techniques, the students were provided an additional outlet of support and the caregiver could learn these techniques to help their children during and outside of sessions. By involving the group, the distressed student also received peer support, and the caregivers witnessed and provided additional support, thus building trust within the therapeutic relationship with each group member.[3]

I found the implementation of these techniques to positively impact the development of my therapeutic relationship with the students. With Osheen, I learned over time what certain facial expressions meant and how I could support him. If their camera was left on but they were muted, I would acknowledge Osheen's feelings and invite the whole group to join in support techniques. I incorporated these techniques differently each time, either by substituting a support technique within the intervention itself or taking a moment to provide verbal and visual support without instrumental accompaniment. Osheen seemed to be grounded when his father would provide him physical sensory support as evidenced by his regulated breathing, relaxation of his facial expressions, and shift in his facial affect in response. I would make sure to invite the whole class and their caregivers to join in these techniques, and the caregivers always participated. This created a collective space in telehealth for all of us to grow together.

My work with Sofia's class led to many fruitful interactions, with students expressing themselves through singing and movement with their caregivers. To create a more personal session, I composed my own goodbye song towards the end of our time together titled "Bye Butterfly," referring to their graduation from preschool and going to kindergarten. My goal was to highlight the change that the class was experiencing and to provide closure for all involved. Sofia also invited me to the graduation ceremony that took place over video chat. This allowed one last goodbye, and I was able to thank the students and their caregivers, teachers, and staff for this wonderful opportunity.

Growing in Our Authenticity

We are both grateful for the opportunity to have explored telehealth as a medium of service delivery at such a fundamental moment within our clinical development. Our undergraduate program provided us opportunities to continue our clinical training through telehealth when it was no longer possible to do so in-person. Our program additionally created an academic course related to service delivery through telehealth that provided us both skill development and a support network of peers.

As we engaged in our clinical work, we realized that we already had the foundations from our education and previous clinical experiences to recognize the core elements of building therapeutic relationships. Even as students who felt like we didn't know how to navigate the newness of being a music therapist in training, we in fact had a starting point and a support system that helped us implement sessions and trust the music experiences we were providing. We learned to feel more comfortable trusting our intuition to try new things in therapy spaces and to gain a sense of confidence in ourselves.

Regardless of whether or not our clinical training had been done fully in-person versus a mix of in-person and telehealth, we would have been on a similar journey of recognizing the importance of who we are as individuals and music therapists and understanding how these identities impact our clinical work. As much as it felt so out of control and impossible in the moment to have to pivot and do our training online, we now realize we had a bit more control in our learning experience. No matter the medium through which services were provided, we were working to bring authenticity into our practice and develop trust with clients by finding ourselves, trusting our instincts, and building self-confidence. While this process began in these practicum placements, it continued into our internships and will be a career-long journey.

While we both tended to be self-critical in our learning journey, we had support from others and were able to learn how to reflect on our work and improve in future sessions. Answering questions like *What does this client need now? How can I meet these needs?* helped us learn to trust that we are capable of meeting their needs and supporting them, even when we're worried about whether or not we're doing a "good enough" job. Telehealth wasn't necessarily the biggest concern for us in our training, but it was certainly another barrier we weren't excited to navigate at the time. Yet, we learned to look at it as an opportunity that impacted us in a good way. In the end, we wouldn't be the therapists we are today if we didn't go through the experience of our clinical training through the pandemic. It was a difficult and necessary step within our academic education, clinical training, and personal growth.

Summarizing Ideas and Questions for Discussion

1. Many music therapists in training experience a number of barriers in their journeys to becoming a professional, barriers that require us to seek internal and external supports to help us persevere.

   a. For music therapists in training, what were barriers you had or have had to overcome in your clinical training that you feel have helped you become the therapist you are? What support systems have you found helpful? What support systems do you think are available to you that you have not tapped into?

   b. For professional music therapists, what barriers did you have to overcome in your training, and what support systems helped you be resilient? What might be support systems you accessed then that you could access now in times of need?

2. Learning to identify and integrate our most authentic selves in the therapeutic space is also a journey that can be supported by practicing self-awareness, engaging in supervision, and growing through experiences.

   a. Who are you as a music therapist when engaging with your authentic self?

   b. What conditions are helpful for that authentic self-actualizing in session? When do you feel you are your most authentic self in sessions?

   c. In what ways do you feel being authentic impacts your sessions? How do your clients respond? How does your music respond?

Notes

1 Gaddy, S., Gallardo, R., McCluskey, S., Moore, L., Peuser, A., Rotert, R., Stypulkoski, C., & LaGasse, A. B. (2020). Covid-19 and music therapists' employment, service delivery, perceived stress, and hope: A descriptive study. *Music Therapy Perspectives, 38*(2), 157–166. https://doi.org/10.1093/mtp/miaa018

2 Knott, D., & Block, S. (2020). Virtual music therapy: Developing new approaches to service delivery. *Music Therapy Perspectives, 38*(2), 151–156. www.doi.org/10.1093/mtp/miaa017

3 Annesley, L., Curtis-Tyler, K., & McKeown, E. (2020). Parents' perspectives on their child's music therapy: A qualitative study. *Journal of Music Therapy, 57*(1), 91–119. www.doi.org/10.1093/jmt/thz018

Unit 2

Aligning Personal Values and Emerging Clinical Identities as a New Professional

Chapter 5

Discovering Self Through Reflexivity and Shared Social Identities With Clients

Alex Peuser

Abstract

Shared and/or similar social identities between music therapist and clients can provide opportunity for great insight and also introduce complicated clinical decision-making and boundary setting. Clinical supervision, personal therapy, and critical developmental growth can help music therapists become aware of these dynamics and how they can impact both growth and harm in the therapeutic process.

Tags: Clinical Supervision

This case details my experiences as a music therapy intern within a residential psychiatric treatment facility for children and adolescents, where I created and implemented a group for LGBTQ+[1] clients on the campus. As an intern, my evolving therapeutic mindset was trauma-informed and person-centered while using music *in* therapy more than music *as* therapy. Today, that approach has expanded to include aspects of social justice.[2] Certain facets of my personal identity also influenced this case. Using the ADDRESSING Model,[3] I am a younger disabled Millennial who holds no religious affiliation, although I was raised in the Catholic tradition. I am a transracial adoptee from South Korea who grew up in the middle class, and I am a queer person. Each of these intersecting identities played a part in how I understood myself and the individuals within this group. These identities also influence how I reflect on this work today.

Sanctuary Model Supervision

My internship aligned with the Sanctuary Model of care predicated on seven commitments: nonviolence, emotional intelligence, democracy, social learning, growth and change, social responsibility, and open communication.[4] As an intern, this model was helpful in creating an egalitarian

DOI: 10.4324/9781003123798-8

understanding between my supervisor and myself.[5] It allowed for safety to be identified by the supervisor and supervisee while exploring any parallel processes the supervisee may be experiencing in clinical work. It was during the identification of safety in my first supervision session that I shared I was gay (which was how I described myself at the time) and that I wished to focus on treatment and techniques with LGBTQ+ adolescents. If it were not for this time to identify and operationalize what safety meant to me, I am not sure I would have shared this information so early or so freely.

Proposing SAFE Spaces

Navigating an internship – or any work setting – as a queer individual poses a unique set of challenges. The first few weeks are filled with many unknowns. *Can I be my authentic self with this person?* At the time, I was only concerned with whether or not I could be *Out* with clients. However, there is definitely more to living authentically than being *Out*. It took a little more development and experience for me to understand that. *What should I do if a client asks me about my sexual orientation or identity? How do I maintain a professional boundary while also being my authentic self?* All of these were questions I had within the first few weeks of internship. Fortunately, I had the support of a supervisor – and the agency at large – who saw the value of authenticity and who helped me navigate each of these questions by frequently checking in about how my answers to these questions were evolving. My supervisor also consistently reminded me that I did not have to do or say anything I was not ready for, which I found to be equally important when facilitating a music therapy group or participating in clinical supervision.

Within my first week of internship, clients asked me either general or very specific questions regarding my sexuality at least once a day. While slightly caught off-guard by these inquiries, they seemed to stem from a place of curiosity and understanding as opposed to judgment. Furthermore, their questions were bold and unashamed, which was a departure from my own experiences growing up as a queer kid in the Midwest only a few years earlier. Being asked these questions so frequently made me curious about the demographics of the clients on campus. After some investigating, I discovered the campus intake screening indicated that approximately 16% of the clients on campus were a sexuality or gender minority.

I decided that I wanted my internship project to focus on a group for LGBTQ+ individuals. I did not entirely know what I wanted this to look like, but I knew how much I would have valued a group of this nature as an adolescent. I thought about how different my own coming out experiences may have been different if I were able to have positive queer representation at an earlier age. And while I recognized that spending time in residential treatment is not the same as living in the real world, it felt important to provide a space that was not heteronormative in order to make up for some of the missed experiences. Now, I wonder if an experience such as this was as formative as I imagined it to be.

When preparing to propose this group I was aware that there could be some resistance to a group of this nature. There was no major hesitation from my supervisor, but she was straightforward that a group of this nature could be unwelcomed by some members of staff and on-site residents. With that said, and I appreciated her candor, my supervisor wholeheartedly supported this group and worked with upper administration at the facility to ensure its success.

As I reflect on the development of this program, I am more aware of the advocacy that was required for this group to go forward. I wonder whether or not my feelings of apprehension and awareness of resistance to this group were a result of my own insecurities, a means to maintain safety for myself, or a bit of both. As I think about this group in today's sociopolitical climate wherein the safety of queer people in everyday society remains in question and even actively threatened, I wonder what other barriers to success this group would have faced that I was not aware of as a student.

After a month of research and planning[6] with my supervisor, we decided that the group would be titled SAFE Spaces (or Sexuality Advocacy For Everyone). The purpose of this group was to a) provide a space on campus to talk about sexuality openly, b) educate individuals on LGBTQ+ issues, c) build community on campus, and d) share our experiences as queer individuals. These groups met for the remaining duration of my internship (60- to 90-minute group sessions once a week for seven weeks). Individuals were referred on an invitation basis via their primary therapist or as a self-referral.

Each week revolved around a central theme, which was selected based on group member input. Topics included understanding the LGBTQ acronym, coming out, healthy relationships, and discrimination and peer support. Group discussion would sometimes help determine the topic for the following session. And for me, each session offered rich material for supervision.

Processing Countertransference in Supervision and Therapy

There were several instances during the implementation of SAFE Spaces where my own experiences as a queer person – including growing up in heteronormative spaces narratives with internalized homophobia and heightened self-monitoring – undoubtedly impacted the clinical experience for myself and clients. Many of these instances I was fortunate enough to explore with my supervisor, and at times my personal therapy. I have also come to realize there were experiences left unpacked until writing this case study.

Just before beginning the group, I remember being extremely nervous. I felt the self-imposed pressure to be the queer role model that I did not have growing up and to use the group as a corrective experience that could address the adversity I experienced in childhood. *Can I truly be the person that I needed to see during my youth?* When my supervisor asked how I was feeling about the group, I casually said I was "fine," but I was also so scared. This was a group that I had developed with the belief that I was the only one at the agency with the life experience to be beneficial to clients. I was concerned with not being "enough" for the individuals in the group and, at the same time, of being too open with the clients in a way that could get me into trouble with the organization.

To help prepare me for the work, my supervisor and I discussed what made up a "safe space." What stuck with me from this discussion is that the space also had to be safe for me, and I was not required to disclose anything I did not feel ready to share. I realize now, just like life does not exist in a vacuum, neither did this group. Therefore, the acceptance and support for the group offered by my supervisor, co-intern, and other colleagues was integral in fostering safety. I now see that the experiences and support of everyone involved fostered a supportive environment that was more ideal than what most queer individuals experience daily.

During the second group session we planned to discuss coming out and the coming out process. To do this we participated in a music listening experience centered around the music video for *Heaven* by Troye Sivan. The music video's depiction of queer love, attraction, and sensuality was important, but I was unsure if the material was appropriate for the audience of our group. The chorus of *Heaven* asks a simple question: "Without losing a piece of me – how do I get to heaven?"

In supervision, my supervisor, myself, and my co-intern spent a great deal of time discussing whether or not the music video was therapeutically appropriate and necessary to be brought into the session. I remember my supervisor asking me plainly why I felt this material may be inappropriate and, at the time, I stated this was due to the sensuality depicted. However, upon reflection this concern was likely a manifestation of my internalized homophobia. We determined the content of this video and the lyrics to the song were no less appropriate than any other material these individuals may be bringing to the group space anyway, and that our concern was rooted in a need to appease a heteronormative society. In the end, the decision to use this content was left to my own discretion, but the collaboration and support I received in supervision was necessary for me to feel comfortable and empowered in my decision-making.

Week 4 focused on the theme of Bullying and Discrimination, which was not in the original plan for this series. However, after we had formed this group, there was an increase in phobic bullying from clients and, in some cases, microaggressions from staff. I spent this time holding space for the participants to share their experiences and feelings regarding these types of attacks. This was the most challenging group for me as a facilitator. As someone who experienced the many instances of discrimination that participants were recounting, I did not realize how triggering this session would be for me. I also did not realize how activated I was at that moment. During the session I did my best to hold the many emotions of the group members, but there were also times where I was more than the blank slate we are taught to be in school. I allowed myself to share this experience and my emotions with the group.

Following this session, my supervisor and co-intern worked with me to find a sense of safety again by validating my queer identity, which is something they both did explicitly early on in our relationship. I was not pushed to share things I was not comfortable with sharing, and my supervisor reiterated her compassion, support, and open-door supervision policy. It felt as though we had an unspoken understanding.

Lived experience is very important in extending empathy and at times enhancing the therapeutic alliance, but to do this type of work while having the lived experience requires additional supports and boundaries to be in place. I was fortunate enough to have an internship in the same city where I pursued my bachelor's degree, and I was still considered a student so I could continue work with my therapist at the university counseling center. In addition, the Sanctuary Model emphasized self-care as an active practice. Therefore, taking a break to decompress from a stressful session was not only encouraged but generally required. I also had the support of a co-intern who was and is one of my closest friends. We held each other accountable to our self-care plans and safety plans.

That said, even years removed from more predominant experiences of discrimination, I have not adequately taken the time to acknowledge how those experiences shaped me. It's possible that perhaps, if I had the capacity at the time to explore these experiences more in-depth and things further, I would have felt less guilt in expressing myself as a queer individual in a professional setting. Similarly, if I had more understanding of how my intersecting identities – primarily my queerness and being a person of color – impacted my work I could have been more prepared to sit with these challenging emotions. In hindsight, I see that I was not developmentally ready to explore these topics in supervision and how that impacted my experience of and capacity to facilitate this group.

Establishing and Maintaining Boundaries

I've dedicated a lot of reflection about boundaries in clinical work that is so connected to my social identity. In school I was taught how to be professional through a cisgender, heteronormative, and Western framework. By following these guidelines, I was able to maintain a "professional" boundary while implementing the group but while leaving parts of me out of supervision and clinical spaces.

At the time, I did not know how to be queer and professional because of how oppressive systems shaped my sense of professionalism. Parallel to my personal process was the group's process of forming their queer identities in a heteronormative world. In work so closely connected to the experience of living as a historically and systematically marginalized individual, self-disclosure is both an act of courage and an act of defiance with liberatory implications for all involved in the therapeutic alliance.

The group's conversation in the Week 2 (Coming Out) session included individuals sharing their experiences of coming out, their fears about coming out to close family members, and questions regarding my process of coming out. I did my best to maintain boundaries and to reflect clients' questions back to their experiences. One client stated:

> I came out when I was about your age, and I was met with a lot of support which I know is not the case for many people. I was scared, and there are still times when I experience this discomfort. What has your experience been like?

Another client asked: "Can I be queer and religious?" My responses to these questions were complex. Since coming out was the focus of the group, I allowed myself to share slightly more than I would have otherwise, and as a non-religious person I struggled to know how to be unbiased; however, given the intimacy of these topics, I determined it was most critical to bring the conversation back to the clients within the group and sidestep self-disclosure.[7]

Still, I realized I was perhaps not as open as I could have been and turned to clinical supervision following the session to explore what was happening in my internal world. Sanctuary supervision requires the supervisee to name their levels of safety and identify an agenda for supervision at the onset of each session. My agenda was to share my concerns about whether I had handled the clients' questions in an appropriate manner. *Did I share too much information about myself? Was my neutrality appropriate?* My supervisor acknowledged my feelings and reminded me that it was okay to not have all of the answers. I am curious now to see how this supervision would have been different if my supervisor were also queer. *Would we have gone deeper than discussing my therapeutic skills, or could we have done that anyway and I was simply not ready?* I imagine it would have been the latter.

Now, I realize I kept all of my responses just below surface-level and did not dive into the pain and fear I once felt regarding my own identity. As a queer person, I am accustomed to being asked questions related to my identity but generally from an antagonistic perspective. In hindsight, these clients were being as inquisitive as I once was. Instead of asking questions like this to the depths of the internet, they were asking me.

This process taught me a lot about being a music therapist. I made the choice not to engage in these conversations with clients largely due to my own discomfort and developmental readiness and learned there would be times that I would not be the best fit for the individuals seeking my services or in my care. However, I realized I could remain a resource for these clients by helping them find the appropriate supports.

I also learned how to create balance in ways that followed the Sanctuary Model through identifying safety, emotions, experiences of loss, and thoughts about future sessions. It was also done by identifying triangulation between myself and clients, maintaining awareness of how our cultural makeups were both distinct yet shared. In some ways creating this balance and holding these boundaries felt counterintuitive because I knew how I would have felt if the roles were reversed. I wondered if perhaps my trajectory would have changed if I had more positive queer role models earlier on.

In one of my therapy sessions, I was reminded that these boundaries exist as a means of protection and growth for all individuals involved. In a parallel process, my psychologist also took on a mentor-type role (as I was interested in becoming a clinical psychologist), so I was able to see how this process could be helpful and safe while being in a similar position. The boundaries that I enacted facilitated safety for both the client and myself. However, I also yearn for a time where even the smallest part of me is not afraid of the potential consequences of self-disclosure as a queer person. At one point in the program, I was informed in supervision that one individual in particular had experienced intrusive thoughts and vividly sexualized dreams involving me. This individual was concerned they would be removed from the group as a result. I was not surprised to hear this based on the interactions I had previously with this individual. However, I did feel concerned. *Was I responsible for this? Is it because of this group that this individual was experiencing these outcomes?* While I recognized transference could emerge at any time as an authentic and healthy dynamic in the therapeutic process, I was afraid this experience would be used as a reason to discontinue this group early or to no longer support initiatives of this sort on the campus. And yet I did not share these thoughts with my supervisor. Entry-level training taught me about many of these scenarios but did not prepare me how to support myself while moving through these experiences. Consequently, I did not view supervision as an area to be vulnerable and to continue my growth as a therapist, but rather as a time to check on my professional competencies and clinical skills. More actively utilizing supervision to address my emotional reactions to this transferential experience could have better prepared me to maintain both the client's and my safety.

Retrospective Reflections – The Importance of Healing

I did not always have the insight and awareness of what to bring into supervision, which definitely impacted how I showed up for clients and the overall implementation of the group. And, as previously mentioned, I do wonder if my supervisory experiences would have differed if supervised by a queer individual. I also wonder how this group would have been different if I were to unpack my own positionality in relationship to this work during the planning phase of group implementation. I have since taken a considerable amount of time in my own therapy to explore queerness and some of the adversity that comes with those experiences. If I had been similarly vulnerable in supervision – or even privately with myself – some of my therapeutic choices would have been different.

There were times in the group, such as in a song sharing experience done in the first week, where I brought in music I thought would be beneficial to exploring session content. In retrospect, I would have engaged in these song sharing experiences differently. While the artists I shared had personal meaning for me at the time, I did not recognize how I was projecting my queer experience onto group members without regard for how queerness is relative to each person and their unique circumstances.

During the week we talked about Chosen Family, I found it difficult to explain as it was something I had yet to experience. Yet, it is a prevalent theme in the LGBTQ+ community. In this session, we watched a Mercedes-Benz commercial depicting many different types of people from all aspects of life coming together to create their own "family." This is something queer individuals may do as we go about the process of figuring out who we are. An improvisatory music experience that was supposed to mirror the creation of chosen family ensued. Clients had the opportunity to create and direct their own ensemble that suited their needs and musical tastes.

There was not much processing that occurred following this experience. I believe this is mainly because the topic was not one that these individuals who had little autonomy in their lives were ready for. This was another example of unchecked countertransference. *Perhaps this was something that I was instead missing in my own life*. I did not process this in supervision or in personal therapy at the time. It was actually a recent conversation with my current therapist that makes me think this type of community is what I was missing then. In hindsight, perhaps this whole session was created to prepare these individuals for a future where they knew how to cultivate this type of family. At the time, this community was something I was lacking, and I did not know how to find it on my own.

Final Thoughts

I wonder how much of this experience was beneficial for the individuals in the group and how much of it was a part of my own journey toward self-acceptance. Or, perhaps it was as foundational for the group members as I believe it to be for myself. If I were to implement a group of this nature again, I would engage in supervision differently. I did not have the self-awareness at the time, nor had I embraced myself to a great enough extent to allow for some of this insight.

Additionally, some weeks I found it challenging to be present with the individuals in these sessions because conversations or the topic at hand became too close to my personal experiences. These were weeks that I relied heavily on supervision, peer support from my co-intern, self-care, and personal therapy. This is not to say that I regret providing a space for this work to occur. Instead, it reinforces my belief that open and positive experiences regarding gender expansivity and sexuality need to happen early on to mitigate some of the internalized phobia that manifests as self-doubt, hyper-awareness, and caution that I experience today. As I write this chapter now, I realize how much unrecognized guilt and shame I held regarding my own identity. I believe internalized phobia kept me from taking therapeutic risks and from taking up figurative space within supervision and in sessions.

I acknowledge that this work would not have been possible for me without the support of my supervisor, co-intern, and therapist at the time. The objectivity provided by each of these individuals helped me to recognize and process countertransferences and instances where I may have been tempted to cross boundaries from therapeutic to seemingly helpful. Admittedly, not all of the necessary processing took place during the span of this group. Much of it came after the fact and while writing this chapter. I believe this is largely because I was not ready to reflect on past experiences of trauma as related to my identity. The group that was offered was adequate and important to many individuals, but as I gain more life and clinical experience, I now see how much deeper this group could have been.

Summarizing Ideas and Questions for Discussion

1. Using Hill's *ADDRESSING Model*, complete a cultural sketch on yourself and a client.[8]

   a. Compare your sketch to that of your client's. What are strengths and areas of growth you see between them?

   b. How might your identities impact how you facilitate a session with this client?

   c. What additional skills or knowledge do you need to facilitate this session well?

2. Music therapy interns and music therapists can find clinical work suddenly activating difficult and/or intense feelings, thoughts, and memories stemming from their past.

   a. What has the *ADDRESS Model* helped you become aware of as sensitive areas related to your past? What boundaries might you benefit from setting around those areas, and what might be the process through which you process those areas in your personal work?

   b. As a supervisor, or as a future supervisor, how might you adapt your supervision style to assess for the supervisee's safety (e.g., emotional, physical, spiritual, and psychological safety)?

Table 5.1 Pamela Hays' Addressing Model Framework[3]

Cultural Influences	Reader's Cultural Sketch
Age and Generational Influences **D**evelopmental Disabilities **D**isabilities Acquired Later in Life **R**eligion and Spiritual Orientation **E**thnic and Racial Identity **S**ocioeconomic Status **S**exual Orientation **I**ndigenous Heritage (remember we all occupy indigenous land) **N**ational Origin **G**ender	

Notes

1 This author uses the acronym LGBTQ+ to discuss past sessions as it is congruent with their understanding of this community at the time and the known characteristics of group participants at the time. This author recognizes that this community is more expansive, and that language is changing to provide more inclusive and accurate representations.

2 Alvarez, J., Babb, A., Barriga, J., Bluvhstein, M., Brill, B., Cookey, N., Crossman, R., Fornero, S., Guirguis-Younger, M., Gary, H., Imarenezor, E., Jenke, A., Johnson, R., Joyce, M., Lok, S., Maglio, A.-S., McDonald, A., Nicholls-Allison, W., Pearson, T., . . . Williamson, C. (2019). *A movement for justice: Socially responsible practice.* Adler University. https://srp.adler.edu/doc/A_Movement_For_Justice.pdf

3 Hays, P. A. (2016). *Addressing cultural complexities in practice: A framework for clinicians and counselors* (3rd ed.). American Psychological Association.

4 Bloom, S. L., Yansoy, S., & Harrison, L. C. (2013). A reciprocal supervisory network: The sanctuary model. In D. Murphy & S. Joseph (Eds.), *Trauma and the therapeutic relationship: Approaches to process and practice* (pp. 126–146). Palgrave Macmillan.

5 Peuser, A., & Kailey Campbell. (2022). Sanctuary model supervision: Reflections and implications for the music therapy profession. *Dialogues in Music Therapy Education, 2*(1), 90–111. www.doi.org/10.18060/25609

6 Whitehead-Pleaux, A., Donnenwerth, A., Robinson, B., Hardy, S., Oswanski, L., Forinash, M., Hearns, M., Anderson, N., & York, E. (2012). Lesbian, gay bisexual, transgender, and questioning: Best practices in music therapy. *Music Therapy Perspectives, 30*(2), 158–166. www.doi.org/10.1093/mtp/30.2.158

7 Harris, B. (2019, October). Queer as a bell: Music and the psychotherapeutic relationship. *Voices: A World Forum for Music Therapy, 19*(3). https://doi.org/10.15845/voices.v19i3.2674

8 These discussion questions were modeled after discussion questions developed by my mentor, Abbré McClain, PsyD.

Chapter 6

Finding Intimacy Through Supervision

Joy Kaminski

Abstract

New professionals face a challenging transitional period immediately following internship when they independently determine who they are as a professional and how that self-concept aligns with their personal values. Clinical supervision can be a critical space for nurturing and cultivating that developmental growth.

Tags: Clinical Supervision; Professional Development

What does it mean to feel enlivened in music therapy work each day? How is intimacy in music therapy defined? Is it normal to dread work each day? What is the difference between struggling at work and burning out? These were the questions I wrestled with for quite some time after completing my entry-level training in music therapy and transitioning to professional practice. Critical to helping me engage with these reflective inquiries was supervision, through which I became more aware of and better able to express my values.

At the start of this process, my practice was product-oriented and activities-based, which I came to find was inconsistent with those values. By the end, my practice had become more process-oriented and humanistic. This alignment between who I was and how I practiced helped me to discover those feelings of enlivenment and intimacy I was seeking.

Before Supervision – Discovering My Limitations

I entered the profession as a 23-year-old white woman, raised in a middle to upper-class neighborhood. In my first job, I primarily served white school-aged children, children who were growing up similar to how I did in not having to think about their privilege much, if at all.[1] I bought a lot of song books and structured my sessions to exactly the themes or academic concepts the children were working on. I was doing what I had seen in practicums

DOI: 10.4324/9781003123798-9

and what I had experienced in my upbringing. This approach felt comfortable and familiar, and I naturally gravitated towards it. Teachers seemed to be happy and excited that I might be able to help the children learn some important academic and social concepts through the energizing medium of music.

I initially thrived on this energy for quite some time, but as the days went on, I found myself feeling farther and farther away from myself. I had this constant critiquing voice in my head: *You should be writing more of your own songs. Be more creative. Don't play that song again.* I had hardly any planning time within my day, so my work bled into my personal time. My job seemed to be closing in on me both personally and professionally. I was struggling with finding a way out as I needed a paycheck.

About this time, I received a referral from a past supervisor about a music therapy position at a psychiatric hospital. Moving from working with children in a school to working with people with mental illnesses and trauma histories was a big change. I was already feeling stressed and drained at my other job, and this new position offered better pay and benefits (which my current job didn't give me). I didn't think very much about what the differences would be between the people I would work with in this new setting versus the old one. I hadn't been taught in my training about how to make such clinical transitions, and it was hard to think much about what I might be signing up for given how low my resources were then. Any trepidation I had was soothed by my previous supervisor's confidence in me and my desperation to get out of my old job.

I began work at the psychiatric hospital as I had started with the schoolchildren. I found activity books that were made for working with people with mental illness. Each session plan was clearly structured and laid out. *This should be simple, right? Just follow the plan, and how hard could this be? These books were written by professional music therapists, right? With much more training and understanding than myself.* I didn't know any other way, so I figured I would stick to what I knew.

However, I was now working in a very different environment with people from a variety of racial, ethnic, and socioeconomic backgrounds. Many were homeless, struggling with substance use, and disconnected from their families and other support structures. I was suddenly forced to be more thoughtful about how my upbringing might be different than what many of these patients had experienced. Growing up, I had always had food, safe shelter, and physical safety. It felt painful to acknowledge my privilege, to know and see how different my upbringing was from many of the patients around me.

I also felt intimidated by some of the interactions I had with patients. In my first week, a patient spit right in my face when I introduced myself to her. I can still remember how the spit slowly dripped down my face as the patient glared at me as if to say, "You don't belong here." After my shift that day, I went home and cried. I didn't have these painfully bold experiences in my old job, and I was shocked by the way that many patients freely expressed their inner experience, be it enthusiasm, curiosity, mistrust, aggression, or anything else. While I knew the adults that I'd be working with at the psychiatric hospital would have different ways of relating than the children with whom I had previously worked, I was startled by how much more the patients' needs and conflicts were front and center.

The burnout feeling emerged quite quickly in the new job.[2] My first few weeks, the patients seemed interested in getting to know a new person and in seeing what I would have to offer in sessions, but as time went on something started to feel sour. Patients seemed to be drifting farther and farther away from me as I reached out to them harder and harder. I would come home feeling drained and dreading this work that kept demanding my focus and attention each day. I knew I valued and respected each person who walked into our therapy space, but I didn't quite know how to show that value and respect.

One of the turning points happened during a warm-up activity at the start of a group on the acute floor for adults under age 60. Oftentimes there were 15–20 people in a group, and it was quite difficult to truly hear anyone. On one particular day, I was having clients toss a ball to pre-recorded music. If the music stopped and they were holding the ball, they had to answer a "get to know you" question about themselves. I kept a large emphasis on keeping the music upbeat. I thought at the time that helping my patients have fun was a good clinical focus. I remember the moment a client, John, angrily exclaimed, "This song again?!" while he slammed the tambourine down on the floor before leaving the room.

I felt horrible. I can still picture the anger and frustration on his face as he walked out of the room. John and I had developed a meaningful connection outside of the group, so why was it that as soon as we entered the music therapy room our relationship went down the tubes? It seemed he couldn't understand why I was facilitating a group this way, that there were more possibilities in the space than this game with a ball and music. He didn't know the answer either. He just knew he had to get out of the music therapy group room.

And in that moment, I realized I needed to let go of the rigid session plan and explore other ways of practicing, ways that could help me discover an intimacy with patients, myself, and my practice. John's frustration had motivated me, and that moment, along with so many other moments like it, led me to realize I needed clinical supervision.

Beginning Supervision

Before starting supervision, I was very isolated. In my local community there were very few music therapists working in psychiatric settings, and I didn't have the support that I needed. So, I turned to professional forums on social media and found myself feeling unfulfilled when people provided specific answers in response to clinical questions. Each human being is so complex and different, how could one person's exact needs be met through a social media post? I was looking for something different although I didn't know what it was exactly that I was looking for.

I began noticing one person, Michelle, whose comments really stood out to me. She encouraged others to ask the client what they felt like they needed and frequently responded with questions rather than answers. I messaged Michelle and asked her if she provided supervision, specifically to help me find a new way of structuring music therapy groups. At the time, I was searching for a different way of connecting with my patients, but I was unsure of how to do that. I felt I had a solid understanding of activities-based work and I knew I could stay within my scope of practice running my groups that way, but I was ready for a change. I knew I needed more support so that I could safely and ethically explore this new way of practicing.

I remember the first time I called Michelle for supervision. I felt so tired and burned out and truly unsure if I wanted to stay in this profession, and having never met Michelle in person, I was skeptical whether she could truly help me. We started discussing how to restructure my groups. Unable to hide my distress, I described what I was doing for each of my groups and explained how burned out and frustrated I felt. Michelle assured me that there was another way of practicing, and she provided a couple of suggestions for ways to run a group without having to do so much planning, including starting with a check-in about how they were feeling. She encouraged me to let the group naturally flow and to not get caught up in making sure that each person speaks up or participates in a certain way.

We also explored what it would look like to verbally reflect back what patients had verbally shared. This was scary because I often had difficulty understanding what patients were saying due to their more disorganized, tangential, or psychotic statements. Yet, I wanted them to feel seen and heard even when I was feeling confused. With Michelle's encouragement, I started seeking to understand the essence of what a patient might be saying. I listened to their words and to their body language. I was craving more intimacy and closeness in my work, and I felt ready enough for this next step that I was willing to try despite my fear.

I slowly began running my groups in a more process-oriented way, and started bringing to supervision questions and concerns about what I was experiencing: *How do I respond when it feels like a patient is flirting with me? I feel so agitated every time I meet with this patient – what could be going on here? What do I do when a patient won't speak in group, but always pulls me aside outside of the group? What do I do when a patient tells me I didn't play the song "right"?* It was hard to break free from the product-oriented work I had been doing for six years. It was easier to stick with more concrete themes such as seasons and holidays rather than face the anger, sadness, and confusing feelings that would inevitably arise in this process-oriented approach. As John's face stayed with me, I realized that "easier" wasn't that easy after all. I was at rock bottom and about to leave the profession entirely, so this seemed like a last-ditch effort to see if I could stay in the profession of music therapy.

Once I found my footing in being with whatever content the patients introduced, Michelle encouraged me to think about songs and improvisations more as containers or holders for feelings. In the past I had categorized music by concrete, rigid themes rather than open-ended emotional containers, because I wasn't sure I knew how to handle those emotions. I was surprised, then, to find that I was capable of doing this work. I didn't need a highly detailed session plan to guide what I'd say and do in each moment of the session. Asking the patients how they were feeling that day led to meaningful music making and conversations – I was getting to know them better and allowing them space to get to know each other better by starting with where they were. I hadn't known if I was capable of doing process-oriented work because I had never seen a music therapist practice in this way.

I also began engaging in personal therapy to help me explore my perfectionism and low confidence issues, as these issues were impacting my presence as a music therapist. I wanted to see more nuances and counter my tendency toward binary thinking. With these supports, I slowly began to feel more comfortable with process-oriented work. I was becoming better at valuing my emotions and the emotions of my patients, and when I struggled with expressing myself, I paid attention to how my body was feeling. Parallel to this professional growth, I was feeling more in tune with myself, and I began to feel an even greater calm even outside of work. I was no longer spending all my evenings outside of work planning activities. I was more present in the moment at both home and work.

Negotiating Power and Privilege

In the first months that I began participating in supervision, I found myself chronically struggling in my relationship with an older Black woman named Mabel. Mabel was in her 70s and diagnosed with schizoaffective disorder and obsessive-compulsive disorder (OCD). She had been institutionalized on and off since childhood because her symptoms were so severe that she was unable to function independently, even with more informal or familial help. After so many years of interacting with staff and patients in the various institutions where she lived, Mabel had developed some regimented patterns of interaction. These interactions with staff were often distressing and injurious to others.

Mabel received group music therapy for 45 minutes each week. Prior to starting supervision, Mabel would sing one or two of her preferred songs and then I would attempt to proceed with my session plan. At the time, I thought that I was giving her space for her songs, and I thought that we were working towards her goals of increasing flexibility by also expecting her to be able to listen to my activities-based songs.

As time went on, Mabel would often interrupt other group members and myself, saying the names of the songs she wanted to hear over and over again. We all then became engaged in what I experienced as a group tug-of-war. Mabel wanted to hear her songs, other group members wanted to hear their songs, and I still had my activities-based session plan that I had hoped to get to. The group was in conflict, and I was struggling with how to move through this conflict.

Mabel often requested to hear the nursery rhyme song "London Bridge is Falling Down," and I remember judging her and thinking: *This is an adult group and I'm not doing nursery rhymes. Why would this woman crave this simple, silly song so much?* In retrospect, I can see that I was being discriminative towards Mabel due to her age. I had labeled her song as "silly" because it was a nursery rhyme. I had an idea in my mind of what kind of songs older adult patients "should" want to hear, songs that were "age-appropriate" and not nursery rhymes. When I worked with the older adults using themed sessions related to the seasons and holidays, it was an activities-based way of working on reality orientation goals. But then when we were together, Mabel didn't seem to want to know what holiday or season it was. It felt like she needed and craved connection and belonging in the here-and-now regardless of what season or holiday it was, and that we had different expectations about what was going to be of help to her in music therapy.

I remember Mabel's voice pleading, her body rocking incessantly back and forth asking for the song "London Bridge, London Bridge" over and over again. I tried to lean into Michelle's advice to more fully welcome Mabel's songs. So, we played "London Bridge is Falling Down" together. Her eyes gently met mine and she began to sway her body in unison with me. I stayed present with her and sang with her. Finally, she lifted up her hands and said, "Ok, ok, that's enough now. The song's over – you can stop."

This moment with Mabel has stayed with me. It was one of the first times I had allowed myself to more fully be with her in the music. Subsequently, something intangible eased between us, as I had finally stopped from trying to make her do and simply allowed her to "be." By extension, it slowly began feeling more natural to let Mabel take the lead singing her songs in the group.

Looking back now, I can see that there were power dynamics being negotiated between Mabel and me. Having been institutionalized since childhood, she did not have the freedoms that I had. Her ability to move freely was greatly restricted: she couldn't eat when she was hungry, go back to her bedroom when she was tired, or use the bathroom when she was ready. I had reinforced a dynamic of staff being in power and the patient being told what to do by coming in with a set activities-based plan. I also reflected on the potential of the institutional power dynamic being further exacerbated by my unearned power and privilege being white. I don't know how Mabel experienced this, but I had not considered at the time these potential power dynamics. And given how my supervisor and I both shared white identities, it may not have been as present to either of us how this could have been impacting my interactions with Mabel. I wish I would have more fully listened to Mabel sooner.

During our supervision sessions, Michelle encouraged me to take a closer look at the lyrics of "London Bridge is Falling Down" and explore them in context of Mabel's diagnosis and treatment history. I remember Mabel's voice elevating as she sang *Take the keys and lock her up, lock her up, lock her up*. The song lyrics made sense to me as an expression of what Mabel may have been experiencing. Perhaps she was feeling as if I was "locking her up" by not fully welcoming her songs or quickly judging them.

Once this insight became clearer, I was wracked with guilt and shame over how annoyed I had been with Mabel. But Michelle welcomed my feelings of annoyance as we talked about them as part of my countertransference. It was frustrating to feel helpless and captive to Mabel's relentless demands for her songs, and when I didn't know how to tolerate the feeling of helplessness, it turned into annoyance. Helplessness may also have been part of what Mabel was feeling in these difficult moments in the group. Instead of seeing her preferred songs as not in "my plan," I began welcoming her songs, trusting that the path to greater wellness would lie in Mabel having the opportunity to make choices and me responding more mindfully to those choices.

At this stage, I found myself feeling more confident and prepared. My time in supervision was beginning to feel more exploratory and less directive. I was able to be more thoughtful about my patients, their music, and be responsive to subsequent challenging clinical situations.

Finding Myself

After about a year of supervision, I realized I needed to remove more prescriptive interventions and directive groups from my schedule as they were no longer aligning with my self-concept as a professional. Many of my groups became simply called "Music Therapy Group," and we followed the general format of asking the clients how they were feeling either through words, songs, or percussive improvisation. The goal was for clients to use songs to hold their emotions and use those moments in the music to relate or connect with other group members.

As these connections began happening, I was surprised to find how calm my body began to feel and how confident I was becoming. I was no longer constantly looking at the clock and wondering when the session would end. I embraced silence and accepted that group engagement became richer and more diverse when I allowed myself to be led by the clients. I asked patients more questions so that I could better understand what they were saying.

Patients opened up more as I listened instead of waiting for my turn to talk. They shared their sadness authentically and openly, giving us a window into their real world. I remember one group where I asked a patient if there was a song speaking to him. He said, in the most serious and saddest of ways: "Any song would be too beautiful for my life." He explained that there was no song that could hold his level of sadness and despair. It was so hard for me to hear his profound sadness. I could feel the despair running through him and me in that moment.

For the first time in a session, I allowed a tear to roll down my face. Any song that I could have played would have felt artificial at that moment. Allowing that tear to fall seemed to be the most real thing that I could have done. The other group members sat there quietly holding the space. It felt good to be outwardly emotional without judging myself. I began to not be afraid of emotion both in myself and in my patients, to welcome sadness and anger as much as I had welcomed happiness in my old activities-based way of working. I realized I didn't need to immediately fix or change it, and that it was more important to first learn how to just be with the sadness together.

Conclusion

At the earliest stages of my career, I struggled to understand who I was as a professional and found myself becoming burned out, even disillusioned. I knew I needed to completely change my practice to stop dreading work the next day, but discovering my authentic practice was not easy. Clinical supervision became a pathway for discovering my identity as a music therapist; within that supportive space, I confronted my fears, actively questioned my foundational understandings of health and relating to others, and ultimately discovered a way to practice that was meaningful and intimate. It was deeply freeing to individuate from the philosophies of my entry-level training and discover new philosophies that aligned with how I understood what it means to be healthy and in music.

Summarizing Ideas and Questions for Discussion

1. The first few years of practice can be a challenging time when, as a music therapist, we confront fears and anxieties about our work and our evolving professional identity.

    a. How do you define music, therapy, and music therapy?
    b. How do those definitions align with your personal values?

    c.   Where and how do your current definitions align or deviate from your personal values?

2.   Clinical supervision can be a vulnerable space for substantive, even radical, professional growth.

    a.   What are experiences of clinical supervision that have been helpful for you in the past?

    b.   What are experiences of clinical supervision that have been unhelpful, or even harmful, in the past?

    c.   How would you describe a supervisory relationship that is challenging yet supportive? What would it feel like to be a part of such a relationship?

Notes

1 Kendall, F. (2012). *Understanding white privilege: Creating pathways to authentic relationships across race* (2nd ed.). Routledge.
2 DeCuir, A. A., & Vega, V. P. (2010). Career longevity: A survey of experienced professional music therapists. *The Arts in Psychotherapy*, *37*, 135–142. https://doi.org/10.1016/j.aip.2009.12.004

Chapter 7

Expanding Practice by Exploring Clinical Limitations

Cathleen Flynn

Abstract

Music therapists in training and new professionals may experience pressure to feel and appear consistently competent in their practice, yet an essential component of professional development is recognizing the limitations impacting the clinical encounter. Acknowledging those multi-layered clinical limitations can help music therapists be better positioned as reflexive clinicians who can adapt to evolving situations and emerging contexts.

Tags: Supervision; Therapeutic Relationship

Content warning: mention of violence and homicide

So much is possible in the music therapy encounter, yet I have found clinical limitations in my work that, when left unacknowledged and unattended, have weakened therapeutic relationships, reduced treatment effectiveness, and dampened connection to my practice. Clinical supervision provided me an avenue for exploring how clinical limitations, rather than being something to shy away from, could reveal significant aspects of the therapeutic process and allow me to cultivate meaningful experiences with patients.

In this case, I navigate two interdependent roles – clinician and supervisee – in a shared process of emotional attunement involving me, Rosa (a hospice patient), and Jen (my clinical supervisor). Multiple sociocultural locations texture my perspective of this case. I am a queer, White, neurotypical, non-disabled, cisgender female and see each of these identities as potentiating and limiting forces in my work. My clinical experience is distinctly shaped by American approaches to music therapy training, and I practice psychodynamically while also drawing heavily on existentialism and feminism. At the time of this case, I worked at a hospice in the rural southeastern United States.

DOI: 10.4324/9781003123798-10

Clinical Limitations

Based on my clinical experiences, I define a clinical limitation as any factor that constrains what is possible in a therapeutic encounter. Although "limitation" may have negative connotations or conjure unchanging phenomena, I suggest limitations are neutral, frequently dynamic constructs that can reveal information relevant to treatment. Any feature of a music therapist, patient, physical setting, or sociopolitical context can constitute a clinical limitation. Music therapist limitations may include skill or technique, aspects of identity or experience (e.g., cultural identities or life experiences), psychological aspects, and access to resources (e.g., research and adequate salary). Patient limitations may include variable readiness and/or interest in therapy, compromised states of consciousness, and access to resources. Physical setting limitations may include organizational structure, available equipment, and treatment environment. Sociopolitical context limitations may include reimbursement, insurance dictates, government regulation of healthcare, and the healthcare industry climate in a community.

I take a broad view of factors impacting therapeutic encounters (e.g., competency, countertransference, cultural identity, and resource availability), highlighting how in everyday practice they may be experienced by the music therapist as ambiguous, multivariate limitations requiring supervisory support. Examinations of limitations are largely absent despite increased attention to historically under-examined factors like dominant cultural narratives[1] and intersubjectivity.[2,3,4] Depictions of music therapy as a miraculous treatment foster a tendency to idealize music therapy practice, making it tempting to deny limitations altogether; at the same time, some music therapists are haunted by self-doubt[5] and an exaggerated sense of the limits of their potential.

My learning as an early career professional involved both accepting limitations and addressing them through skill-building, such as verbal processing and familiarity with new musical artists. But skill-building and acceptance have been only part of the equation: when limitations have constellated in complex ways, I have experienced difficult emotions requiring commitments to ongoing reflexive practices such as supervision and personal psychotherapy. Since clinical limitations can be like optical illusions – best visible from a distance with relaxed focus – I needed skilled assistance to address them. This case illustrates how supervision helped me tend to limitations in ways that gradually expanded what was possible in therapeutic encounters.

Supervisor and Supervisee

At the time of this case, I had been meeting virtually with Jen twice a month for one year prior to meeting Rosa. Jen, a depth psychologist also trained as a music therapist, presented on a topic of interest to me at a conference, so I contacted her when I wanted professional supervision for the first time. I had been board-certified and practicing at a bachelor's level for one year and was pursuing a master's degree at the time. On a conscious level, I sought her support for problem-solving and short-term oversight of a challenge that arose during graduate studies; I had a thesis idea and wanted a supervisor from outside my work and school institutions to help me think through a clinical research project. But I had also been feeling intermittently numb in my work, saturated by the perceived demands of my job and patients. I experienced dread at the beginning of many workdays and guilt about my dread, thinking I must be doing something wrong to feel that way. Though I was not entirely conscious of it at the time, I think I hoped supervision would ease that discomfort and help me feel more connected to my work.

Jen told me her approach lent itself to a longer-term relational commitment between the two of us. I felt nervous, not knowing how things might unfold, but knew I wanted to work with her. Jen and I made a plan to meet, and from that initial conversation onward my sense of how supervision could support me developed in unexpected ways.

Through our supervisory alliance and her relational psychoanalytic approach, Jen readily attuned to and inquired about the emotions I experienced in clinical work. I had mostly lived in my head up until that point and thought my strong emotions – particularly the unpleasant ones – were largely something to avoid. Over time, supervision became a place to consider how that avoidance severed my connection to the work, explore how patients were impacting me, and wrestle with my emerging professional identity.

I was lucky to have strong relationships with my coworkers, but the amount of time and skilled investment required to explore my experiences in depth was not available from a peer or boss. Even in a collegial environment, it was easy to feel isolated as I traveled throughout the day to patient residences and participated on multiple teams. A critical difference between ongoing supervision and informal consultation with colleagues was Jen's cumulative understanding of my strengths and struggles that grew from our shared investment in the relationship. Further, Jen's position outside of my institution kept her curious; she could not rely on assumptions about what was possible based on lived experiences on-the-ground with me, so my own perceptions were the central guide. That understanding and curiosity were the dynamic resources necessary to address clinical limitations as they arose in my work with Rosa.

Patient and Practitioner

Rosa was a retired Christian minister in her mid-80s receiving hospice care for pancreatic cancer. We worked together for ten months prior to her death at a skilled nursing facility. Rosa was a second-generation German American who had traveled extensively during her career as an evangelist, theologian, and missionary. She had created chosen family in each of her communities, the latest being her care facility. Her terminal diagnosis demanded she step down from a leadership role on the facility's resident council, but she remained focused on the social and political life of the community while integrating the hospice team into her interpersonal sphere. As cancer metastasized and increased her fatigue while decreasing her mobility, I received a referral from the hospice nurse who sensed Rosa's depression in the face of these changes. Rosa agreed to meet out of curiosity, uncertain whether or not she wanted music therapy.

In addition to writing medical record notes after sessions, I wrote subjective reflections to help me track what to discuss in supervision. I re-read those notes in the months following Rosa's death and filled out reflective fragments with more narrative to depict the experiences as I remembered them. The following section is a condensed version of this narrative to outline the trajectory of our work and highlight aspects most significant to my clinical limitations.

Reflections on Rosa

As I entered Rosa's room for the first time, I felt examined. She smiled, spoke words of welcome, and gestured where to sit like so many patients I'd seen before, but I was strangely aware of my movements, facial expressions, and voice . . . my shallowly buried insecurity sounded a thin, echolalic string of inner questions about my adequacy and acceptability. She had prepared for the session by marking a song in her hymnal, and asked: "Can you play it?" I was eager to please her and said I could try. After an earnest sight-reading attempt, she informed me she did not really like the song but felt the lyrics communicated things I should know about her life. I had been working professionally for a couple of years, but felt like a new student who should be taking notes.

I left our first interaction feeling intimidated, as if I would need to measure up to be deemed worthy of an invitation back. She accepted my offer to borrow a preferred instrument for a week, perhaps ensuring I would come back or asserting a measure of control in the process. From those first moments, she and I began co-creating a world pre-constructed by our respective histories but evolving through our immediate interaction and began navigating a terrain of ambivalence and power/powerlessness.

In our third month of work, Rosa shared her distrust in the willingness or capability of others to truly care for her. Staff often asked if she needed anything; after they left, she would say: "They don't really mean it, that offer to help." I recognized she might have been sensing a real incongruence in some staff, yet I was also aware of how her history might shape this perception. She discussed a sense of independent self-reliance from early childhood. I wondered internally about those attachment patterns, acknowledging she was probably also suspicious of my sincerity. I did not in that moment have the skill or courage to formulate my thoughts into an exploratory question, but held the curiosity in mind. Rosa asked to end that session with a children's song. I wondered if this was an invitation for me to engage with a younger aspect of herself, a request to shift to something novel and far away from what we were discussing, or something else entirely. Not knowing, I readily followed this unexpected lead and noticed a sense of vulnerability alive in the playfulness of the song.

When I arrived for our next session, Rosa was watching news coverage about a man who had abducted and murdered multiple people. She was engrossed and we listened to the coverage together as I completed the customary process of arranging furniture to create a place for myself and my instruments. Rosa expressed sympathy aloud for the man, stating she could "understand the hunger" for power over others and the desire to violently act out, and that she sometimes felt "that hunger." Although I asked her to tell me more about her experience of this hunger, Rosa appeared to feel my internal withdrawal and contraction. I was afraid to hear her, a woman who had committed her life to vulnerable others, sharing fantasies of dominance and even violence; this was a threshold I was not yet ready to cross. In retrospect, I realized Rosa must have felt abandoned or rejected in the face of my fear. After fumbling for ground in words and music for the remainder of the session, we ended our time from a place of subtle but significant awkwardness and disconnection. I suggested a familiar song to close, and she acquiesced.

Rosa refused the next four sessions I offered. After the second refusal and at Jen's suggestion, I acknowledged with gentle words the issue of my inadvertent emotional abandonment, but she declined the invitation to discuss it. I validated how difficult it might be for her to process it with me. She seemed to find a sense of power and safety in rejecting my offers to meet. I swam through many responses – guilt, anger, indifference, panic, disappointment – in supervision. Jen's attunement to these varied reactions became a buoy through which I could stay present with myself and Rosa in those challenging weeks.

Eventually Rosa agreed to a session again, and the next three months of our work involved the gradual re-establishment of trust. We explored themes of connection/disconnection, harm, and help. She shared about a heartbreak faced as a child, made more painful by her father's difficulty empathizing with her distress. And four months after my own failure to adequately empathize, Rosa offered an empathic reach that deepened our connection. Rosa asked how old I was. After I decided to disclose my age and inquire about her curiosity, she shared that she had been fired from a job at the same age. I initially perceived this as meaningful simply because of her choice to disclose information about an experience of vulnerability. In supervision, we explored how Rosa's disclosure revealed a parallel between her experience and mine wherein she "fired" me for several weeks. It was Rosa's most direct acknowledgment about what had happened between us.

About a month later, Rosa's disease process quickened. Sessions became more receptive as she became weaker and more confused. She gave the hospice nurse a piece of music for the hymn "I Was There to Hear Your Borning Cry" and requested I learn it; she asked to hear it nearly every session, sometimes multiple times, for the remainder of our work. During the last six weeks of her life, sessions became shorter as her wakeful hours decreased. In what was our final session, she requested I adjust her blankets and moisten a sponge for her mouth (a common comfort measure taken during imminent death when body hydration changes). These gestures were acutely intimate for a woman who had doubted others' capacity to give care and similarly doubted her capacity to receive it.

When Rosa died, I grieved what we had created through our attempts, and failures, to find one another in our work. Many potentials and limitations characterized our process, each one rich with material upon which a relationship was built.

Tending to Clinical Limitations

A fundamental force alive in the work I shared with Rosa was the relational space, or intersubjective field, between us. I had been board-certified for a year before encountering the notion that psychological material between me and a patient was always co-created. I had received cautionary statements in my training about the detriments of the practitioner not leaving their emotional "stuff" at the figurative "door." This caution framed emotional experience as entirely *within* either the practitioner or the patient, rather than something *between* us.

Ambivalence and the dynamics of power/powerlessness were two aspects of Rosa's and my intersubjective experiences frequently discussed in supervision. I had difficulty understanding how I simultaneously desired and feared greater connection with Rosa, and Jen helped me consider how Rosa was likely experiencing a similar conflict. Rosa would reflect on her waning sense of agency at the same time I felt her authority in sessions. Disease factors (e.g., fatigue) and cultural factors (e.g., generation and gender) further contributed to this complex intersubjective field. Although there was a 60-year age difference between me and Rosa, we both grew up in religious and educational settings that subjugated girls' desires for power or physical domination. Jen's questions about what I initially imagined about Rosa (i.e., that spiritual virtue or old age meant she would be gentle) helped me consider how Rosa and I co-created our dynamic.

I felt confused, anxious, disappointed, frustrated, and despairing, but also felt deeply touched, elated, and humored at various points with Rosa. Jen's attunement to these emotions helped me find the meaning within them even as I struggled, as a new professional, to get outside of my head. Attunement is "a two-part process that begins with empathy – sensitive to and identifying with the other person's sensations, needs, or feelings and . . . communication of that sensitivity to the other person."[6] Through this attunement, I was able to navigate four regions of clinical limitations in my work with Rosa. In exploring each region here, I will illustrate how our supervision process helped me tend the limits of what was unfolding between me and Rosa.

Musical Limitations

With Rosa, music had limited the therapeutic encounter when I hid behind it in our session. When Rosa voiced her violent fantasy, I chose a familiar, previously preferred song to close. I felt uncomfortable and deflated at the time and, in retrospect, see the choice as an attempt to stabilize my ego. Instead of sharing my uncertainty and concern about ending the session from a place of disconnection, I pacified myself with a song and hoped it would pacify Rosa too. My reliance on the concept of a closing song limited our encounter by positioning the music between us to create distance within a difficult encounter.

After this experience, it became important for me to consider how I sometimes used music to obstruct rather than facilitate connection. My decision-making was not fundamentally bad as it served a protective function for me, nor was I able to make a different decision in that moment, but it also was not therapeutic for Rosa because it cut off our connection instead of further cultivating it. Over-reliance on particular musical processes, like my need with Rosa to end with a familiar song, limited my responsiveness to present-moment needs.

Jen and I explored instances in which music distanced rather than connected me and Rosa. Addressing my musical limitations as a practitioner meant investigating the emotions and psychological content at play in those instances. This was accomplished in part by expanding my repertoire to include songs with a wider range of musical and lyrical affects, such as rage, isolation, and numbness.

Interpersonal-Verbal Limitations

Here, I discuss interpersonal-verbal limitations jointly and frame them separately from musical limitations. I recognize the risk of representing these phenomena separately as both are part of musicing in music therapy, but I do so to encourage systematic reflection on these interrelated domains.

At this point in my career, I found verbally relating and responding to patients to be a challenge since my music therapy training was geared toward paraverbal and nonverbal encounters. I had internalized several discourses around me that framed music therapy as more psychologically safe and accessible than verbal therapies; this perception impacted how I approached and what I expected from verbal processing. Another complication was learning how to support patients who did not readily express

expectations or needs in music therapy because they belonged to generations, cultural groups, and/or families who responded to struggle through
silence or avoidance. The interpersonal-verbal limitations in my work with
Rosa existed for all of these reasons.

Rosa had difficulty voicing her disappointment in me for inadequately
empathizing with her destructive side. At the time of her second session
refusal, she declined my tentative offer to discuss how I emotionally abandoned her when I felt disturbed; instead, she communicated her hurt
through continued refusal to meet. Harm resulted from my failure to more
fully empathize and because of this situation's resemblance to childhood
experiences with her father. It was difficult to discuss with her the impact
of my limitation because it required being vulnerable in admitting how
I had hurt her despite my best intentions.

In supervision, I began organizing my thoughts and imagining the conversation. By articulating the impact of my limitation on Rosa, I resisted
some of my own habitual ways of moving through the world. Both Rosa
and I grew up in cultural and familial contexts that prioritized thinking
over feeling, so it would have been a familiar route to leave unspoken what
we felt toward one another and the process. In supervision, I practiced
sharing my feelings about Rosa and the process Jen and I were forging.
Supervision became a parallel process wherein talking about my limitations softened their anxiety-ridden edges. Jen offered in various forms the
question "What are you and Rosa not saying to one another?" as a way of
helping me identify the interpersonal-verbal limitations at play.

Psychological Limitations

Whereas interpersonal-verbal limitations can be responsive to technical
adjustments based on insight gleaned in supervision, I have found psychological limitations take more time and energy to address. While Rosa
and I worked toward reckoning with the unsaid between us, that did not
mean I suddenly became comfortable with her rage or mine. It took several
years of personal psychotherapy to explore, embody, and articulate my
relationship to rage and destruction. Similarly, Rosa's avoidant attachment,
marked by hyper-independence and distrust to offers of care, did not dis-
appear even when we openly explored how it impacted our work.

Psychological limitations, which are not consistently conscious, required
my supervisor's deepest level of attunement because of the vulnerability
they evoked and how profoundly they shaped my life experiences. Supervisor attunement to these areas necessarily touches the thin boundary
between supervision and psychotherapy. Jen and I periodically dialogued
about that boundary to keep the focus of supervision on my clinical work
while staying attentive to the aspects of my personal psychology that manifested with Rosa.

When a boundary was troubled between me and Jen, we worked to repair our connection as is done in the therapeutic relationship. In one supervision meeting, I dissociated when exploring a psychological limitation in my work with another patient around the same time I worked with Rosa. Jen noticed my shift in engagement and, while we did not have adequate time to fully process what happened, we scheduled an extra follow-up meeting. Her curiosity urged me to also be curious about how that limitation was impacting our dynamic. I verbalized feeling overexposed and she empathized, sharing her uncertainty about the blurry boundaries between supervision and therapy when we explored the deep personal impacts of my clinical relationships.

This dialogue about the limits of our supervisor/supervisee relationship renewed my commitment to supervision. This discussion of boundaries also helped me imagine how I might utilize similar care with Rosa (and other patients) when psychological limitations brought out unexpected elements in our work. Her compassion for the not-yet-accessible parts of my psyche helped me hold compassion for the not-yet-accessible parts of patients like Rosa.

Limitations of Setting

Multiple sociopolitical and physical setting factors limited Rosa's and my work. Providing care in skilled nursing facilities means working around fixed meal, activity, and personal care schedules, and accepting that sessions will frequently be interrupted for medication distribution, social visits, or team rounding. Additionally, my coming and going from Rosa's space required furniture rearrangement and positioning myself at the doorway to her private bathroom, which she sometimes expressed embarrassment about. She was courageous to allow me to take up intimate physical space when it was so limited. While these physical setting limitations may seem insignificant, they contributed to our unfolding experience.

Besides the visible attributes of her room and residential community, invisible sociopolitical structures limited our work. Over the course of our work together, large corporations purchased both my employer and Rosa's community, destabilizing their organizational identities. Rosa expressed deep concern about the legacy of her community, which she would not live to see adapt to this change. While Rosa may have benefited from weekly therapy, my caseload did not always allow for sessions more than twice a month, which is still more frequent than many hospice music therapists can schedule patients. Supervision helped me cope with the frustration I experienced providing music therapy in a profit-driven healthcare industry that often seemed at odds with the hospice philosophy of care and my personal values. Jen gave me space and supportive feedback to discharge my dissatisfaction with what was *not* possible so I could become more available for what *was* in the limited settings where Rosa and I met.

A Closing

To reduce harm and promote good in music therapy, I needed to negotiate my limitations alongside those of Rosa and her settings. Negotiating limitations with the support of an attuned supervisor increased my tolerance for "the value of not-knowing."[7] Addressing these limitations made me more present, compassionate, and flexible in my practice.

As I close, I wonder whether the significant aspects of this therapeutic relationship may make it seem unrepresentative of everyday clinical encounters, but I find experiences of uncertainty and intensity *are* ordinary in the daily life of the music therapist. Even the seemingly mundane presents to me as textured and layered when I reflect deeply on my experience of shared relational-musical spaces with patients. By tending to both limitations and potentials, I have been better able to face wholeheartedly a wide range of human experience in myself, and to witness it more fully in others. May we all be well-supported in our tending.

Summarizing Ideas and Questions for Discussion

1. All therapeutic encounters are limited by aspects of the practitioner, the patient, and the setting (physical and sociopolitical).

   a. Think about a patient or group you have worked with. What wasn't or didn't seem possible given clinical limitations? How did these limitations impact you at the time, and what do you make of them now?

   b. In your current clinical environment, which limitations are unchanging session-to-session? Which limitations change, and how do such changes happen?

   c. As a supervisor, what do you see limiting supervisees in their work? What do you experience as limiting the supervision process?

2. Emotional attunement from a supervisor helps the practitioner work with clinical limitations and maximize therapeutic potential.

   a. How does it affect you when a supervisor or colleague asks about your emotional experience of work with a patient?

   b. What influences what you want and need from a supervisor?

   c. As a supervisor, what facilitates your attunement? What makes attunement difficult?

Notes

1 Hadley, S. (2013). Dominant narratives: Complicity and the need for vigilance in the creative arts therapies. *The Arts in Psychotherapy, 40*(4), 373–381. https://doi.org/10.1016/j.aip.2013.05.007

2 Arthur, M. H. (2018). A humanistic perspective on intersubjectivity in music psychotherapy. *Music Therapy Perspectives, 36*(2), 161–167. https://doi.org/10.1093/mtp/miy017

3 Birnbaum, J. C. (2014). Intersubjectivity and Nordoff-Robbins music therapy. *Music Therapy Perspectives, 32*(1), 30–37. https://doi.org/10.1093/mtp/miu004

4 Trondalen, G. (2019). Musical intersubjectivity. *The Arts in Psychotherapy, 65*(101589). https://doi.org/10.1016/j.aip.2019.101589

5 Pickett, C. (2020, August). *The occurrence of imposter phenomenon: A survey of music therapists* [Master's thesis, Saint Mary-of-the-Woods College]. https://scholars.smwc.edu/handle/20.500.12770/158

6 Erskine, R. G. (1998). Attunement and involvement: Therapeutic responses to relational needs. *International Journal of Psychotherapy, 3*(3), 235–244 (p. 236).

7 Freshwater, D. (2009). Reflexivity and intersubjectivity in clinical supervision: On the value of not-knowing. In C. Johns & D. Freshwater (Eds.), *Transforming nursing through reflective practice* (pp. 99–115). Blackwell Science Ltd.

Chapter 8

How Much Giving Is Enough?

Yu-Ching Ruby Chen

Abstract

Music therapists working long-term with patients in acute settings can have their boundaries challenged in multiple ways. One potential result is split loyalties, wherein the music therapist feels caught between sustaining care with the long-term patient at the expense of providing care to patients with more acute symptoms. Split loyalties can also be a re-enacted dynamic from the music therapist's history. A culturally reflexive process of critical self-reflection and clinical practice can help the music therapist negotiate that boundary loss.

Tags: Therapeutic Relationship; Treatment Planning

The Sixth Admission

Diane was admitted to the hospital again. Her breathing had become more labored, even after her doctor increased her usual breathing treatment and supplemental oxygen. She lived with multiple chronic illnesses, including chronic obstructive pulmonary disease (COPD), anxiety, and depression. She had been going to the hospital more frequently in recent months and was staying longer in each admission. The frequency of recent hospitalizations raised the question of whether there was something more to Diane's medical condition, which had been stable for decades until these recent admissions. As it turned out, an X-ray found a spot in her lungs, and a biopsy was recommended to rule out malignancy during this admission.

Upon reviewing the medical chart, I noticed Diane had on multiple occurrences refused daily care, such as labs, therapies, medications. Sometimes the behaviors were labeled as "aggressive" when documented by nursing staff. I suspected that the music therapy order was the team's effort to improve Diane's compliance.

As both the only music therapist providing service at this hospital and an immigrant from Taiwan, I was not sure if there was another person within

DOI: 10.4324/9781003123798-11

the system who shared my social identity. Growing up in Taiwan, being friendly and respecting others were highly valued qualities in social situations. I am also a private person, and in order to maintain friendliness without dismissing a conversation, I learned to keep my thoughts vague, especially when I interact with older relatives because we must respect our elders. After experiencing burnout, I learned the importance of protecting my personal time and developed strong boundaries between my personal life and my work life. Protecting my personal space has not affected my ability to be emotionally connected with people, either socially or in sessions.

In my practice, I assess with curiosity by focusing on the person's various lived experiences and the cultural sources of their values and ethics. I also strive to find commonalities in our feelings and reactions regardless of the differences we may present; in an environment where I regularly meet people under circumstances that are stressful and extreme, I find connecting through the mundane details in life humanizing and appreciated.

Starting to work with Diane was initially challenging. Being a white woman living in a suburban neighborhood, Diane represented a cultural demographic that I had a growing uneasiness with after an incident in which my safety was threatened. This incident occurred in the area where many of my former clients lived, and I developed a remote association of hostility with this demographic after the incident. This uneasiness was further amplified when I read about Diane's behaviors in her chart. Yet, I knew my experience of feeling threatened by this demographic was not a fair judgment of Diane, and I chose to focus on learning more about her regardless of what others had said and the feelings I was projecting. I wanted to know about the things she liked to do, the people she cared about, and her support structures. I wanted to know what the behaviors noted in her chart meant in the context of her personal experiences.

A Formed Bond

Diane appeared calm when I greeted her in her room. She tensed up slightly, perhaps trying to understand the reason for my visit. As soon as I introduced my role as a music therapist, her eyes lit up. She identified herself as a "music lover" and named several favorite country music artists, including George Jones, Randy Travis, Tammy Wynette, and, most notably, Dolly Parton. There was a genuine excitement in her tone of voice.

In initial sessions, I usually give patients freedom with their musical choices, level of engagement, and style of participation. Diane did not hesitate to take the lead. We found a nice balance between music listening and verbal discussion about the songs. Since I did not know every song Diane identified, both live and pre-recorded music experiences were used. She did not seem to prefer one method of music delivery over another, but she was specific about the artists on the songs she wanted to listen to. It did not take long before I noticed that Diane was smiling more with a shift in her posture. The energy in the room changed. It felt like she was allowing me to get to know her as a person and not as a patient by sharing the music she loved with me.

As I learned more about Diane, I felt puzzled. Nothing about this interaction suggested that she was an "aggressive" person. The incongruence of my experience and the team members' notes about her disruptive behaviors made me wonder what exactly happened during those incidents. After observing positive responses in our session, I felt a sense of obligation for music therapy to help soften the tension between her and the care team. I was hoping the frequency of behavioral notes would decrease with the addition of music therapy. Relatedly, I saw my work with Diane as an opportunity to prove that music therapy is needed in the acute care medical setting. Even though the hospital system had been an avid supporter of creative arts therapies for decades prior to my employment, I gripped on to this self-assigned responsibility tightly. Perhaps it was a way to pay my respect to my elders, all the predecessors in the music therapy community who had nurtured the field in this clinical space and who had personally mentored me.

It was early on when I discovered something about Diane that furthered my commitment to her care. In one of our usual sessions, Diane shared she had a lot going on but did not wish to elaborate. Instead of directly discussing what was on her mind, we followed our usual session structure: listening to songs selected by her and discussing why these songs are meaningful to her. Some of the songs she chose included "He Stopped Loving Her Today" by George Jones, "He Walked on Water" by Randy Travis, and "I Will Always Love You" by Dolly Parton. When I brought up the common theme in these songs (i.e., the ending of relationships), Diane hesitated and became silent. When she spoke again, she revealed years of being emotionally abused and financially exploited by family members. To make matters worse, Diane had lost her only child to cancer just a couple of years prior to this admission. He was her only support system. She said: "I thought I did not have the right to be happy again." Now she was facing the possibility of a diagnosis similar to her son's while still experiencing grief. She finally acknowledged that she was terrified of the biopsy. She was not ready for the diagnostic test and would rather stall by refusing care.

My underlying uneasiness had dissolved. Instead, I felt a tremendous amount of empathy and sadness for her. Perhaps the behaviors indicated in the notes were there to protect herself. She was trying to hide a vulnerable and frightened person behind a tough armor. The grief was likely intensified when she was facing a similar diagnosis herself. Whether or not Diane chose these songs purposefully, they helped me understand her experience and gave her a way to express the pain through something beautiful.

I opened a dialogue about how emotions can muddy our thinking process, especially when we have to make important decisions. I validated the fact that losing a son to cancer was probably one of the reasons why her fear was so intense. Diane added that she did not want to go through this process alone. Knowing she had nobody in her personal life to rely on, this statement felt so heavy we had to let silence fill the space. After a moment, I noticed her posture and affect softened, then she told me she was ready to rest. There was no sense of burden in her words. This was a freeing experience for Diane, to be able to acknowledge the fear itself. We closed our session and set a plan for next.

I don't think I understood the impact of this session until more deeply reflecting while writing this case. Making this connection with Diane through music was a tremendous and humbling experience, both as a person and a clinician. In that moment, we were simply entranced in the sense of release from the hospital, from cancer, and from the need to protect. I remain struck with how this profound healing experience could just as easily not have occurred had Diane declined my service due to her wariness towards hospital staff, or had I allowed my past experience to prevent me from investing in her case.

At the next session, Diane surprised me by proudly announcing that she had decided to proceed with the biopsy, and she felt relieved after signing the consent form. Out of curiosity, I asked what helped her finally make the decision. She said it was the support from the unit staff, nurses, and therapists. Their words of encouragement made an impact. Diane said: "I realized I am not alone; this is my village . . . I'm ready to expand my world, just don't know how yet." To support this new phase of her process by affirming the support from her caregivers, we moved back into the music with "Never Alone" by Jim Brickman and sang about staying present with loved ones through the unknown.

The next time I saw Diane was after the biopsy. She was feeling foggy but was open for a session. She seemed shaken up and spoke about how scared she was during the procedure. She repeated to herself: "It's now in the past." I used our usual music listening and verbal discussion structure to gently bring her to the present moment to move through the emotional impact.

Supporting Diane Through Changes in Health

Conversations with staff a year after Diane's admission evoked vivid accounts of what they deemed as inappropriate behaviors: excessively calling for assistance, sometimes as frequently as every minute. From an administrative perspective, there is no way a facility can handle this level of demand from a single patient. This behavior quickly fatigued staff and the response to her calls began to delay which, in turn, led to Diane feeling ignored. Thus, a destructive cycle began wherein to receive the care she needed, she increased the frequency of requests which, in turn, led staff to respond less and less.

I recognized that her behaviors were coming from the fear of not receiving treatment and being forgotten, and I bore witness to her pain. When she described the experience of neglect and abuse by family members, her tremors increased. When she discussed going through medical procedures alone, she became sweatier and more fidgety. She never cried audibly in our sessions, but the tears that silently flowed down her face were noticed.

Diane spoke about how hard it was to start over again developing rapport and trust with new care staff on different units with each admission, a difficulty I empathized with given my fatigue when adapting to unfamiliar surroundings. When Diane finally felt more comfortable with the new unit, it was usually around the time for discharge. For someone already carrying a heavy emotional burden, this process was exhausting and further decreased her ability to adjust to changes.

At this point, Diane had identified music therapy as a service that made hospital stays easier. Therefore, I visited her daily whenever she was readmitted to the hospital. As the only music therapist in the hospital, I naturally became the one person she could have continuity with regardless of the unit she was admitted to. Having access to something familiar seemed to help Diane be more tolerable of unpredictable changes and feel supported.

There is very little in a hospital operation that I have control over, but it was within my power to serve as the one consistent and predictable element for Diane through this process, and I decided to see her for as long as she needed. Most of the staff worked under a tight schedule with limited flexibility, but I had a flexible schedule wherein I could purposely schedule Diane at the end of the day. Some days I stayed past my scheduled work hours for sessions. As a person who had made conscious efforts to separate work and personal life, I questioned these decisions, but at the time I believed they were right because of music therapy's potential to bring her relief.

Partly informing this decision was the knowledge that Diane was working against time as her condition continued to decline. I was noticing cognitive changes, such as an increased length of time when decision-making and increased repetition with memory-sharing. I was motivated to give Diane moments of living with dignity and peace through these health declines. It was a responsibility I gripped tightly.

Meanwhile, Diane continued to request staff's attention frequently while refusing necessary medical care. Her behavior was also affecting discharge planning. Due to increased debility, Diane either required home health care or skilled nursing facility placement. However, her behaviors did not stop at discharge, and many facilities and agencies declined to accept her. This lengthened her stay in the hospital and increased the stress of hospital staff. Diane, who had been deemed medically ready for discharge, did not respond well when staff shifted attention to patients with more acute symptoms.

When she started losing capacity to make medical decision, Diane appointed her grandson as her healthcare power of attorney, but the joyous reunion did not last long. When her grandson became engaged, Diane went into yet another spiral. A life event that most people celebrated with joy had triggered feelings of abandonment. Diane said: "I feel like I am losing him." She was so aware of her declining health that she was uncertain whether she would live to be present for the wedding. The future was becoming an increasingly ambiguous concept the more she became aware of her own mortality.

Diane's mental health suffered as she sank deeper into a helpless place. She was convinced she was unable to participate in physical and occupational therapy, which led to continued declines. I reinforced her strengths with comments on how she physically moved to music and sought to empower her to participate in her own care by continuing to make song choices. And whenever Diane was able to take a positive risk, I celebrated with her. In one session during this period, she made self-affirming comments that showed an emerging acceptance of ambiguity: "I don't know what tomorrow will look like, but I will do my best." I treasured these moments like catching a sliver of sunlight in a dark, cloudy sky. I truly believed that Diane genuinely desired to change when she experienced these successful moments.

Moving Beyond Boundaries of Safety

Diane's final admission occurred at the same time the world began grappling with the COVID-19 pandemic. Our entire hospital system became inordinately stressed as staff, becoming ill by the hundreds with this unknown disease, struggled to maintain operation of the facility while fearing their mortality. As staff attention turned to managing the crisis, Diane's behaviors became even more challenging to handle. I continued to visit Diane daily, but the demand from her was starting to weigh on me as well. She requested longer sessions with comments like "You are the only reason my day got better" or "Other people will never appreciate you like me." While seemingly appreciative, I could sense a hidden agenda to extract additional music therapy sessions by provoking my emotional responses to her regardless of my schedule, assessment, or caseload. Her requests for my time were getting harder and harder to manage.

My caseload more than doubled after the initial shock of the pandemic, and yet the average length of session with Diane increased from 30 minutes at initial admission to 85 minutes at the final admission (see Table 8.1).

Table 8.1 Length of Music Therapy Sessions Across Admissions

Admission	Mean (minutes)
1	29.4
2	40
3	52.5
4	74
5	85.6

Note: Co-treatment sessions were excluded to show the progression of time increase in individual sessions.

This lengthened session time during a period of increasing demand across the hospital meant I was taking access to services away from other, potentially more acute patients.

I had set a trap for myself. The daily visits with unlimited session length were now interfering with my ability to take care of my other patients, many of whom had heightened acuity. The only way I could continue to see Diane at the same frequency and length was to extend my work hours or drop patients who were appropriate for treatment. This threatened the healthy work-life balance I had cultivated, and I realized needed to start setting session time limits with Diane.

With this decision came a sense of guilt, the very guilt I was trying to avoid by acquiescing to Diane's ongoing requests for more sessions. Diane begged for me to stay longer when it was time to end. *What if she was genuinely crying for help? What if I ruptured our relationship?* I felt like I was failing Diane.

I carry certain beliefs and value systems from my upbringing. Similar to the expectations of maintaining friendliness and respect for others, it is often frowned upon to display showy behaviors. As a result, I learned to become a "social chameleon." I wanted to develop my music therapist identity in the United States with the intention to adapt and not let my social identity influence my work. I thought I could separate my Taiwanese values from the American professional expectations, yet I did not see how my values were affecting my clinical decision-making. Since early in my childhood, I was taught to never question elders, to please them and seek compliance, which explains my tendency to seek proof for self-worth through external validations. This tendency made me vulnerable to Diane's words. I have been working on self-reflection for some years to better understand myself and to keep this tendency from entering clinical spaces, but I struggled immensely here.

Several factors, in addition to the general stress of the pandemic, were impacting my resilience and ultimately my capacity to manage this case. The increased size and acuity of my caseload had worn me down; it felt like trying to stand steady on a sandy beach but stumbling when the waves swept over my feet. I took the Professional Quality of Life Scale[1] at the beginning of the pandemic and again some months later, with the results suggesting I was experiencing burnout. In order to be functional and carry out work responsibilities, I could not be vulnerable or expend energy in the ways necessary to fully process the challenges of this case.

I was also feeling isolated facing this dilemma. I did not have access to professional supervision due to financial stress, and I did not have access to peer supervision due to the hospital's administrative structure. I hesitated to bring this topic up with peers outside the hospital system because I was sensitive to everyone being under pandemic-related pressure, and I did not want to be perceived as incompetent.

During the time I was writing about this case, my father was hospitalized on the other side of the world. Feeling desperate and helpless, I had to put all my trust in the hands that took care of him and accept that not every care team member would advocate for his needs when he couldn't speak for himself. It hurt to think about how my father may have felt when his needs were overlooked.

This new perspective brought me a deeper compassion for Diane, and a new appreciation for my role as a music therapist in a medical setting. Her behaviors may have been considered inappropriate, but they were signs of psychosocial needs. She was a survivor and continued to suffer from the consequences in the forms of anxiety. She was a loving, caring person who did not deserve what she had been through.

In our final session, Diane thanked me for working with her to expand her openness to new ideas. She shared that she kept close to her heart the key message from our first encounter: she was never alone. I often evaluate session outcome and effectiveness through observable behavior changes, but since Diane never changed her behavioral patterns, I initially thought my treatment was ineffective. Her comment was a reminder to set goals that are meaningful to patients themselves and not just what I think should happen. I was glad that she eventually found moments of peace through music and trust through our relationship. Most important of all, it was comforting to know that these hospital admissions were not as cold and frightening for her because our paths had crossed.

Summarizing Ideas and Questions for Discussion

1. People entering and exiting systems (e.g., hospitals, schools, clinics, centers) may experience false narratives forced upon them, which risk carrying labels with negative stigmas.

    a. Think of a time when you had an experience with a client that was different from how they were framed in clinical documentation or verbal referrals. How did you reconcile these two perspectives of the same individual with yourself and with the treatment team?

    b. Consider the language that can be used to negatively describe an individual in your clinical setting. How can that language be transformed into discourse that is compassion-based?

2. Supporting a patient does not require breaking personal boundaries to accommodate unrealistic demands or disruptive behaviors, and yet there are times where we find ourselves having already violated those boundaries.

   a. How should a music therapist navigate unrealistic demands or requests?
   b. What can a music therapist do to repair a therapeutic relationship that has been ruptured?
   c. When boundaries are established based on values that may not be shared with a patient, how much flexibility should be considered while still honoring the boundaries?

Note

1 Stamm, B. H. (2009). *Professional quality of life: Compassion satisfaction and fatigue version 5 (ProQOL).* https://proqol.org/use-the-proqol

Unit 3

Attuning, Adapting, and Maturing in Practice

Connecting, Disconnecting, and Reconnecting Through Changes in Therapeutic Context

Crystal Luk-Worrall
Illustrated by Anna Oboratova

Abstract

Changes in social context and personal circumstances often feature in long-term therapeutic work. These changes pose ongoing challenges, but also present opportunities for music therapists to support clients, and at times their families, in building resilience through their therapeutic relationships. Music therapists are tasked with being attentive to clients' needs as these contexts and circumstances shift, and subsequently adapting treatment conceptualization when appropriate.

Tags: Treatment Planning; Therapeutic Relationship

During the COVID-19 pandemic, I became accustomed to the error message "Your internet connection is unstable" when running online sessions. The solution is usually to reboot the internet or to restart the computer. However, when it comes to disruptions in therapeutic alliance, there is neither an error message nor a quick fix. Instead, it requires the music therapist to continuously evaluate their approach and support the client and their loved ones to reflect on the purpose of the work.

This case outlines my long-term work with Josh, a 5-year-old boy, and his family through the COVID-19 pandemic. It consists of the initial treatment planning process and two reconceptualizations of treatment in response to the changing social context and the family's needs. The first phase of treatment features individual sessions at Josh's family home. The second phase features online sessions with Josh and his mother, Julie. The third phase features family sessions with Josh's parents, including his father, Dean, and younger sister, Ellarie.

This reflection is written in celebration of the resilience Josh and his family developed during our time of engagement, highlighting:

- The parallel growth between myself, as a newly qualified practitioner, and Josh's family

DOI: 10.4324/9781003123798-13

- How we navigated the challenges and opportunities presented by the changing social context and family dynamics
- The negotiation between my preferred therapeutic approach and Josh's therapeutic needs

My Therapeutic Orientations

My music therapy training, based in the United Kingdom (UK), prepared me to be psychodynamically-informed while also covering a wide range of therapeutic approaches. I found myself gravitating toward the optimism in the humanistic approach that people have the innate need to better themselves.[1] I admired Winnicott's respect for his clients' insights on their personal growth and was drawn to his proposal of therapy being a "potential space" where the therapist supports the client to explore both reality and fantasy through play.[2] I believe therapy is a collaborative process and resonated with Rickson's stance that music therapy is facilitated by "family members and other experts."[3] This leads to my work with Josh.

Meeting Josh

Josh, referred by his mother Julie, was one of the first clients I worked with after completing my entry-level music therapy training. Josh had a diagnosis of moderate learning disability and limited mobility below his knees due to complications at birth. He could sustain attention for things he was interested in for a long period of time but required support in following routines set by adults. Josh particularly struggled with strict instructions. Julie shared that Josh once found being supported by a "bossy" teaching assistant so stressful that he refused to go to school daily.

Josh's behaviors escalated just before the referral. He began throwing things across the room, screaming for prolonged periods of time, and hitting his 3-year-old sister Ellarie when things did not go his way. These behaviors made it difficult for the family to manage everyday tasks, but also became a barrier for Josh to develop healthy relationships with others. Being an early childhood educator herself, Julie believed these behaviors rooted from Josh's limited capacity in acknowledging and expressing his emotions. She hoped that music therapy would give Josh a space to learn to express himself and connect with others healthily.

Josh's struggle with "bossy" adults struck a chord with me. I grew up in Hong Kong in the 1990s when the Confucius value of respecting elders unconditionally intersected with the Western influence of encouraging critical thinking and creativity.[4] Many parents, mine included, began adopting an authoritative style of parenting. Reasoning and nurturing conversations were promoted. At home, I was encouraged to be curious and reflective, while the public educational system leaned toward the authoritarian approach.[5] There was an assumption that only compliant children were good children. At school, I had to do as I was told without question, or I faced the consequence of being humiliated in front of my classmates.

The stark contrast between interactions with my parents and my school-teachers was confusing. I struggled to understand why I was not allowed to express my individuality at school and was baffled by the absolute power presumed by my teachers. It is fair to say that I harbored an aversion towards authoritarian figures as I grew up. When I heard Josh's background story, I found myself identifying with his disinclination towards authoritative figures. It was important for me to become aware of how my childhood experience converged with Josh's struggles. This awareness allowed me to be informed by my countertransference when working with Josh rather than allowing those countertransferences to project my needs onto Josh's therapeutic process.

First Encounters

I remember the first session vividly. Josh was excitable when he met me, choosing to come into the playroom on his own without Julie. He began the session by examining the instruments and attempting to make them stand upright in a line. I picked up my guitar, wanting to provide some musical structure for his play, but Josh quickly asserted himself, saying: "No, no, no!" He put a pair of wrist bells around my wrists and demanded: "Quiet!" I held my hands together in front of my face as if I was hand-cuffed. Josh seemed pleased. Josh continued to line up the instruments but became stuck when the egg shaker would not stand. After several tries, he threw it across the room out of frustration and did the same with any instrument that would not stand.

I was struck by the cruelty he exhibited to these instruments. I reminded him not to hurt the instruments, but he ignored me. At this point, Josh's aversion to stern commands came to mind. I wondered if he experienced me as another bossy adult. Knowing how I would have detested it as a child, I adjusted my response. Each time Josh threw an instrument, I gave the instrument a voice (e.g., "Ouch" and "Oh no"). Josh began laughing. He eventually came close to me, took off the wrist bells, and told me: "You can play now." I felt I had passed the test. After the session, Josh asked Julie when I would visit again.

On reflection, I was glad that Josh stopped me from playing the guitar. The guitar was my safety blanket. I often reached for it when I felt unsure of how the session might unfold. By not playing the guitar in this instance, I was able to immerse myself in Josh's play and embrace our mutual anxieties. I noted Josh's exertion of control over when I could play and when I was only allowed to be a witness. I wondered how often Josh was able to play and interact with others at his own pace in the presence of the demands of everyday life. As such, I felt it was essential for Josh to have experienced a sense of control and empowerment in this early session.

After two more sessions and a discussion with Julie, we collaboratively decided to focus on the following goals:

1. Provide a space for Josh to experience self-agency and a sense of control
2. Provide a contained environment for Josh to express himself, especially with difficult emotions such as anger, frustration, and aggression
3. Promote Josh's confidence in social interaction through play

In the next few months, the egg shaker Josh banished in the first session became one of his favorite instruments to play. Referring to it as "Humpty," Josh would hold the egg shaker as I held the xylophone as the wall Humpty Dumpty would sit on in the nursery rhyme (see Figure 9.1). I would shake the wall as Josh laughed in anticipation until eventually dropping the egg shaker on the floor.

As this work continued, it became clear Humpty was something more than an egg shaker. Josh appeared to be projecting onto Humpty his frustration and anger about not being able to stand physically. Humpty became a representation of what Josh perceived to be the "bad" part of himself. This created an opportunity for me to support Josh to discover empathy for himself by offering a nurturing presence and guiding Josh's play with Humpty. As a newly qualified music therapist, Josh's progress gave me hope in what we could achieve together and confidence in believing that the way I had interacted with him was helpful.

Figure 9.1 Josh balancing "Humpty" the egg shaker on the xylophone "wall"

"Your Connection is Unstable"

Four months after our first session, the first national lockdown in the UK was announced in response to the COVID-19 pandemic. Julie felt that music therapy, even conducted online, would provide some needed consistency and interaction for Josh. I was transparent that telehealth would be a new adventure for me. Julie understood and we were determined to make it work. We agreed it would be appropriate for her to remain in the room during the session to support Josh's engagement and to ensure his safety.

The first few sessions were challenging, to say the least. Our internet connection was poor, with the first few minutes often spent shouting "Can you hear me?" at each other. Josh's sister Ellarie, being home-schooled at that point, often waltzed into the playroom, wanting to join in and eager for my attention (see Figure 9.2). Josh was keen to share his sessions with her most of the time, but this inevitably caused me to divert my attention and created a different dynamic in the sessions.

Without consciously shifting the goals of the session, I adapted from creating space for symbolic play to simply engaging Josh through the sessions. Because I was not physically in the room, I felt I had to constantly make my voice heard so Julie and Josh knew that I was present. I seized

Figure 9.2 Ellarie and Julie joining in the online session

any opportunity to respond to Josh musically. Josh responded well to conducting and copying games, but only for a few minutes at a time. These moments of engagement were often interrupted by continued internet disruptions, and with every disconnection, I had a sinking feeling that our therapeutic alliance, too, was disconnecting.

It finally became too much.

Two months into lockdown, Josh was finding it difficult to engage. He threw himself on the bed, kicking, screaming, and throwing everything within his reach. He ignored anything Julie or I said. I could see Julie beginning to feel deflated as she moved away from Josh and sat quietly in the corner of the room. Eventually, Josh became tired. He lay in his bed with his face buried in his pillow and stopped moving. I verbalized:

"It's not the same anymore, is it?"

Josh kicked the bed in response.

"Are you okay?"

No answer.

"Are you able to sit up?"

No answer.

"Are you sad?"

A kick on the bed frame.

"This is really hard."

Another kick followed.

Julie went up to Josh and placed his face on her lap while gently patting his back. I had learnt from experience that my body identifies significant moments in therapy before I could articulate why. My gut churns and time slows down. This was one of those moments. I could hear my lecturers' advice, "When in doubt, breathe out," at the back of my head. With that breath, I felt the fragility of the moment and Josh and Julie's vulnerability.

I searched within myself for a song that allowed me to be with Josh and Julie. The song "My Bonnie" came to mind. My mother used to sing it to me before bed as a lullaby. Since English was my second language, I used to think that the lyrics were *My _body_ lies over the ocean, my _body_ lies over the sea . . . oh bring back my _body_ to me*. It felt fitting as Josh, Julie, and I were paralyzed by a myriad of emotions. On one hand, we all needed a moment of privacy to acknowledge our distinct, unique emotions. On the other hand, there was an overarching sense of loss among us. I hoped the song could encapsulate our shared experience and bring us comfort as it did to me when I was a child. As I sang, Josh remained still, and Julie sobbed quietly. I clutched the guitar for comfort while holding back my tears as I recalled the times Josh and I shared in the playroom. It was as if we had all been waiting to acknowledge the changes in our relationships and in our lives imposed by the pandemic.

Minutes later, Josh turned his head with a smile and announced: "I made it!" Julie and I, still in a lull, were stunned. He handed Julie a shaker, picked up his toy guitar, and directed: "Crystal, time to sing goodbye." I looked at the watch and he was right. To this day, I still wonder what Josh had gone through in his mind to allow him to recover from such a powerful emotional experience. Before leaving the meeting, Julie, seemingly with embarrassment, apologized, saying: "We didn't get to do anything other than singing goodbye." Unbeknownst to her, I also felt compelled to apologize for my failure to run the session. I questioned whether I had made a wrong decision in offering telehealth for Josh, and whether the benefit of staying connected outweighed the frustration we experienced.

I reflected on the session in supervision. Every supervision session, since the pandemic started, had felt like a confession because I felt as if I was not doing music therapy as I was taught. In training, I was taught the importance of keeping the boundary of the therapeutic relationship and the therapeutic space. However, I had foregone both. It was no longer just Josh and I in the room, nor were we in a room where I could protect the space.

My supervisor encouraged me to view my work with Josh within the wider social context impacted by the pandemic. In that sense, our sessions were a miniature representation of how Josh, Julie, and I responded, both practically and emotionally, to the limitations posed by the pandemic. I was able to see that Josh's life would have been significantly impacted regardless of our shift to telehealth, and that our sessions continued to be a protected time dedicated to facilitating Josh's self-expression.

We also reflected on my role and Julie's role in the online sessions. Notwithstanding the limitations of telehealth, I was given a unique opportunity to witness Josh's interactions with her. This allowed me to build a therapeutic alliance with Julie by offering different perspectives on Josh's presentations. As for Julie, not only was she there to keep Josh safe, but she was also another expressive adult in the room and an expert in being with Josh.

I realized that up to this point, Julie and I had not explicitly discussed her role in the sessions. While I had considered Julie an active member of the session since we transitioned to telehealth, I wondered if Julie experienced it that way. I arranged a review meeting with Julie to discuss how we could adjust therapeutic goals and utilize her expertise to support Josh, given the new context of the work.

Rebooting

In the meeting, Julie shared that she was able to think about the sessions more objectively after that cathartic experience. She talked about how it was both valuable and embarrassing for her to have someone outside of the family witness Josh's behaviors and her struggles. She was relieved that she was no longer alone in witnessing Josh's tantrums, but also felt she had to "keep it together" during the sessions and was exhausted both mentally and physically afterwards. I often found that Julie's and my experience of being with Josh mirrored one another. Dare I admit that Julie's presence in the last session gave me a sense of relief and pressure to "put on a good session" at the same time?

The boundary between Julie and I had always been a delicate one. Julie's patience and gentleness with Josh resonated with me, and I felt she had an understanding of the way I worked. We formed an alliance over the joint responsibility of supporting Josh's engagement in the sessions and drew on each other's strengths in moments of ambivalence with Josh. However, precisely because of our irrespective responsibility to Josh, there was an unspoken understanding that we would uphold the boundary of our relationship – to remain close enough so I could bear witness to Josh's interactions with Julie, but distant enough for me to offer insights from a different perspective. As such, I often found myself treading the fine line between supporting Julie and supporting her to support Josh.

With that in mind, I invited Julie to reflect on her emotions using simple language in future sessions when she felt able to. It would allow us to acknowledge her feelings, model healthy expressions, and demonstrate her resilience towards difficult feelings about Josh. Julie was excited by this idea and felt she had more clarity on how to be a source of support. We agreed that our goals for the sessions in the next few months would be:

1. Facilitate good experiences in online interactions during a time of physical isolation
2. Create opportunities for each person to choose their preferred activity
3. Give Josh an opportunity to witness healthy reflections from Julie and myself

The sessions to follow felt much more contained.

We took turns deciding what activities to do together. Julie began to offer short verbal comments, like "I am sad" or "This makes me happy," to model and normalize emotional expression. I narrated my observations with short sentences like "Mummy, it looks like Josh wants some quiet time" or "Oh no, Mummy is left out!" At first, Josh showed little interest in our verbal comments but over time, Josh would sometimes glance at us in acknowledgment.

Family Sessions

As the government gradually relaxed the COVID-19 restrictions, Julie and Dean returned to work part-time. The family did not have alternative childcare, so Ellarie began joining the sessions. The sessions were supported either by Dean or Julie, depending on the couple's work schedule. I had not corresponded with Dean much before this, but was excited that he would be more involved in the therapy process.

Admittedly, I was not quite prepared for the new relational dynamic in the sessions. Ellarie, now 5 years old, had flourished into a willful young lady determined to have her voice heard in the session. Dean's support was largely functional, distributing instruments and keeping order between the siblings. When Ellarie and Josh began fighting or one of them disengaged, Dean often covered his face, shook his head, and then looked at me expectantly as if to say, "What do we do now?" Although Josh seemed genuinely excited to share the sessions with the rest of his family, he struggled with the constant negotiation with Ellarie and would turn around to play on his own in response. At times, I felt that we were simply getting through the activities for the sake of it. There was little joy in it for anyone as Josh and Ellarie spent most of the sessions fighting for attention, which often led to either one of them getting dysregulated and the other leaving the room.

Being aware that the goals I set with Julie previously were no longer appropriate, I invited both Dean and Julie for another review meeting. To my pleasant surprise, Dean came with questions and insights. He was upfront about not understanding what he and the children needed to achieve in the sessions and suggested if I was more directive, we would "get more done." Before I answered, Julie responded, "It's not about getting things done." Dean thought it should be a space for the children to learn to get along and follow instructions while Julie insisted it should be a playground for expression and creativity. Regardless, the couple admitted that it had become progressively difficult for the children to have fun together after being stuck at home with each other for months.

As I listened to Dean and Julie, I found myself caught in the crossfire of order and chaos once again. I thanked them for their contributions and honesty. I conceded that it was easy to lose track of what we wanted out of the sessions in a time of constant change, but we all wanted the children to enjoy the sessions together. I agreed with Julie that expressions from the children, and adults for that matter, should be welcomed. However, there seemed to be too much flexibility in the structure of the recent sessions that had provoked competition between the siblings.

At this point, Dean shared an insightful observation. When the siblings were actively responding to the same musical instructions, like when I led a game of "Stop and Go," they seemed to have a sense of unity, like they were working towards something together. Julie agreed, suggesting that perhaps the children needed to learn how to be together again before participating in turn-taking activities. We concluded that the goals for the sessions to follow would be:

1. Shared enjoyment as a family through playing as a group
2. Support Josh and Ellarie to accept other people's lead
3. Provide opportunities for the siblings to witness healthy reflection from adults

While I recognized that a more directive voice in the sessions might offer better containment for Josh and Ellarie, it did not come naturally to me. I chose to train in a psychodynamically-informed, improvisation-based music therapy program because I wanted to champion freedom of expression through music and steer away from exerting authority over my clients, due to my childhood experience. To take on a more directive role in the sessions felt like a departure from the music therapist I wished to be.

I confided in my supervisor, who asked, "What do *you* need from this work?" It took me a while to answer, as it had not crossed my mind to tend to my need in the therapeutic relationship. I realized I wanted to do right by the family while staying true to the nurturing and curious therapist I aspired to be. The ever-changing dynamic of my sessions with Josh's family was representative of how the pandemic challenged me to be more flexible with my practice. My supervisor and I explored the difference between being directive to satisfy one's need for power and being directive to channel the children's anxiety. We also discussed whether there was scope for me to actively promote Josh's and Ellarie's curiosity towards each other's emotional responses and model that with Dean and Julie.

The structure of the sessions to follow was more organized. I moved swiftly from one activity to another to minimize opportunities for Josh's and Ellarie's anxiety to develop. There were still moments when the children became overwhelmed and disengaged; however, Josh was becoming more aware of Ellarie's engagement in the sessions. The song "My Bonnie" became a recurring feature of the sessions. Josh would sing it whenever he noticed that Ellarie became upset and left the room. On several occasions, Josh had successfully lured Ellarie back to the playroom with the song. I was amazed that what used to be a song with personal meaning to me had become a meaningful resource for Josh to express himself.

As a degree of normality from the pandemic slowly returned, I visited the family's garden for outdoor sessions in the summer of 2021 (see Figure 9.3). Dean and Julie felt that promoting healthy interactions within the family continued to be their priority, so we carried on with the goals set in the previous review. Dean became a lot more playful in these sessions and began using his sense of humor to defuse tense moments between the siblings. Julie and I continued to comment on the siblings' emotional responses to support them to develop empathy towards each other.

Josh had been listening. In a recent session, Ellarie moved away from the circle after Josh chose the xylophone she wanted. Josh commented: "Ellarie sad." He put the xylophone on her seat and started singing, "My Ellarie is over the ocean." When Ellarie did not come back this time, I was worried that Josh might not have the resilience to accept that and would become dysregulated himself. Instead, Josh urged his parents and I to put down our instruments and added: "When people sad, they want quiet time." In a simple sentence, Josh embraced the overarching goals of the

Figure 9.3 Family session in the garden

therapy, to express himself and to relate with others healthily. I glanced towards Julie. She was smiling. It was a smile of relief, joy, and pride. Her persistent modeling of reflective comments in and out of the sessions had paid off.

Concluding Thoughts

Julie's early comment of "We didn't get to do anything" and Dean's wish of "getting more done" prompted me to ponder on the emphasis that we as a society have placed on *doing*. It was as if the session did not happen if we did not do anything. However, as I reflected on my work with Josh and his family, I found that moments of *being* and *not working* were equally valuable. I believe music therapy happened when Josh banished Humpty across the room as it did when we sang "Kumbaya" to make Humpty well again, and it happened when Julie cried with Josh in her arms as it did when she smiled at Josh's achievement. The apparent dysfunctional moments were integral parts of Josh's life. Having the privilege of witnessing these moments allowed me to identify potential areas of growth in the work and to remain attuned to the family's evolving needs.

While much of music therapy practice is about maintaining relationships, in long-term work, disconnections, disruptions, and detachments are inevitable. In fact, they are essential in modeling resilience in interpersonal relationships to our clients. I believe relationships are defined by disconnections as much as connections. Our work as music therapists is therefore as much about acknowledging and overcoming moments of disconnection as it is about progressing.

At the time of writing, I had been working with Josh's family for 65 sessions over 20 months. While I cannot claim credit for Josh's growing ability to empathize and his developing awareness of others, I am proud of what he has achieved. I am also grateful for Julie's and Dean's contributions to the treatment planning process and their willingness to be reflective in our therapeutic alliance.

Our journey continues.

Summarizing Ideas and Questions for Discussion

1. Changes in circumstances and social context are likely to feature in our relationships with clients in long-term work.

   a. How would you ensure your case conceptualization and therapeutic goals stay relevant to your clients' needs, given the ever-changing nature of social context and clients' personal circumstances?

   b. How would you manage the challenge posed by the evolving therapeutic boundaries and relational dynamics between you, your clients, and those who care for your clients?

2. Our core values are developed through our lifespan and are informed by our cultural background and lived experiences.

   a. How did your upbringing, cultural background, and lived experience impact your therapeutic stance?

   b. How would you balance your therapeutic preferences and your clients' needs?

Notes

1 Rogers, C. (1951). *Client-centered therapy: Its current practice, implication and theory.* Constable.
2 Winnicott, D. W. (1971). *Playing and reality.* Routledge.

3 Rickson, D. (2021). Family members' and other experts' perception of music therapy with children on the autism spectrum in New Zealand: Findings from multiple case studies. *The Arts in Psychotherapy, 75*. https://doi.org/10.1016/j.aip.2021.101833

4 Morris, P., & Sweeting, A. (1991). Education and politics: The case of Hong Kong from an historical perspective. *Oxford Review of Education, 17*(3), 249–267. www.jstor.org/stable/4618592

5 Baumrind, D. (1971). Current patterns of parental authority. *Developmental Psychology, 4*(1, Pt.2), 1–103. https://doi.org/10.1037/h0030372

Chapter 10

Regaining Trust in the Music
Music Therapy with Emily

Conio Loretto

Abstract

In everyday practice, music therapists must balance the creative nature of their work with the clinical responsibilities of their role. Internal and external factors, both professional and personal, can influence clinical work and upset the balance. Clinical reflexivity is critical to being an effective clinician who maintains a balance between authentic practice and organizational expectations.

Tags: Treatment Planning; Therapeutic Relationship

When she arrived at her first music therapy session, eleven-year-old Emily came bounding in with unbridled energy. She moved quickly around the room, which was set up with instruments ready for her to discover. She played the instruments vigorously in quick, impulsive bursts. Sometimes, however, she knocked them over, threw them, or banged them against the wall. I improvised music at the piano to both welcome Emily and to hold her musical responses. Admittedly, it was hard to keep up with her chaotic presentation. As with most first sessions, I wondered: *Where will this all lead? Will I be able to connect with her? Will she grow?* Little did I know that the journey to follow would not only lead Emily to significant growth, but that I too would grow; that my faith in music therapy would first be tested, but then ultimately strengthened in unforeseen ways.

Intensive Treatment Model

I met Emily a little over 20 years into my career as a music therapist. I oversee the music therapy program at Emily's school and have as one of my responsibilities the design and implementation of systems for delivering services. I have always maintained the precept that music therapy should not be static, but rather evolve to meet the unique, ever-changing strengths,

DOI: 10.4324/9781003123798-14

needs, and interests of the individuals we serve. As such, many dynamic applications of music therapy have been developed by the team I work with.

At the time I met Emily, we were trialing a new service delivery model to capitalize on the impact of music therapy more fully, specifically in relation to the development of social skills. The model was introduced to us by administration when they learned of significant outcomes reported by clinical teams in similar settings when treatment sessions occurred at a high frequency (e.g., daily) over a predefined time frame (e.g., over 10 weeks). Curious, our administration asked us to design a similar model and trial it to inform clinical work across disciplines at our school. The request came out of an appreciation for the effect music therapy was already having and the potential of strengthening our impact. Though initially hesitant to make a change, we came to embrace the opportunity and took on the challenge in earnest.

After thorough research, we developed a framework we coined the Intensive Treatment Model.[1] We began offering sessions to individuals or groups at a frequency of four or five times per week for a set duration of 12 weeks. Previously, sessions had been offered one to two times per week throughout an entire school year. We hypothesized, based on our research, that the increase in session frequency (with a pre-determined end date) would result in outcomes that were more concise and consistent. We also theorized that skills were more likely to be generalized outside of the session when developed in this more intensive manner. In order to illustrate outcomes, sessions were to be video recorded, reviewed, and coded.

Approach to Music Therapy

The philosophical foundation of my work is deeply rooted in humanistic[2] and music-centered[3] theoretical orientations and is strongly influenced by the Nordoff-Robbins approach.[4] There are four philosophical principles I subscribe to in my work:

- **Potential and possibility.** My approach is strengths-based, looking at what a person can do and building on that as the basis for change. Instead of assessing deficits and designing interventions to "fix" someone in therapy, I am a guide, leading individuals in therapy toward a deeper understanding of themselves, their relationship to others, and how they interact with the world around them.
- **Music making.** The act of creating music, and creating it with another person (or group of people), is the primary vehicle for connection. As the quality and depth of the interrelated music making grows, so too does the person in therapy who is making it.[4] This can be seen in both quantitative outcomes (e.g., the development of specific developmental skills) and qualitative outcomes (e.g., enhanced confidence and self-esteem).

- **Innate musical sensitivity.** In Nordoff-Robbins literature, a person's intrinsic musicality is referred to as the "music child"[5] and exemplifies the inborn, universal sensitivity to music inside every person. For various reasons, the music child may be difficult to reach. I strive to engage a person's music child while simultaneously expanding their understanding of their abilities so they can reach their highest potential.
- **The musical relationship.** The way someone creates music, and creates it with another person, is perhaps the most crucial part of the therapeutic process[4] in music therapy. It is through this relationship, when trust is established, that new musical frontiers can be explored and a heightened awareness of oneself and one's capabilities can emerge.

This set of guiding principles translates into a way of working that includes an ongoing assessment of each individual, in each moment, within each session. *What is the quality of the individual's natural, musical responses? What is their emotional presence? How are they relating to me? Or the instruments found in the room? Where are we right now and where can we go?* Based on the assessment, I improvise music to seek, gain, and keep contact from moment to moment with the individual.[4] Or, composed music may be introduced to provide stability and structure. Regardless of form, the music is used to meet the individual where they are, evoke new or enhanced responses, and develop greater expressive freedom and interrelatedness.[5]

As we began trialing the Intensive Treatment Model, our team contemplated how our humanistic, music-centered way of working would intersect with it. It was important for us to hold tight to our foundation as we began to focus more closely on specific quantitative outcomes. We knew one could not happen without the other. Our administration was not looking for us to authenticate our work, but rather challenging us to strengthen the clinical impact of it. We surmised that the nature of our approach did not need to change, but rather the lens by which we were examining it. We could still practice in the way we had always practiced, but would now hold up a more greatly focused magnifying glass to assess outcomes using the video coding process.

Meeting Emily in Music

Emily is a day student at a residential school for individuals who have complex conditions, including autism and multiple disabilities. She is diagnosed with Down syndrome, autism, and with visual and hearing impairments. She is nonspeaking, often emoting deep, guttural sounds to communicate how she is feeling. When meeting her, one cannot help but be taken by her excitable, playful nature and the mischievous twinkle in her eyes. She is bright and curious, and her sensory system can often become overwhelmed as she takes in and organizes the world around her. As such, her attention can be fleeting. When transitioning between activities or she is unsure of what is expected of her, Emily may simply stop moving and drop to the ground or strike out towards someone in her immediate path.

Emily received individual music therapy for 48 sessions over 12 weeks. The sessions were facilitated by myself and Rebecca, another music therapist on our team. I was typically seated at the piano and had the primary responsibility of creating the music to reflect and guide the therapeutic process. Rebecca's role was to be physically and emotionally present with Emily, guiding her into the music and presenting various opportunities for her to explore while modeling expectations. At the start of each session, we set up chairs near the piano and had various instruments available, ready to be played. These included larger instruments, like standing drums, a cymbal, and xylophone placed strategically around the room, as well as an assortment of smaller rhythm instruments, including hand drums, tambourines, and maracas.

In early sessions, Emily entered, went directly to the chairs set up for her, and hastily knocked them to the ground. She would then move to a larger instrument, like the drum, and play it by using her hands or a drumstick in quick bursts of rhythmic energy. Her playing was loud, forceful, and impulsive, and usually ended with her knocking the instrument to the ground. Sometimes she would bang on the wall with a drumstick that she would toss once the impulse was realized. Similarly, she would energetically play handheld instruments before tossing them across the room. She would emote low-pitched vocal sounds or sometimes giggle. She moved swiftly around the room, spending no more than a few seconds with an instrument. Her energy could best be described as chaotic, but also somewhat playful as periodic sly glances let us know that she was curious about the music that was happening and our efforts to engage her.

For us, Emily's presentation was not out of the ordinary; we had met many children in music therapy who presented similarly, though each of them retained their unique qualities. The way Emily approached the session was reflective of her overwhelmed sensory system and fleeting attention. The forceful sounds she made on the instruments were certainly indicative of her hearing loss, but also of her unchecked emotional state. Thus, we approached the session as we typically would by meeting Emily right where she was and communicating to her that she was being seen, heard, and valued for whatever she had to offer in each moment. We sought to simultaneously pique her interest, foster her curiosity, and hold her focus so mutual expressive possibilities could be realized.

The music I was improvising at the piano matched the impulsive energy Emily was emoting to keep pace with her. I played sharp, dissonant chords with moments of silence in between that highlighted the instrumental and vocal responses coming from Emily. The improvisation was typically grounded by two chords a whole step apart (i – VII7), with notes outside of the tonality strategically added to provide musical surprises to spark Emily's interest. The character of the music was somewhat dark and mysterious to reflect what I perceived as Emily's emotional state, but also playful in order to engage her. At times, the music did feel jarring, but I deduced it was necessary as the unpredictability would grab Emily's attention. Any vocalizations Rebecca and I shared typically echoed Emily's vocal sounds. Sometimes we added lyrics to the improvisation that repeated Emily's name as an attempt to hold her attention or to acknowledge her musical responses (e.g., *Emily plays the drum* or *Listen to Emily play*).

We quickly noticed that Emily's music child emerged in the moments when she was knocking over a chair or hitting the wall. Yes, she was knocking over a chair, but timed it to punctuate the end of a musical phrase. She hit the wall in time with the basic beat of the music. Working within a school setting, I often have to contemplate whether to embrace or ignore/redirect behaviors that could be deemed maladaptive, as embracing them could be contrary to a child's educational or behavioral plan. There are times I have had to realign my philosophical approach to ensure a child's safety and wellbeing. But in Emily's case, the decision was easy as within these moments her innate musical sensitivity surfaced in ways we could not deny. Moving forward, every expression, whether played on the drum or a chair, became incorporated into the improvised music.

At this point, our musical exchanges felt like a chase. Emily would send out a burst of musical energy that I would respond to, but the second our exchanges started to form Emily would run to another instrument and we would start anew. It felt increasingly difficult to hold the music making and I started to contemplate what might need to change. It felt like we were trapped in a circular, push-and-pull pattern that was not going anywhere. I was perplexed: *What would break this pattern? What did Emily need? What was our next step?* Before I could ponder and ultimately answer these questions, an unexpected dynamic emerged alongside the creation of Emily's formal treatment goal.

Treatment Planning

In order to define her goal, Rebecca and I forecasted what we thought Emily's sessions would look and sound like at the end of our 12 weeks together. We asked ourselves what would serve Emily best and contribute to her ability to be more socially engaged both in school and at home. Working within the parameters of the intensive format, we were tasked with defining a measurable outcome to be tracked via video review. Emily was slowly becoming more purposefully engaged in the music making, and we envisioned Emily committing to the experiences of the session with more focused intention. We anticipated breaking the circular pattern we were stuck in by continuing to strengthen the connection between Emily, us as her therapists, and the music we were creating together.

With this in mind, we defined Emily's goal as increasing the amount of time she was "purposefully engaged in the act of creating music." "Purposefully engaged" was operationalized as a working list of observable actions that demonstrated Emily's connection to the experience on a deeper level. The list included actions such as staying within the proximity of the instrument she was playing, keeping her focus on the activity at hand, and responding to musical suggestions presented by the therapist (e.g., closing a musical phrase or matching the basic beat). To collect data, we video recorded each session and, to maintain objectivity, trained a music therapy intern to code one session per week. Coding involved reviewing the entire session and timing the intervals where Emily was "purposefully engaged" as determined by our list of actions.

What I have learned over the course of my career is to trust the process, that my work does not need to be driven by outcomes because clinically focused music making leads to growth. It might not be the growth anticipated, but it is growth all the same. I held tight to these notions as we began video coding Emily's sessions. And yet, after we defined her goal, I began feeling the pressure of meeting it. For example, Emily would sit in a chair to play the drum, but the moment she stood up and knocked it over, I literally imagined the stopwatch clicking as I knew at that point Emily was not achieving the goal. It worried me. I found myself getting frustrated with Rebecca. *Why isn't she working harder to make Emily stay with the drum? Why isn't she getting Emily to sit down?* In retrospect, my frustration with Rebecca was likely displaced frustration with myself. I began introducing strategies contrary to my philosophical beliefs. For example, because Emily was continuing to knock over instruments, I suggested we remove all of the instruments from the room or that we preemptively knock them down before she could.

The quality of the music I was improvising began to reflect my frustration and concern. It was disjointed and disconnected, and at the same time very strict. It lacked responsiveness to Emily and was instead quite rigid in order to achieve the desired end result. Sometimes I just stopped the music altogether to verbally redirect Emily towards what was expected of her. As Rebecca and I met to process each session, I ultimately shifted the conversation from what we were doing musically to what we could be doing to better manage what I was now referring to as Emily's "behaviors." Suddenly, this humanistic music therapist, whose career was built on trusting the process of making music as the impetus for change, was focusing solely on outcomes and the end result. And in my quest to show Emily's progress, very little was actually happening. Emily became less focused and increasingly resistant to our attempts to engage with her as they were rooted in changing behavior as opposed to making music. My clinical approach at this point had strayed from my long-held philosophical beliefs.

Finally, during one of our post-session meetings, Rebecca asked that we contemplate the role of the music. In that moment, it felt like a reset button had been pressed: *Of course! The music! What was I thinking? How could I forget about the music?* I quickly went to the collection of readings I keep close at hand for moments in my work when I need to reflect, be inspired, deepen my understanding, or challenge what I think I know. I recognized that I was clinically stuck. This wasn't the first time I felt this way and certainly would not be the last. This recognition dramatically shifted the trajectory of Emily's sessions.

Clinical Reflexivity: Finding My Way Back

At this point, the concept of "Poised in the Creative Now"[6] proved especially helpful. Developed by Clive Robbins, "Poised in the Creative Now" outlines the polarities of the artistic qualities and practical tools music therapists need to do our work effectively. I used this concept to identify where my thinking was centered within the work we were doing with Emily. I realized how wrapped up I had become in the practical tools (e.g., documentation and professional accountability) and how I needed to balance this with the creative, artistic nature of our work. Again, we were trialing a new system and as the head of the team I felt the need to validate it through our work with Emily. And, in validating the system, so too validating music therapy as a viable treatment modality.

During this time, I was a new father to three children. In retrospect, I recognize how this was influencing my clinical work as well. The expectations I was placing on the children I met in therapy were changing as I placed expectations on my own children at home. This came to light in a group session where I observed myself being less forgiving of a child who was impulsively jumping up and down during the session. As they jumped, I found myself thinking they needed to "follow the rules" and remain seated for the duration of the session. My response surprised me. Typically, I would be more accommodating of what the child was doing, taking a response like that and turning it into a musical experience, like a jumping song or musical game. But in this case, I wanted the child to "follow the rules." In my self-reflection, I recognized that my response was much more parental in nature.

At home, I found myself gauging my success as a parent on my children's behavior. Because I'm gay, I think this phenomenon was even stronger. In my private therapy sessions, I have had to face the expectations I place on myself to be a "perfect" parent with "perfect" (i.e., well-behaved) children in order to prove my worthiness to even be a parent in a potentially judgmental world. I have come to appreciate, however, that parenting, just like therapy, can be messy at times and that my effectiveness is not necessarily reflected in my children's day-to-day behavior. This awakening prompted me to continually discern how my developing role as a parent influences my clinical work.

With renewed faith in the process and a keen awareness of the countertransference[7] issues at play, my perspective shifted. Instead of chasing Emily, I improvised with the intention of meeting and grounding her. I recognized my attempt to musically keep pace with her was counterproductive and contributed to the "chase." I created musical phrases that were less dissonant and more open and inviting. I centered improvisations around modes that were more stabilizing, but also intriguing based on the unexpected movements of the scale. I sought to create an aesthetically pleasing musical environment that Emily would want to be a part of. The lyrics of the improvisations shifted from announcing what Emily was doing (e.g., *Emily plays the drum*) to inspiring what she could be doing (e.g., *Emily can play the xylophone*). Rebecca and I also sang singular words to color the improvisations (e.g., *Beautiful, beautiful . . . Emily can play*). The focus was no longer on changing behavior, but rather on creating a musical landscape where we could meet and see together where the music would take us.

Emily's expressiveness and her ability to relate to us progressed. I am certain she could sense the easing of the expectations I was placing on her. Her trust in me grew in concert with my renewed trust in the music making. Her scattered, impulsive responses became more controlled and purposeful. She began to align her musical responses to the phrases of the improvisation by starting and stopping in time with them. She started to match the contrasting dynamic levels and tempi we brought forth and at times introduced her own expressive elements. The duration of the music we were playing together increased steadily as she relished the co-responsive music making, as seen in her more relaxed emotional presence, smiles, and joyful giggles. When she attempted to retreat from the session, the music was able to call her back in with a quick shift in energy or by simply pausing and waiting. Emily became playfully interactive as we created music and created it together. Rarely, if at all, did she knock over instruments or play the wall. And, while initially our musical expressions felt parallel (i.e., she was playing an instrument while I improvised alongside her), our two separate expressions met and became woven into a rich musical tapestry.

Conclusion

At the end of our 12 weeks together, data revealed that Emily was "purposefully engaged" for an average of 80% of the session. Interestingly, the data directly reflected where my thinking was and how it was influencing her progress. Noted in Figure 10.1, the initial measure of Emily's purposeful engagement was just below 50%. We were initially surprised, yet also encouraged by this baseline assessment. In early sessions, this number began to rise. But, when we introduced her formal goal around session 19, Emily's engagement began to lessen. As we reached session 26, her engagement was steadily dropping, which coincided with my strict focus on outcomes. With the renewed focus on the process-oriented nature of the work after session 26, Emily's level of engagement flourished.

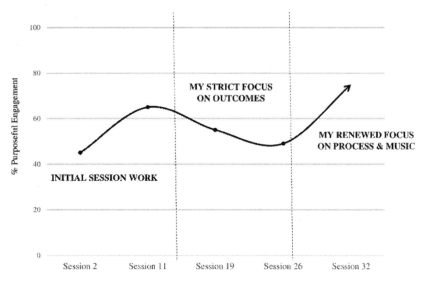

Figure 10.1 Select data points from Emily's sessions

Following each session, Emily returned to her classroom to join in circle time with her classmates. This was traditionally a challenging time for her, but on the days she attended music therapy, her teacher noticed she was more apt to stay within the circle for the duration of the experience, pay closer attention to the activities at hand, and be more cooperative with her peers. In fact, Emily's teacher observed a marked difference in her participation in circle time on the one day per week she did *not* have music therapy. Based on these anecdotal observations, Emily moved into a group session for another 12-week intensive rotation that afforded her the opportunity to build meaningful relationships with her peers.

It was exciting to laud Emily's progress when it came time to compile her final report. Through music therapy, she found a regulated state that allowed her to build meaningful relationships, first with the music therapists and then with her peers. The music provided a framework where interactions could be structured and could grow. She found purpose in the music making, which brought about greater focus and control. Layers of emotional expression were realized and acted upon. Emily discovered new levels of social competence and confidence. We shared these results in a case study presentation to Emily's treatment team where the dynamics of our work were illustrated. It was a deeper explanation of therapeutic processes than we had ever shared before, which undoubtedly broadened our colleagues' appreciation of not just what we do in music therapy, but why we do it.

The Intensive Treatment Model is still part of how music therapy services are delivered in our program today and continues to evolve. We have come to appreciate that the model is not appropriate for each child, how a one-size-fits-all approach does not have real-world application. Sometimes session work at a frequency of four or five times per week is overwhelming for a child. We have found that the intensive approach is most fitting for a child who is considerably unstable and meeting their needs is more urgent. Our assessment process now includes determining if the intensive process is indicated or not.

Summary

The journey with everyone who lands on my caseload provides an opportunity for solidifying what I know about music therapy, discovering something new, or challenging what I think I know. Being open to this type of reflexive growth has allowed my clinical perspective to deepen. There were several takeaways from my time with Emily that continue to inform my everyday practice.

- **Feeling "stuck" is an inevitable part of being a therapist.** Rebecca and I experienced unexpected twists and turns as we endeavored to connect with Emily and guide her toward co-responsive music making. But I do not regret them, as navigating them was simply part of the process that led to the outcomes Emily achieved.
- **Clinical reflexivity is crucial.** Self-reflection (and having tools at my disposal to help me do so) was critical in identifying the forces at play that were influencing the therapeutic process. Reconciling the expectations I placed on the outcomes of Emily's sessions, alongside the role my countertransferences played, became an important part of our journey together.
- **Be open-minded.** It would have been all too easy to feel threatened or defensive when administration presented the Intensive Treatment Model. But, in our trial of it, our team discovered an effective way to deliver services, explored how we define outcomes, and strengthened how others view music therapy within our agency. Wonderful advancements can come from being flexible and open to the possibilities of what music therapy can provide and be.
- **Always trust the music.** Perhaps the most important reminder of my time with Emily. When trust in the music making was restored, Emily discovered a heightened sense of herself, her abilities, and the connections she could share with others.

Summarizing Ideas and Questions
for Discussion

1. As music therapists, it can be challenging to balance the artistic, creative qualities of our work with the clinical responsibilities of setting goals and reporting outcomes.

    a. Reflect on a time you have navigated this balance in your session work. What did you learn about yourself, the music, and your clinical approach(es)?
    b. Are there specific strategies you use when preparing for, facilitating, and reflecting on your session work to help you maintain this balance?

2. It is important to identify resources that can help you when you are feeling stuck with a particular session on your caseload, as this is an inevitable part of being a music therapist.

    a. What has been especially helpful when you feel stuck in your work? Make a list of resources in your toolbox and describe how they help you remain empowered and restored.
    b. In what ways are you (or could you be) a resource to other music therapists?

Notes

1 Loretto, C., & Deyermond, E. (2012). *Overview of the intensive music therapy program at the center for discovery*. Unpublished Manuscript.
2 Ruud, E. (1995). *Music therapy and its relationship to current treatment theories* (3rd ed.). MMB Music Inc.
3 Aigen, K. (2005). *Music-centered music therapy*. Barcelona Publishers.
4 Bruscia, K. E. (1987). *Improvisational models of music therapy*. Charles C. Thomas Publisher.
5 Nordoff, P., & Robbins, C. (2007). *Creative music therapy: A guide to fostering clinical musicianship* (2nd ed.). Barcelona Publishers.
6 Turry, A. (2019). Supervision in the Nordoff-Robbins music therapy training program. In M. Forinash (Ed.), *Music therapy supervision* (2nd ed., pp. 351–364). Barcelona Publishers.
7 Turry, A. (1998). Transference and countertransference in Nordoff-Robbins music therapy. In K. Bruscia (Ed.), *The dynamics of music psychotherapy* (pp. 161–209). Barcelona Publishers.

Chapter 11

The Ever-Changing NICU
A Journey Through Crisis

Elisabeth Bombell

Abstract

During times of crisis, music therapists play an essential role in helping to stabilize patients and their families and prepare them for the more intensive work to follow. Critical care settings like the NICU are filled with unknowns and unexpected challenges that require families to access their internal and external coping supports. Drawing from patient and family cultural locations, such as spirituality and relational patterns, can help them tap into the resources necessary for developing resilience.

Tags: Treatment Planning; Therapeutic Relationship

Imagine yourself as an expectant parent, finally reaching that halfway point of your pregnancy. For 20 weeks you have begun to envision what it may be like when your baby arrives: perhaps you have begun making plans for the remaining months of pregnancy, creating a birth plan, or designing a nursery. The 20-week mark might be a point of comfort, particularly if you have had difficulty becoming pregnant or maintaining pregnancy in the past. Imagine your emotions moving through this period, and now being rushed to the hospital with the risk of delivering your baby as early as 24 weeks' gestation.

This was the experience of the Martin family as they birthed, stood with, and advocated for their son Sam, admitted to the Neonatal Intensive Care Unit (NICU) for extreme prematurity. The Martins' experience in the NICU required hope and resilience as they navigated doubt from medical staff, a lengthy admission, and several external stressors. During their journey, I was challenged with facilitating connections in music that were sustainable, accessible, and honored the cultures, experiences, and resources of the Martin family.

Background

The Martin family consisted of Sam, Sandra (his mother), Steven (his father), and Sam's four siblings. When Sam was just 22 weeks' gestation, Sandra was

DOI: 10.4324/9781003123798-15

admitted to a different hospital and placed on bedrest and high-risk pregnancy precautions due to risk of preterm labor. For Sandra, this meant she had to lay with her head below her feet and endure uncomfortable medications, lack of privacy, and fear for Sam's survival. At 22 weeks, Sam was considered "nonviable," which meant that if he had been born there would be no lifesaving measures provided. NICU levels of care in the United States range from level I to level IV; at the highest level of care, neonates require access to resources such as ventilators and lifesaving medications. While viability is dependent on which NICU resources are available to pregnant women, in most areas of the United States, viability ranges from 22 to 24 weeks' gestation.[1]

When Sandra and Steven were informed by their medical team that Sam had a limited chance for survival at their hospital, she requested a transfer to a trauma center with a higher-level NICU. After remaining on bedrest and labor-suppressing medications for another two weeks, Sam was born at 24 weeks and 3 days gestational age[2] in February 2020. Sam's age at under 28 weeks' gestation classified him as extremely premature, also called a micro-preemie.[1]

At the time of Sam's arrival, I had worked in the NICU and Pediatric Cardiac Intensive Care Unit (PICU) for about four and a half years. To situate myself, I am a white, cisgender, heterosexual woman with no children or experience with childbirth or parenting. I am religious, identify as Catholic, and am actively involved in music making at my church. I work to honor the differences between myself and the families I work with. When this case began, I was two years into my graduate degree and focusing my clinical reflexivity on how to honor culture and identity in music making. I was also learning about the sensitivities of preterm infant neurodevelopment and how to acknowledge and empower parents as their child's musical caregiver. Theoretically, I align within a humanistic perspective, with a focus on family-centered, resource-oriented, and cultural-relational models. Family-centered care in NICU music therapy means acknowledging trauma, embracing varying levels of parent participation, focusing on empowerment, and weaving in culturally appropriate approaches.[3]

Meeting Sam's Family and Honoring Their Connection to Spirituality

I originally received a referral for the Martin family because of Sam's extreme prematurity. About two years before Sam's birth, the NICU staff developed a micro-preemie protocol, which includes unique standards of nursing care, early involvement of developmental therapies, and automatic referrals to supportive services like music therapy. My first meeting with Sandra was about one week after Sam's birth. Sandra was open during our conversation about her birth journey and music preferences, which had strong connections to her spirituality. It is not typically my practice to bring up spirituality and religion in my assessment unless families have shared a connection between music and their spiritual practice themselves. For Sandra, these two parts of her life were interwoven, and when I asked about her music preferences she organically shared about her spiritual practices as well.

Regarding their birth journey, Sandra chose to transfer to our facility before Sam was born because of the treatment resources available. Giving birth in our birth center allowed Sam to be immediately brought to a high-level NICU for lifesaving intervention. Sandra had also experienced the previous hospital as negative and not offering her much hope. It was important that Sam's care, from his prognosis to how providers engaged, be marked by sensitivity and compassion. Sandra was seeking out opportunities to engage with Sam in a meaningful way and desired a team that would honor them as a family unit.

What I noticed first about Sandra was her attentive care and strong advocacy for Sam. Always at Sam's bedside and involved in taking care of him in any way that she could from day one, Sandra appeared unafraid and ready to face whatever was thrown at her. For some parents, extreme prematurity can be wrought with a rollercoaster of emotions: fear and anxiety juxtaposed with joy and excitement for their baby, and a guilt or hesitation to bond out of concerns the child may not survive, thus impeding parental role attainment.[4] Sandra, however, shared that she would not let this rollercoaster get in the way of her involvement or attachment with Sam.

Sandra found support not only in her family and friends, but also in their cultural and spiritual background. Sam's family identifies as Kemetic Africans, and in our initial session Sandra shared a strong sense of spirituality from a variety of perspectives. I felt a sense of curiosity when Sandra shared about their spirituality and identity as Kemetic and was excited to see how music played a role in their practice.

However, I also had to ground myself in my space as a white Catholic woman. On the one hand, my faith modeled for me the value of learning about and respecting different religious beliefs and spiritual practices. On the other hand, I was not the expert here, and I was tasked with addressing my own cultural competence and humility. My first step was to open myself to what Sandra wanted to share about her spiritual beliefs, practices, and experiences. I had initiated a strong relationship with Sandra based on compassion and trust, and I leaned into that foundation to provide her space to share what she was comfortable sharing about her spiritual practice. When Sandra independently made the connection between music and her spiritual practice, it was a cue that her spirituality should be honored during our time together. We began talking about a number of topics, including how she consumed music; what qualities of the music felt grounding; how her values and beliefs were represented in the music; and what made her a musical being in general. In that discussion, Sandra shared the parts of her spirituality that she wanted to lift up in music therapy.

Honoring Sandra's spirituality meant acknowledging my differences and openness to the unknown. Before we could intentionally integrate her spiritual beliefs and practices into music therapy, I had to internally grapple with any implicit biases I had and how they could impact my reactions. My faith modeled for me the value of learning about and respecting different religious beliefs and spiritual practices, but it also meant my personal experience in religion and spirituality was fundamentally different from the Martins. I identified my knowledge gap when it came to traditionally African religions and spiritual practices and wanted to strike a balance between doing my research and letting Sandra guide what being Kemetic African meant in our sessions. I researched the phrases and values she identified as being central to her and her connection with Sam and was receptive to the important aspects of her spiritual practice as a whole. We became collaborators in addressing how to honor the integrity of her spiritual practices while making adjustments that were needed to protect Sam's neurodevelopment.

Of note, Sandra discussed Ma'at, the central theme and foundational ideal of Kemetic spiritual practice.[5] Her practice of Ma'at was guided by several principles: truth, balance, order, harmony, righteousness, morality, and justice. Music played a particularly prominent role when focusing on balance through meditation, a practice she maintained through Sam's NICU admission.

This theme of spirituality and meditation continued when Sandra talked about her identity in music. She chose "Trigger Protection Mantra" by Jhene Aiko as their song of kin. A song of kin is used to promote bonding and comfort between parents and their premature infants. Ideally, the song of kin represents great significance for the family, either as a song passed down generationally from parent to child, or one that has significance in the parent's pregnancy journey, childhood, and/or NICU experience.[6] "Trigger Protection Mantra" had been a grounding song in Sandra's life, particularly during her admission prior to Sam's birth. She referenced using the lyrics *calm down* to soothe and connect with Sam both during and after his birth.

At this point, my head was spinning. Mantra work and its repetitive structure had the potential to be fruitful in finding balance between Sandra and Steven's spiritual needs and Sam's neurodevelopmental needs. This opened up many possibilities for where we could go in music therapy: receptive methods for Sam and improvisational methods with Sandra, each centering around this meditative practice.

Supporting the NICU Journey

As a starting point for accessing Sandra's resources in meditation and mantra work, we moved into creative music therapy experiences that had grounding elements and improvised vocals. Sandra helped structure these experiences by identifying her music preferences and Sam's song of kin. The lyrical content paired with a repetitive frame helped her feel centered, and including these preferences communicated to Sandra that her practices and traditions would be honored in our shared space. These experiences also gave space for Sandra and Sam to connect through singing. Because of Sam's age, we centered the voice and, when appropriate, used one instrument to keep the structure simple and minimize risk of overstimulating him.

Our work together manifested in two phases. The first phase was Separation and Stability, defined by the separation experienced between Sandra, Steven, and Sam and their search for stability. The second phase was Presence and Preparation, defined by peaceful family moments in music and preparing for Sam's discharge home.

Separation and Stability

Infants born as early as Sam are incredibly sensitive to any stimulation, often resulting in physiological instability.[7] Our music that session, when Sam was about 27 weeks corrected gestational age, needed to be calming for Sam while reflecting Sandra's music preferences. I wanted to facilitate music that would physically comfort Sam, help Sandra access her inborn resources, and promote meaningful mother/son interaction.

I brought the gato box for our first session because the repetitive and rhythmic structure mimicking a steady heartbeat would be grounding for Sam and provide space for Sandra to engage musically however she felt comfortable. Beyond my intention to create comfort for Sam and expressive space for Sandra, I had no specific plan for the rest of the session. Instead, I remained open to how Sandra chose to engage, and made clinical decisions from there. Sandra had been intentional and thoughtful about her meditative and spiritual practice, had already built a strong connection with Sam in music with her song of kin, and appeared excited and eager to engage in music therapy. I had to ground myself and not mistake her energy for stability. I didn't want to push her away by asking her to do too much too soon, but I also wanted to leave the door open for her to fully engage how she wanted and needed to.

I began by educating Sandra about what to expect in our session; how we could use our voices to contain, comfort, and connect with Sam; and how to pair music with developmentally appropriate physical supports like positive touch. I then introduced the music to Sam before inviting Sandra to sing. This may sound counterproductive, as my goal is always to allow parents to be the musical caregiver; however, I also wanted Sam and Sandra to have positive moments in musicking, especially during their first days and weeks together, and I needed to assess what Sam's threshold was.

Sam tolerated the heartbeat rhythm on the gato box without any signs of overstimulation or changes in his vitals, and so I modeled tonal vocal holding for Sandra. After singing a pattern of toning within a minor third interval, I invited Sandra to join if and when she felt comfortable. We sang the pattern together a few times and then I faded away, allowing her voice to establish her role as "Mom" while I supportively maintained the rhythm on the gato box. Sandra then sang the lyric *calm down* from their song of kin, which is a slow descending minor 2nd. Sandra followed this by sustaining on the same interval the meditative vowels *om* (i.e., connection to the earth) and *ra* (i.e., connection to the sun or light). Throughout, I kept a grounding 3/4 pattern on the gato box, playing on beats 1 and 2 and pausing on beat 3 to give Sam space to process.

Space and silence were important as they allowed time for Sam to catch up, process, and breathe. Silence is a push-and-pull that gives music and sounds context and separates them from noxious noise.[8] Sandra, Sam, and I developed a rhythm together that continued for about 10 minutes, until Sam demonstrated changes in his vitals that indicated he needed a break from stimulation.

This moment was very powerful. I sensed a release in Sandra, as if a held breath had finally been let go. After making music with Sam, she shared feelings of joy and thankfulness for an uninterrupted moment of engagement with Sam. I was excited to continue this momentum with Sam and Sandra, but after our second session, the COVID-19 lockdown and subsequent restrictions began. We managed to have one session with both Sandra and Steven present, but after that they were only able to visit one at a time.

With only one parent allowed to visit at a time, I had to come up with new and creative ways for us to make music together. I drew upon the meditative music Sandra had been drawn to and began providing environmental music therapy (EMT). EMT is the practice of creating music in and around an environment to change the perception of that environment. Rather than focusing on noise levels – such as reducing noise levels as in the case of the NICU – EMT practices involve musically interacting with the environment to address how sounds are interpreted and meaning is made.[9] With our interactions limited and the hospital environment at large drastically changed, EMT approaches could help address the stress present for patients, families, and staff; sustain the therapeutic relationship Sandra and I had begun to build; and support the musical relationship shared between Sandra, Steven, and Sam.

In our sessions, I reflected music in the environment by playing within and around alarm tones when they rang and responding to how Sam and his parents were interacting. If Sam was crying, my playing became faster and reflective of his distress until he could calm with the music, and if Sam was transitioning from his bath to his bed or into his parents' arms, I musically reflected with key changes or with new melodic structures. I also intermittently sang some of the phrases Sandra used in our first session, such as *calm down* when Sam was upset or when tensions were high in the room, which sustained our connections during uncertainty until we were able to move into a new space.

Presence and Preparation

For the Martins, stabilization came with routine and medical improvement. When Sam became more medically stable, Sandra and Steven were able to have a more active role in his care. They made more connections with him, physically and emotionally, embraced joyful moments, and began to talk about what it would mean to go home with Sam. Through this process, Sandra and Steven could (a) access and engage with their emotions about being new parents in the NICU, (b) begin to process the events they had experienced prior to, during, and after Sam's birth, and (c) connect and bond with Sam as a whole family.[7]

We found a routine in music therapy that reflected their schedule, as Steven spent Mondays and Sandra spent Wednesdays with Sam. Sandra described this time as ships passing in the night, often only seeing each other in the parking garage when one arrived and the other left to be with Sam's siblings. Our sessions were largely structured around moments of physical connection between Sam and his parents when they were holding him. I came with my guitar and began by slowly introducing the music, building from the base note to arpeggios on guitar and then adding vocal toning which moved into short and repetitive melody phrases. I was deliberate in this way in order to assess Sam's tolerance for stimulation that day and his vital signs for indicators of relaxation or distress. At the same time, I was assessing his parents' and their responses to his affective state. Once Sam was comfortable, I could engage his parents in a more expressive process.

For a few weeks both Steven and Sandra, in their respective sessions, participated in improvisational songwriting by sharing their in-the-moment thoughts about Sam's progress and what they were discovering about their love for him. Over time these improvisations developed into a melody that new lyrics were added to each session by Sandra and Steven. Since sessions with them occurred separately but had similar structures, I wanted to support them to connect with each other through songwriting.

I first spoke about this idea with Sandra, who was eager to participate and wrote the first verse with me that day. Sandra and I spoke about what the structure of the song should be, and Sandra wanted the qualities of a lullaby with a repetitive mantra style alternating throughout. We started with a 6/8 time signature using the melody that developed out of their improvisations and wrote a new verse each week. The verses were simple and always ended with the same phrase or iteration of a phrase that included "Superman," Sam's nickname.

In my next session with Steven, I brought up the songwriting idea and offered him the opportunity to write every other verse to collaborate with Sandra. I thought that surely this was a way for him to connect with Sandra and assumed that he would share her excitement, but I was wrong. Steven had different ways of experiencing music therapy than Sandra did. While Steven would occasionally share a phrase of love or encouragement for Sam, he preferred these little improvised lullabies not to be shared outside of the session or even to return in the following session.

In hindsight, there were two dynamics I had missed. First, I had the stronger therapeutic relationship with Sandra, having worked with her closely since Sam's admission. With my work with Steven deepening, I had to be mindful of re-orienting my clinical lens from his perspective and not assuming Sandra's needs were also his. Second, having observed Sandra and Steven only briefly seeing each other in the NICU, I had assumed Steven would desire or need to have a connection with Sandra through music. However, they were already making connections in their life outside of the unit, even as they felt pull towards being with Sam. For Steven, music therapy was not about Sandra, but rather a moment of space, respite, and relaxation with Sam.

While Steven's choice to not participate in writing a lullaby was not part of my plan, it opened the doors for another opportunity. Sam's expected discharge home would be close to Father's Day, and Sandra decided to create a gift for Steven out of the lullaby we had been writing together. After finishing the lullaby, we met to review the song, clarify and edit some details, and decide on instrumentation. I brought several instruments to our session, with specific attention to instruments that would support and recreate some of the sounds found in her preferred music (e.g., the hapi drum, tone bars, gato box, ocean disc, and tubanos). Sandra expressed interest in maintaining the integrity of the lullaby with the acoustic guitar plucking pattern and added tone bars in the bass of the chords as grounding tones, bringing her preferred style and the lullaby style together.

Sam's lullaby included themes of spirituality, motivation, meaning-making, strength, and resilience. The four verses held the same structure: his name, three statements, his name again, another statement, a reference to his nickname, and ending with his first and middle name. It was important to Sandra that his middle name be included, as it derived from the *om* and *ra* phrases she used for meditation.

Musically, arpeggiated guitar was played throughout. Sandra chose to include the tone bars and played the tonic each time Sam's name was sung. At the end, with Sam's full name, Sandra chose to add the dominant and subdominant played with each syllable of his name. The placements of the tone bars at the beginning of musical phrases grounded Sandra and pairing them with Sam's name helped center him within the composition.

The first and second verse were musically structured similarly, with the same accompaniment and melody line. Topics of these verses centered around Sam's strength and resilience and his story of defying the odds and bringing their family joy. The third verse, which reflected their connection to spirituality and Sam being guided by their ancestors, was marked with ascending vocal embellishments to the melody. Conversely, the fourth verse returned to the original melody and with decreased guitar accompaniment, allowing for acapella moments in the vocal line. This change represented space for the possibilities that Sam had in his future, which was the topic of the lyrics.

In collaboration with Sandra and Steven, we have decided not to share the specific lyrics of the song in this case. The music parents create with their babies in the NICU is intimate and exclusive, as there is little room for privacy between parents and their baby when experiencing a hospital stay.[10] For the Martins, the song was a sacred moment that held a great deal of emotional weight and memory for a time that was both difficult and beautiful. For a music therapist in the NICU, these intimate moments are part of my every day; however, for Sandra and Steve who were forging a lifelong relationship with their new son, these moments were their whole world and they wished for that to remain in the family.

Concluding Thoughts

In our final sessions, Sam's mom and I created a video using pictures from Sam's NICU stay and a recording of his lullaby. Sam was discharged in the days surrounding Father's Day, bringing music therapy and his NICU stay to a well-timed close. I was not able to be part of presenting the video to Steven because of Sam's discharge, but both Sandra and Steven have expressed to me how important music therapy was in providing intimate, spiritual, and joyful moments while they were in the NICU.

Through a number of challenges, periods of separation, and difficulties, Sam's family demonstrated resilience and strength at every turn. The fleeting moments that are natural to NICU care require flexibility and frequent reassessments that, when examined on a broader scale, lead to the goal of family unification and independence in preparation to go home. In music therapy the Martins created sacred space in environmental approaches, found their voice in improvisational methods, and created legacy through songwriting.

Summarizing Ideas and Questions
for Discussion

1. As music therapists, we are constantly adjusting to factors both inside and outside of the therapy space while also learning about how those factors are impacting patients.

    a. How do we set realistic expectations for ourselves and for patients during times of crisis?
    b. In what ways can music be flexible to a dynamic, ever-changing intensive care environment?

2. In a family-centered care model, music making in the NICU is directed by the family's experiences, resources, and culture.

    a. In what ways can a parent be involved in music making? What are ways parents can be actively involved versus passively involved in session?
    b. What are actions you can take to better understand the family's cultural locations? How can the music therapy process be informed by those locations?

Notes

1 March of Dimes, PMNCH, Save the Children, & WHO. (2012). *Born too soon: The global action report on preterm birth* (C. P. Howson, M. V. Kinney, & J. E. Lawn, Eds.). World Health Organization.

2 Gestational age, measured up to 40 weeks, refers to the week of development Sam would be if he remained in Sandra's uterus. If Sam is born at 24 weeks gestation and is 4 weeks old chronologically, he would be referred to as 28 weeks corrected gestational age. I refer to their age as their corrected gestational age throughout this chapter to give context as to Sam's neurodevelopmental progress.

3 Ettenberger, M. (2017). Music therapy in the neonatal intensive care unit: Putting the families at the centre of care. *British Journal of Music Therapy, 31*(1), 12–17. https://doi.org/10.1177/1359457516685881

4 Fernández Medina, I. M., Granero-Molina, J., Fernández-Sola, C., Hernández-Padilla, J. M., Camacho Ávila, M., & López Rodríguez, M. D. M. (2018). Bonding in neonatal intensive care units: Experiences of extremely preterm infants' mothers. *Women and Birth, 31*, 325–330. https://doi.org/10.1016/j.wombi.2017.11.008

5 Karenga, M. (2004). *Maat, the moral ideal in ancient Egypt: A study in classical African ethics.* Routledge.

6 Loewy, J. (2015). NICU music therapy: Song of kin as critical lullaby in research and practice. *Annals of the New York Academy of Sciences, 1337*, 178–185. https://doi.org/10.1111/nyas.12648

7 Lammetink, F., Vinkers, C. H., Tataranno, M. L., & Benders, M. J. N. L. (2021). Premature birth and developmental programming: Mechanisms of resilience and vulnerability. *Frontiers in Psychiatry, 11*, 531571. https://doi.org/10.3389/fpsyt.2020.531571

8 Shoemark, H. (2017). Empowering parents in singing to hospitalized infants: The role of the music therapist. In M. Filippa, P. Kuhn, & B. Westrup (Eds.), *Early vocal contact and preterm infant brain development: Bridging the gaps between research and practice* (pp. 205–215). Springer International Publishing.

9 Rosetti, A. (2020). Environmental music therapy (EMT): Music's contribution to changing hospital atmospheres and perceptions of environments. *Music and Medicine*, *12*(2), 130–141. https://doi.org/10.47513/mmd.v12i2.742

10 McLean, E. (2016). Fostering intimacy through musical beginnings: Exploring the application of communicative musicality through the musical experience of parents in the neonatal intensive care unit. *Voices: A World Forum for Music Therapy*, *16*(2). https://doi.org/10.15845/voices.v16i2.874

Chapter 12

Discovering Artistic Truth in Music Therapy

Cassandra Byers

Abstract

Music therapists provide therapeutic support that can be reshaped by clients to encompass elements of community engagement and music education. Such collaboration with clients requires the music therapist to be flexible across multiple spectrums of practice, and music therapists may feel challenged to negotiate more familiar roles and responsibilities with the roles and responsibilities demanded by the therapeutic process. In such situations, focusing on the therapeutic relationship and musical connections can be essential for grounding care, particularly in processes related to closure.

Tags: Therapeutic Relationship

This case describes Bea, a vibrant violinist who happened to be dying but was far more concerned with living her artistic truth. Bea's hospice journey illustrates the significance of allowing the natural therapeutic process to unfold when goals and objectives aren't immediately obvious. At the time of this story, I had two years of professional work experience, one of those being in hospice. I had never had so much as a practicum placement in the hospice setting, and I had not received any formal hospice supervision from another music therapist. Although I came to hospice serendipitously and quickly grew to love the work, my lack of experience both as a music therapist and in hospice frequently made me feel insecure. In order to combat these insecurities and fill in what I felt to be gaps in my education, I was also in the process of earning my Masters in Music Therapy. I felt that I was rapidly growing as a clinician throughout the program, but my experiences with Bea forced me out of my comfort zone and to fully commit to new ways of considering and practicing music therapy.

DOI: 10.4324/9781003123798-16

Meeting Bea

In hospice care, referrals frequently come from well-meaning staff who are adamant that a patient receive music therapy services "because they like music" or "because they played piano at their church." However, my instinctual response in the early years of my career was to ask, "But what is the *clinical* reason for seeing this patient?"

This reaction is a direct consequence of my academic training, which focused heavily on behavioral goals and measurable objectives with tangible outcomes (e.g., the client will say "hello" when given a cue, the client will identify three coping skills, the client will create a legacy project, etc.). Unquantifiable goals such as "enhance quality of life" were unfathomable to me as a student and early-career music therapist. It seemed that, according to my training, most hospice goals could not be considered music therapy and that any musician could "enhance quality of life."

When Bea came on service, I received these vague referrals from every member of the clinical team, especially because both Bea and I were violinists. Bea was a White woman in her early 80s, a lifelong musician, and devout Methodist Christian. She had lived in an independent living apartment within a continuing care retirement community since her husband died 10 years previously, and she maintained an active social life in her church. Bea had three adult children living out of state, and they made weekly group calls. She held an undergraduate degree in violin performance, a graduate degree in Christian education, and she worked as a music educator and performer for decades. Bea was a hometown musician: knowledgeable, technically proficient, and able to create aesthetically pleasing sounds. She was a well-known local performer and educator, but not major-symphony caliber.

Bea and I were educated in the Western Classical tradition: the more technically perfect your music, the more worthy it is of an audience. Training as a music therapist opened my eyes to the many other ways music making can be valuable to an individual; however, I deeply understood Bea's product-oriented motivations, having been brought up in this same musical culture. Having an outcome-based music therapy education further compounded this mindset.

Bea was diagnosed with chronic obstructive pulmonary disease and was initially resistant to receiving hospice services. She agreed to hospice admission solely to receive assistance with activities of daily living so she could remain in her independent living apartment and avoid moving to the assisted living floor. However, Bea remained candidly unconvinced that "nothing could be done" for her progressively worsening illness.

From Constructing to Co-Constructing Music Therapy

During our first session together, Bea made it clear that she felt the addition of hospice services was highly unnecessary because she simply didn't feel like a dying person. She had little interest in discussing her illness or any emotions surrounding her admission to hospice other than to assert her goal of graduating from hospice. However, the clinical team had gotten her excited about music therapy, so she had been looking forward to meeting with me and connecting over our shared backgrounds as classically trained violinists.

After discussing myriad product-oriented music therapy interventions, I asked Bea what she was hoping to gain from music therapy sessions. She immediately requested weekly violin lessons because she was having difficulty consistently balancing the bow in light of a recent significant weight loss. Upon further discussion, Bea decided her primary goal was to regain a strong tone, with a secondary ambition of returning to a consistent performance schedule within the retirement community. She expressed a firm belief that I came into her life because God wanted her to return to the violin after a year-long retirement from playing.

However, I left the session feeling insecure in my identity as a music therapist, in particular wondering how I could have better described music therapy to Bea since she appeared to view me as a music educator. As a music therapist, I wanted to approach the treatment plan through assigning concrete goals with tangible outcomes and documenting her progress toward these specific goals based upon their assigned interventions week-to-week. I could not conceptualize what the behavioral goal would be if she didn't want to process her feelings about dying. *What will our interventions be if we were not processing these feelings through songwriting or creating a legacy project? Were we just going to sit around and play music?* I felt that my role in Bea's treatment had been misunderstood by both Bea and the hospice team, that music therapy was not being utilized to its fullest potential and was, once again, being relegated to the novelty of having a musician on staff.

Despite these internal negotiations about treatment planning, I decided to depart from assigning goals to Bea and, instead, honor the clear goals she had already decided on. Somewhere in the back of my mind I recalled that a humanistic approach to music therapy existed. Up until this point, I had not given it much thought because, as a student, this methodology felt redundant. It was like another way of saying you use the iso principle, which in my undergraduate program was a given. As I worked through this first semester of graduate school, I gave more attention to the idea of a humanistic perspective. I began to understand how humanism and behaviorism do not need to necessarily exist as mutually exclusive frameworks, and perhaps the iso principle could also mean allowing the client to direct their treatment. With further reflection, I realized I had never had clients whose goals weren't already clearly outlined for them, whether through an individualized education plan, parent, institution, or caregiver who took over once dementia or disease became disabling. Bea signed her own admission paperwork for hospice, arranged all her appointments and transportation, and handled her money and affairs. She was an independent adult, capable of making her own decisions and determining the role of music therapy in her hospice journey.

Bea and I quickly built a strong rapport as both musicians and people. Bea retained a finely tuned ear and incredibly high Western Classical standard for her violin playing, often becoming frustrated with herself for failing to meet these self-imposed expectations. Per her request, I provided guidance on technique and adjusting her playing to her weakening body. Because Bea easily tired, she also requested that I play violin for her or sing some hymns. Afterward she would typically ask me to look up information about the composer or history of the piece on my phone, which often led to us connecting over our shared, and even divergent, opinions on various classical composers or periods of music. Bea mentioned that she enjoyed having someone who was "brought up similarly" with which to discuss classical music, particularly standard violin pieces.

Despite this burgeoning conceptualization of humanistic music therapy, I continued to have intermittent doubts about where this was all going. *How did music lessons have anything to do with hospice? How much should I push Bea to discuss dying? At what point do I insist on "real" (i.e., concrete, measurable) music therapy interventions?* I still couldn't envision how music lessons could possibly bridge such a wide gap between total denial and the reality of this patient's terminal diagnosis. Music therapy was something I was supposed to work hard at, something I had been trained to defend as requiring a college education. Providing music lessons felt like something any musician could do, and my professional identity was shaken by the thoughts I dared not entertain. *What if I was just a terrible music therapist? What if music therapists were just gatekeeping music?* My training made it feel like music therapy couldn't possibly be as simple as providing music lessons or playing someone a song – I had to be doing something *more* for it to be considered music therapy. Reflecting on this case, I recognize how I had lost my connection with music by going to music school and had similarly lost sight of what made me want to be a music therapist in the first place: helping others through music. The concept that Bea's relationship with the music could be doing the work, rather than a carefully constructed session of interventions, never occurred to me.

During one lesson, Bea became exceptionally frustrated because she could hardly produce an audible sound. She set down the violin with a deep sigh and shared, completely unprompted: "You're a musician. You know that we're brought up to believe if we work hard enough at something, we can fix it." She elaborated, sharing that working toward musical goals helped her feel as though she was continuing to improve herself and not "giving up." For Bea, continued musical excellence helped her cope with, and accept this terminal diagnosis, giving her agency over this illness that was out of her control. Bea had suddenly addressed my internal questions by defining for herself what music therapy would be and could be at this stage in her life.

This declaration of purpose was a turning point in our work, and in my understanding of music therapy itself. Now that I understood Bea's therapeutic process in her own words, I was able to visualize music therapy sessions and music lessons as distinct, yet also overlapping experiences. Our time together existed in the overlapping space between music therapy and music lessons. Given my behavioral training background and lack of experience with hospice, I had never considered that meaningful therapeutic gains could be so ambiguous, nor that they could center on *process* rather than *product*. We didn't need to write a song about coming to terms with death for Bea's therapy to be legitimate. Simply being a musician, existing in that space of musical achievement, and making music with others gave Bea an understanding of how she wanted to experience the final phase of her life.

Bea's process continued to manifest in subtle ways throughout the coming weeks. During one session, she spent five minutes frustrated by her progressively weakening body and the next 55 minutes learning how to use Spotify and Instagram, two apps her kids thought she would enjoy. As I packed up my violin, Bea took my hand, looked me in the eye, and asked: "You said you're a music therapist, right? I think that if that had been an option when I was in school, I might have picked that instead." Again, I didn't immediately understand how this visit, which seemed more akin to a social call rather than a therapy session, could constitute successful therapy. It seemed that every time Bea and I connected on a person-to-person level, she revealed some new insight which completely shifted my understanding of music therapy practice. I had underestimated the power of rapport-building in a therapeutic relationship, the human need for connection, and music's ability to facilitate these connections.

Performance and Community

Shortly thereafter, Bea decided that she would like to start performing in the dining hall as she had done in years past. At her request, I provided guidance regarding programming and modified pieces to suit Bea's physical limitations while also playing to her strengths. After several months of playing ambient dinner music for the other residents, Bea approached me about Christmas pieces and if I could possibly accompany her on the piano. Within the hour, this idea had grown into a full-fledged holiday concert. Bea directed the programming and put me through my paces, requesting that I accompany her on violin, viola, piano, and guitar throughout the program. She was in her element, assigning me tasks to include researching the history of each piece to present to the audience, creating posters to advertise throughout the building, and communicating with the memory care director to ensure the residents on the secure unit had the opportunity to attend.

Operating as the creative director of the event, Bea demonstrated a passion and energy I had not yet seen during our time together. Planning the performance gave her purpose and provided an opportunity to publicly show her expertise. After so many months of calling me the expert during lessons, it was Bea's turn to be the expert on putting on a dynamic, educational, and musically excellent show. Programming is not a skill I possess, and I was thrilled to watch her shine in this role.

The morning of the Christmas concert, I received several frantic phone calls that Bea had fallen, sprained her wrist, and broken her left pinky finger. However, Bea insisted that the doctor allow her to wear flexible bandages with her fingers free so that she could perform that afternoon. Calmly, and armed with the chaplain's prayer for success in the face of adversity, she insisted that the show would go on.

The concert was well attended and included dozens of individuals from all facets of Bea's life: former students from decades ago, members of her church, residents of the senior living community, and all the members of her hospice team. Bea received flowers and cards from her guests, and I got a glimpse of the performer from decades past. She graciously thanked them for attending and humbly attributed her artistic success to the power of prayer, God guiding her hands, and returning to weekly violin lessons.

Back in her apartment, Bea flopped down on her couch and exhaled deeply, likely for the first time that day. Smiling from ear to ear, she calmly declared: "That was awful." I insisted that she played with her usual flawless intonation, particularly given her injury, but she stated: "My tone was thin, though. It wasn't up to the standard of what we prepared. But our PR was a success; it was very well attended!" Bea remained smiling throughout this entire interaction, seemingly exhilarated by the experience.

Having seen Bea put herself down quite harshly when her playing wasn't up to her standard of perfection, I was surprised to see how joyfully she responded to this performance. I now wondered if the joy came from how thoroughly her community supported her rather than how she played. Here Bea once more introduced an additional dimension of music therapy: baselines for determining growth and healing could be based on intermusical connections rather than intramusical evaluations.

Over the coming weeks, Bea patiently allowed her hand to heal while looking toward the future. We listened to and discussed classical pieces, I played the guitar and answered her questions about how it compared to playing the violin, and we discussed the changing world outside of her retirement community. After the Christmas concert, my instinct to verbally process or push songwriting on Bea had been largely tempered by my new understanding of humanistic and music-centered music therapy practice. We remained focused on Bea's relationships with music and performing and how this vital facet of her identity contributed to a peaceful, fulfilled dying process.

In the following months, Bea reluctantly agreed to change performance venues to the smaller, more intimate bistro due to the chaos of mealtime impacting her audience's ability to hear her play. After several performances, I noticed that Bea had grown closer to the other residents of the retirement community. I often found her socializing in the bistro rather than sitting alone in her apartment, and she became a regular at several activities she had not attended in the first year of our work together. These performances had also brought her closer to the retirement community staff, who before were just another face in a crowded dining hall.

These observations helped me gain a greater understanding of the role of performance in Bea's life. Thinking back to her seemingly contradictory response to the Christmas performance, I began to wonder if she wanted the other residents to be able to hear her music in the dining room or if she desired the human connection that had accompanied decades of music making. I began to consider Community Music Therapy, an approach that aims to "accompany [clients] as they move between 'therapy' and wider social contexts of musicing."[1] Community Music Therapy considers the person in context of their cultural ecologies, and felt accurate to how we cycled between individual sessions preparing music and the public spaces where she performed.

Once autumn rolled back around, Bea and I switched focus from solo performance repertoire to preparing the chamber ensemble program for her second annual Christmas concert. At the time, I was supervising an intern who played the cello and the possibility of a trio delighted Bea. She threw herself into programming and publicity with even greater fervor than the year before, candidly determined to outdo her inaugural Christmas concert. This time we had a cellist, camera-ready makeup (Bea was appalled at how washed out she looked the year previously), professionally made refreshments provided by the retirement community, coordinating Christmas-themed outfits, and an explosion of Christmas decor. Most importantly, Bea had full use of her hands.

The concert exceeded even Bea's high expectations, checking off every box for her ideal experience. The audience filled the entire bistro, lobby, and adjoining library space. Bea played with a strong tone and did not have to compete against the accompanying instruments. She looked beautiful and festive in the professional photos. Concertgoers mingled to ambient holiday music while consuming refreshments, congratulating her on a beautiful performance, and sharing how impressed they were with all of the little details she had carefully coordinated for the event. This experience fulfilled Bea's vision of the classic holiday recital, an experience she had enjoyed so many times in her life and spent over a year working toward having one more time.

Equally important were the connections Bea had made with her community through the process of putting this performance together. The majority of the audience were her neighbors; although they lived right down the hall from each other, in some instances for years, they had never gotten to know one another until the bistro performances. Bea made connections with residents who had a variety of age-related physical deficits, and I observed that she made fewer comments about how her weakness was a result of not working hard enough to become stronger. As she got to know her peers' stories and that they also had a sense of their bodies being out of their control due to aging, she began accepting that her physical limitations and disease progression were not her fault and were a natural part of life.

Saying Goodbye

Bea transitioned into the active dying process unexpectedly while I was on vacation. I found out from a profusely apologetic coworker who shared that she couldn't bear the thought of me returning from vacation unaware of this death. I agreed, thanked her for letting me know, hung up, and burst into tears. I explained to my confused mother and husband that the violinist I had just had the concert with was imminently dying, and likely so while I was away for the holiday.

My mother matter-of-factly asked: "Well, how are we getting you home to say goodbye?" I immediately began explaining that not only did I desperately need this vacation for my own mental health, but it would also demonstrate incredibly poor professional boundaries to cut the vacation short, over a holiday, in order to be with a patient. The past year had taught me that I had to set this boundary in order to not burn out as a hospice worker. Setting this boundary acknowledged that, although our shared backgrounds gave us a much more personal connection than I typically experience with a patient, I was not the most important person in her life. Between her children and God, Bea had everyone she needed at her side. Although the presence of music therapy would likely enhance the experience, particularly as I already had a rapport with Bea's children, music therapy was not vital, and I knew they would all be well supported by the other hospice team members.

I finally felt grounded in my role as Bea's music therapist and understood that music therapy can be important without being the *most* important. Bea dying peacefully without the presence of music therapy didn't mean that my presence was redundant. It meant that I didn't need to be present and actively contributing to her peaceful death at the moment of her death to prove the validity of music therapy. My presence throughout our time together, through this whole process of dying, was one of many factors that contributed to Bea signing the do not resuscitate order without hesitation and declaring that she was ready to meet God, after 16 months of steadfast refusal to "give up on herself" by declining lifesaving measures.

Surprisingly, Bea was still alive when I returned to work. All three of her children were at her side, and various church friends and relatives had been popping by throughout the week. A number of colleagues declared that she "had waited for [me]." However, this idea made me uncomfortable because I did not want to overstate whatever importance I may have had in her life nor insinuate that I needed to see her for my own closure. Rather,

I wanted to achieve therapeutic closure through honoring her previously established desire for live music during the active dying process.

When I arrived, Bea was unconscious, sweaty, and exhibiting labored breathing. She was surrounded by her children who readily agreed to the session. I had met all of them at various points in our time together, and they remained up-to-date on Bea's performances and accomplishments. Her children were coping appropriately, grieving their mother but ready for her to be with the Lord and free of pain. Eventually, her children shared that she had taught them all how to read music and sight-sing. They pulled out Bea's hymnal, and I facilitated a number of her favorite hymns with her children singing harmonies and the chaplain weaving in prayers and scripture readings. Bea's younger son eventually requested that we sing "Will the Circle Be Unbroken" as a way of acknowledging their loss in context of their religious convictions.

After the song concluded, the room remained still with reflection, and I continued to hold space until we closed the session with another hymn and blessing. I thanked the family for welcoming me into Bea's life, as well as into this sacred space. They thanked me for facilitating Bea's final musical journey. Finally, I thanked Bea for being open to our work together. And with one more long look around the room, taking in all of the little details, I said goodbye and left. Bea passed away the next morning, surrounded by loved ones.

Reflections

Bea is one of many lifelong musicians I have worked with. Our time together shaped how I approach hospice work by pushing me out of my behavioral comfort zone and into the more nebulous arenas of humanistic and Community Music Therapy. Although I carried into this work the philosophy of "Meet the client where they are at," I later realized how I conflated this idea largely with using client-preferred music in sessions. It could also mean slight deviation from my rigid session plan, but these occurrences filled me with anxiety. By rolling with Bea's explicit request for violin lessons and allowing her to define her own experience, I discovered what it actually meant to meet the client where they are at. Since this experience, I've continued to have moments where I question: *Am I just singing songs to this person? Am I phoning it in as a music therapist?* I have always been proven wrong when a caregiver tells me what these passive experiences have meant to them emotionally and/or spiritually.

Bea never defined herself as a dying person. She identified as a musician and performer until her death. Performance was the essence of her being and allowed her agency over her end-of-life experience. Throughout our time together, I spent a great deal of time reflecting on how Bea and my coworkers had misunderstood music therapy, confusing it with music education. However, I was the one who misunderstood music therapy: they knew exactly what music therapy was all along.

Summarizing Ideas and Questions for Discussion

1. Therapeutic closure varies amongst clinical settings, and typically in the hospice setting this means the death of the client.

   a. What does therapeutic closure look like in the setting in which you work?
   b. How does that process of closure align and/or differ from your expectations of what closure would look like?
   c. How have you been challenged to re-position your practice in response to different expectations around closure?

2. Music therapists will use different terminology to illustrate their practice, such as "music intervention," "music experience," and "music activity."

   a. What is the difference between a music intervention, music experience, and music activity? What terminology were you taught and/or do you use?
   b. Why might it be important to make distinctions across these different terminologies?

Note

1 Ansdell, G. (2002). Community music therapy & the winds of change. *Voices, a World Forum for Music Therapy*, 2(2). https://voices.no/index.php/voices/article/view/1590/1349 (para 2).

Chapter 13

The Ebb and Flow of the Therapeutic Journey

Adjusting Theoretical Orientations in Clinical Practice

Kate Myers-Coffman

Abstract

Clinical reflexivity is a process in our daily music therapy practice that challenges us to be responsive to in-the-moment needs of those we work with. One way that reflexivity is expressed is through adjustments to theoretical orientation in response to someone's growth or progression in their therapeutic journey.

Tags: Therapeutic Relationship; Professional Development

It has been a journey to feel grounded in an ever-emerging clinical identity shaped by my lived experiences, expanding understanding of the world and how to exist relationally within it, and constantly developing therapeutic skills. The tasks of learning how to apply a range of clinical theoretical orientations, finding a comfortable flow that is authentic to how I practice, and being in community with others has been exciting and daunting. The more I learn about myself, my values and beliefs, and how others experience the world, the more my therapeutic practice shifts.

My education and social identities have greatly influenced how I've curated an approach to practice integrating a number of theoretical orientations. In my undergraduate degree, my concentration in psychology was heavily psychodynamic in nature. My subsequent music therapy education and clinical training was rooted in behaviorism and further influenced by the cognitive model and cognitive-behavioral therapy (CBT).[1] I was drawn to humanistic, person-centered theoretical readings,[2] and in my doctoral studies I resonated with resource-oriented approaches to therapy.[3] Critical theory frameworks[4] – including feminist, queer, critical race, and disability justice theories – have become central to my work as I recognize the socio-cultural and political contexts impacting health and wellbeing. My experiences as a middle-class white, Hispanic, nondisabled, queer, and genderqueer person in my mid-30s who grew up socialized as a female

DOI: 10.4324/9781003123798-17

impact the ways in which I digest and implement these critical frameworks. Over time, I have learned how to weave between and through these orientations and philosophies in ways that help me attend to the evolving nature of someone's therapeutic process.

Through my humanistic and resource-oriented lenses, I believe that everyone has the abilities, resources, and strengths within them to gain the insights needed to shift their mental health in their desired direction. I aim to be a caring, empathic witness and collaborator rather than a leader. I do not view myself as the expert in either a therapy session or someone else's life. What I have, however, is education and training to offer different perspectives for engaging in one's thoughts, behaviors, and moods as they relate to health and well-being. Based on the clinical context, I may offer to teach individuals about CBT strategies, such as a) thought-stopping, b) evaluating thoughts to see whether they are hurtful versus helpful, and c) identifying the link between thoughts, behaviors, and moods.[1] These strategies can help us make shifts on our own to maintain a general sense of well-being. Therefore, I often provide psychoeducation, guided by the cognitive model, to offer options someone can choose from to help manage their everyday mental health. With a focus on agency, I encourage them to engage in these CBT strategies thoughtfully in and outside of sessions.

Integrating humanism and CBT may seem unlikely due to incongruences in philosophical underpinnings. For example, CBT can be viewed as directive, with the music therapist holding power and knowledge, while humanism is non-directive, with the individual holding power and knowledge. However, in CBT, individuals are choosing their own goals and objectives, and the therapeutic process is collaborative.[1] They control their therapeutic journey, and my verbal and music strategies may introduce new perspectives or directions. This agency is also a critical driving factor in humanism,[2] providing opportunity for philosophical overlaps to be applied in practice.

I approach the integration of CBT strategies in therapy through inquisitive rather than directive statements. For example, in considering CBT concepts of hurtful versus helpful thinking, I would never respond to someone's statement with: "That's not a good way to think." This can serve as an exertion of power and be perceived as oppressive in several clinical contexts. Instead, I might ask: "How does that thought make you feel?" so they can determine for themselves whether a thought and resulting behavior or mood makes them feel good or bad. Therefore, I am able to find and use the common factors across different theoretical orientations to navigate the therapy space with theoretical flexibility. With this being a skill embedded in my daily practice, my theoretical orientations adjusted throughout my time working with Lesley to help get her to where she wanted to go in music therapy.

Meeting Lesley

Lesley identified as an African American woman in her late 20s, living and working as a helping professional in a large East Coast city. She referred herself to a community health clinic for anxiety and depression. She had seen therapists in the past, yet this was her first time trying music therapy. I saw her in individual hourly sessions typically every week or every other week for a year and a half.

When Lesley first came to therapy, she talked about her anxiety and depression and shared that some family members had died from gun violence. Additionally, she grew up in and out of foster care. Her early childhood years were spent with her biological mother. Then, she was under the care of a loving foster mother until her biological mother felt she was ready to mother Lesley again in her early teens. She felt very connected to her foster mother and was not able to re-establish a strong relationship with her biological mother, whom Lesley described as often very hard on her. The adverse events of this unstable family life during her impressionable years and the unresolved grief she felt over the death of family members from 5-10 years prior contributed to her anxiety and depression.

Lesley described herself as more spiritual than religious, though she most closely aligned with Christianity. Her family members were devoutly religious and spiritual, some being Catholic and others Muslim. While she experienced depressive symptoms related to her unresolved grief, she relayed how her spirituality gave her strength and comfort when she thought about her deceased loved ones. She had many brothers and sisters, most of whom lived near her. She shared that because of the stigma of mental health in the African American community, she could not talk openly about her mental health challenges with her family. They knew that she was in therapy, but they did not understand the depths of the challenges impeding her daily living.

Lesley was also active in promoting social and racial justice. We openly discussed my being a white music therapist and her being an African American woman. Despite my inability to fully understand some of her experiences because of our differing backgrounds and upbringings, she trusted me and appreciated my willingness to engage with her when speaking about the impact of race, religion, gender, and systemic oppression as contexts for some of her experiences. She was a deeply empathic person who had trouble finding a space within her community and family to be open about her mental health experiences. It took some time for her to open herself the way that she wanted to in our work together. Our racial differences could have played a role in this, though she also shared she did not have a space outside of therapy to deeply explore her thoughts, emotions, and experiences. Therefore, she was not in the practice of openly discussing her mental health.

Lesley described herself as a "people person,"[5] and felt that being present and connected with people uplifted her. She acknowledged, though, when her moods became very "low" she tended to isolate herself from others, further exacerbating her depressed moods. Additionally, she found her work very stressful, and it often contributed to increased anxiety. Her goal for music therapy was to "get a plan together for the anxiety and depression" and to work on these challenges both in and between sessions.

The Start of Lesley's Therapeutic Journey

At the start of our time together, Lesley had shared that she saw a cognitive-behavioral therapist for her grief, which she found extremely helpful. I asked if she'd like to structure our time together similarly. Lesley was agreeable to this, so we began with CBT-oriented sessions that emphasized collaboration between us on all aspects of her therapy trajectory.

CBT is traditionally a short-term therapy (e.g., 6-14 sessions), with session frequency and length depending on the individual and issues they choose to bring to therapy.[1] The first session of CBT is typically organized into three parts:

1. Initial part: setting a session agenda, doing a mood check-in, discussing the diagnosis or, in our case, presenting issues, and having the therapist offer psychoeducation on presenting issues.
2. Middle part: identifying problems, setting goals, discussing the cognitive model, and addressing a presenting issue.
3. Final part: summarizing the session, reviewing action plans (previously referred to as "homework"), and gathering feedback on the session.

Future sessions are similar, except that in the initial part of the session, the individual's work on the previous week's action plans is reviewed to help organize and prioritize the session. The middle part of the session is aimed at working on a presenting problem through psychoeducation on how to use CBT skills for that issue.

I adopted many of these session structures given Lesley's familiarity with them, though we talked about how we would be more free flowing than the traditional brief-form CBT. For example, I explained that we likely could not do the same amount of verbal processing while also fitting in engagement with music. She expressed understanding and noted her desire to maintain a focus on the musical pieces. So, throughout the sessions, I offered various opportunities to engage with music. I asked Lesley to bring in preferred genres or songs that she felt connected to, offered to do melodic or rhythmic instrumental improvisation, invited lyric discussions, and asked if she'd like to write a song. I provided psychoeducation on several CBT strategies to help with mood management, such as asking herself why her mood might have shifted when she noticed it did, reviewing thought-stopping and non-judgmental thinking, and evaluating evidence for/against hurtful/helpful thoughts.

Lesley actively engaged in verbal and musical exchanges, providing thoughtful insights throughout her sessions, and expressing appreciation for the weekly check-ins on the action plans and being able to set her own goals to work on. She talked about how the music experiences helped her understand her emotions through new perspectives and how the CBT strategies were helping her better manage her moods, specifically the anxiety, outside of sessions. For example, we worked on using music for grounding, relaxation, and being present so that she could use these strategies for mood management in her day-to-day.

She regularly came to sessions with specific examples of when she used strategies introduced in music therapy. She shared how the thought-stopping helped her identify her self-judgments, how the questions about mood shifts helped her draw more connections between cognitions and behaviors, and how she became more aware of the behaviors that would result in negative or positive mood changes. She discussed these thinking processes in relation to music experiences as well, such as how she'd use music listening to match or shift her moods and how she would connect with various qualities in a song (e.g., rhythm, melody, and lyrics).

Evaluating and Adjusting Theoretical Orientations

We worked with this CBT structure for about five months. Lesley was openly and willingly engaging in activities, using her own agency and choice to guide her session work and providing positive feedback throughout her time. She expressed wanting to go musically and emotionally "deeper" in her sessions, yet there was a palpable resistance – or perhaps fear – to this. For example, she typically chose to explore experiences and emotions instrumentally without any vocalizations or verbalizations. She also remained primarily within percussive realms and rarely explored melodic instruments. She felt safe and comfortable at this level of musical exploration but also shared that she was "holding things back."

I, too, felt this sense of holding back. I wanted her to engage her voice more but also knew how tender and intimate it can be to use one's voice in music therapy, and I never wanted to push her. I regularly invited her to sing or engage vocally so that she knew the option was there, but I could sense the disconnect between her verbal expressiveness in our dialogue and processing and her reticence to extend this expression musically. She did not always feel confident exploring various instruments or her voice despite my modeling.

I asked what automatic thoughts she had in relation to this musical holding back and she commented on not feeling skilled enough to play instruments, perform well, and have control in music experiences. We examined these thoughts through Socratic questioning, and she identified that she generally exercises control, planning, and preparation in her daily life and that if she ever feels unprepared, she will "back out" of plans or tasks. These thoughts and behaviors were being mirrored in our sessions.

At the same time, she wanted to "let go" and "be more spontaneous" in her music exploration so that she could go "deep" into her emotions.

She wanted to unpack the "tangled web" her unstable childhood and family deaths left inside her, but "something" was keeping her from doing this unpacking. Lesley did not yet have the skills to dialectically engage in spontaneity and control. While the CBT-informed strategies and structures had helped her functionally manage her moods, I wondered if she might benefit from gradually removing some of the session structure to engage in more organic musical explorations of herself and past experiences. Perhaps this could give her experience in loosening some of her coping-manifested control and exploring how spontaneity feels.

One session, during the initial mood check-in, Lesley shared how she felt "OK," but that she had a "heavy" previous week because it was the anniversary of a family member's death. She had gone to a conference for work that week, which included a poetry-writing seminar where attendees shared grief stories, broke out into groups, and engaged in group poetry writing based on their grief experiences. In her group, she had shared the weight of her loss and grief because everyone was so attuned with each other's feelings. She shared selected lines from her poem with me.

Her words were incredibly powerful – authentic, full of imagery, resilient, and vulnerable. To see her concretize in a poem a level of emotional depth she had not yet reached in music therapy, I was immediately grateful she could access support and solidarity with others at this conference session to share her grief experience. While I had invited poetry writing opportunities in the past, the community element of group writing and sharing with others also experiencing grief seemed to help create the space she needed to explore her emotions in this way.

I also recognized my own countertransference when being moved by her poetry. Poetry writing and songwriting were avenues for processing grief, depression, and anxiety after my mother died when I was 13 years old. While my emerging desire to invite Lesley to engage in songwriting was strong, I worked to balance my personal knowledge of songwriting's potency for grief processing with my clinical knowledge of that potency following years of witnessing how songwriting benefited others. I asked Lesley if she would be willing to try songwriting since she had created this beautiful poem. She was agreeable to this, so I invited her to try writing in a stream-of-consciousness style, free from judgments, just writing anything that came to mind in relation to the three lines of poetry she shared.

While I gathered instruments from the closet, Lesley engaged deeply in the writing. I did not give her any time limits for the writing so as not to disrupt her process, and I started playing guitar and piano in the background while she wrote so she could hear which instrument she felt most connected to (guitar and piano were her typical instruments of choice). On both instruments, I improvised in the key of C in a moderate tempo, using soft chords and arpeggiation for melodic contour. She let me know when she was finished and said the piano was resonating with her. When asked if she'd like to play or if she'd like me to, she said she'd like to try but was a little nervous. I showed her the C scale and told her any white key would sound good. She explored the keys, came upon middle G and A, moving back and forth between these two single keys, and said she liked those two. She asked me to play, so I sat next to her and played a simple chord progression between G major and A major an octave lower. She chose a tempo around 105 bpm, so I began playing and invited Lesley to bring her lyrics into the music through singing, talking, humming, thinking, and any other way she felt comfortable merging them with the music. She began speaking them and partway through the first verse, began singing:

My tears are a part of my history
When I cry, it's no secret I don't feel any peace
My tears are a part of me, here I stand
My tears shape my life and where I want to be

> *Here I stand, this is me*
> *Here I stand, this is me*

My tears show my love for you
My tears express my soul and guide me from within
My tears bring joy, pain, they are grim

> *Here I stand, this is me*
> *Here I stand, this is me*

To confront my pain helps me to heal
Guide me beyond where you stand
Sunlight on my face, this is where it all begins

> *Here I am, here I am, here I stand, this is me*
> *Here I am, here I am, here I stand, this is me*
> *Here I am, here I stand, here I am, this is me*

Her body swayed to the music. The back-and-forth of the two chords felt grounding and meditative, a beautiful support to the repetitive, chanting-like quality of the chorus lyrics. I matched her dynamics on the piano and swayed alongside her to the music, listening for her lead to close out the song.

When we finished, she loudly exhaled and said she simultaneously felt "great" and "so nervous!" She was nervous because she wasn't sure what she was going to do to get the song started, and she wasn't confident in her ability to start a song from nothing, but "the sound of the piano just began moving me." I commented on what I witnessed while she played – how she started with talking, then moved into singing, and as the song progressed, gave more depth by adding range in the melody and varied dynamics. She told me she still felt like she was holding back, and I told her she could build on this more whenever she was ready.

She decided to do another run-through, which we recorded, and she sounded more confident in her melody and her willingness to add more dynamics. She also independently started playing single notes on the higher register of the piano to accompany my chord playing. Her body engagement was more pronounced, confidently swaying with the rhythm from the start of the song and staying with this movement throughout. Afterwards, she said she felt better, and it was good to "just sing it out and hear the emotions in the music." I played the recording back to her and she swayed in her chair, listening intently, eyes in a soft gaze towards the floor. She made a facial expression that seemed like surprise as well as release. When asked what she was thinking or feeling, she said she couldn't imagine doing anything like this, creating something like this. She said she felt like all the tension she had been holding from the past week "got out in that song." She commented how the chord progressions really spoke to her and moved her, which she found "special." While we had engaged in various music therapy collaborations for months, this was the first time she was willing to engage her voice and write her own song. It clearly made an impact on her, and I equally felt moved and excited for her to access this resource.

Witnessing this songwriting process was significant in several ways. First was seeing Lesley's willingness to engage in melodic music making, given her previous resistance to it. She knew the power of rhythm and melody to serve as both a container and catalyst for lyrical content in songs as she often commented on this during lyric discussions. To this effect, exploring a melodic counterpart to her lyrical story with a basic 2-chord holding progression seemed to have served these same functions for her song. Second, in maintaining the emphasis on Lesley's agency throughout her therapy journey, the addition of the piano offered a multimodal way of cultivating a fuller, more panoramic picture and essence of her narrative. Third, the CBT strategies and structures we previously employed seemed to have provided her with the ability to try something new and experience the impact. She examined the validity of her automatic thoughts, which included gathering evidence that supported or disproved her thoughts.[1] Lesley engaging melodically with the piano and pairing lyrics with the musical content allowed her to experience her ability to perform at a level to her liking, despite not knowing "how to play instruments," while also exhibiting control in the process and outcome. Thus, she alone was able to challenge the verisimilitude of her thinking while engaging in more explorative, spontaneously emerging music making.

From this moment on, the music played more of a co-therapist role. We restructured our sessions to include a quick verbal check-in at the start and time to engage in organic music making through original songwriting or improvisation. We used the musical experience to set the agenda for the session, especially in those sessions where she came to therapy with not much to say or no update from the start. Lesley learned to trust the music, our therapeutic relationship, and the safety of the music therapy room to take her deeper inside herself. I, too, developed a deepened trust with music being a co-therapist through knowing that Lesley and I always had a starting point for our time when entering into musical relationship. We discussed life metaphors based on what she experienced in our music making. The resistances she previously talked about in going "that deep" were gone, and she was incredibly invested, brave, and honest in her self-explorations.

The CBT work continued to inform the humanistic work and was often integrated within the songwriting processes. For example, she might use stream-of-consciousness writing to start the development of her lyric writing and then use more conscious cognitive processes to refine them. She would sometimes balance the tensions between thoughts she identified as hurtful and helpful. She could put painful thoughts (e.g., "I am broken, confused, and fighting for control") and uplifting thoughts (e.g., "I am complex, fierce, beauty of love") in the same song and discuss through verbal processing how both felt accurate while acknowledging that the uplifting thoughts promoted a more favorable mood. Lesley had found value in the personal insights and transformative therapeutic experiences gained through both CBT and humanistic approaches, and we were able to integrate these approaches throughout the rest of her therapy.

We maintained many of the CBT elements incorporated into the first five months of therapy, such as identifying hurtful versus helpful thoughts, using thought-stopping and non-judgmental thinking, identifying evidence behind thoughts and statements, and using cognitive reframing to help minimize the impact of hurtful thinking on her behaviors and moods. We took the action plans out of therapy and she chose to replace them with engaging in art and music making in between sessions. Oftentimes, she would bring in entirely completed songs she had written on her own and we'd use our time to bring music to the lyrics or discuss her lyrics. She would tell me what the lyrics referred or translated to, where and how they emerged, and why they were important to include. With the more organic session structure, she developed a trust in our music making to relive, reflect, and reconsider past experiences. We could be solution-focused when she felt it necessary as she had gained the tools to work this way. We could also be explorative and process-oriented.

I believe that the CBT was an appropriate first step for moving into the humanism. It was a structure and approach to therapy Lesley was familiar with, so we could begin to build our therapeutic relationship through it. As well, because many of her emotional challenges impeded her daily functioning, it was evident to both of us that immediately addressing these challenges was necessary before moving into deeper psychotherapeutic work. This is not to say that we might not have been able to get to the same place had we started purely from a humanistic standpoint. However, CBT was developed to be a short-term treatment to shift cognitive patterns causing harmful mental health.[1] Within the developmental scope of Lesley's therapeutic journey, the CBT provided a concrete and familiar structure to facilitate the safety necessary for Lesley to engage in the more explorative work at a later point in her journey.

I believe that adjusting theoretical orientations based on where Lesley wanted to go with her inner work allowed her to process her experiences in diverse ways. Being able to employ theoretical flexibility in a way that seems equally authentic for me as for those I work with is a signifier of a strong, emerging therapeutic alliance. I've come to a place where I feel firmly grounded in my professional identity by the way I implement therapy through these integrated theoretical orientations. I feel empowered to support individuals, like Lesley, in exploring and experiencing the potentials of their therapeutic process.

Summarizing Ideas and Questions for Discussion

1. Music therapists, whether entry-level or experienced, are challenged to employ theoretical flexibility when working with individuals or groups in order to meet individualized needs and preferences.

    a. Which theoretical orientations do you typically draw on in your clinical practice, and which do you feel you could use more experience or practice with in order to meet the needs and preferences of those you work with?
    b. In what ways is employing theoretical flexibility an ethical component to clinical practice?

2. A clear understanding of the opportunities and limitations of different theoretical orientations is needed for music therapists to effectively employ them with flexibility.

    a. What clinical decision-making or clinical reasoning takes place when employing more than one theoretical orientation in a given session?
    b. In what ways is exercising theoretical flexibility in your clinical practice a culturally responsive approach to working with individuals or groups?

Notes

1 Beck, J. S. (2011). *Cognitive behavior therapy: Basics and beyond.* Guilford Press.
2 Cain, D. J., Keenan, K., & Rubin, S. (Eds.). (2016). *Humanistic psychotherapies: Handbook of research and practice* (2nd ed.). American Psychological Association.
3 Rolvsjord, R. (2010). *Resource-oriented music therapy in mental health care.* Barcelona Publishers.
4 Hadley, S., & Thomas, N. (2018). Critical humanism in music therapy: Imagining the possibilities. *Music Therapy Perspectives, 36*(2), 168–174. https://doi.org/10.1093/mtp/miy015
5 All quotation marks denote words Lesley used to describe herself, which I had taken care to note in my clinical documentation. I integrate these quotes into the description of the case to help center Lesley's voice and self-perception.

Unit 4

Embracing Complexity and Ambiguity in Practice

Chapter 14

The Extended Discharge

Relationship Building, Meaning-Making, and Advocacy in Long-term Treatment

Jesse Asch-Ortiz

Abstract

Music therapists, due in part to the deep intimacy developed within inter-musical relationships, are often asked to step outside traditional conceptualizations of the music therapist role. Such moments become opportunities to expand beyond rigid expectations of what "counts" as practice, and more fully engage with supporting individuals on systems-based levels. The intimate relationships that develop through long-term work offer unique opportunities for advocacy when patients are grappling with ambiguous plans for discharge.

Tags: Treatment Planning, Therapeutic Relationship

Content warning: Experiences of racism, ableism, and discrimination.

This case highlights my experience in an acute psychiatric care setting of stepping out of a traditional clinician role while working with Amara, an individual requiring complex care. Due to Amara's combined medical and mental health status, she found herself with unmet needs as she was transferred from a psychiatric unit to a medical care unit. Her admission spanned 11 months, with recurring difficulties in discharge planning and placement. Throughout her admission, I encountered challenging circumstances with Amara that resulted in ambiguity and parallel meaning-making processes. Amara and I navigated institutional and systemic barriers through a resource-oriented and socio-culturally located approach.

My first introduction to Amara was through nursing staff making statements such as: "Oh no, she is not coming here! I've already contacted the director about it!" Per reports from nursing, Amara had been on the psychiatric unit about four years prior and was "a nightmare."

DOI: 10.4324/9781003123798-19

More specifically, she was referred to as "a huge Borderline" with complex medical needs, including having had a tracheotomy, being morbidly obese, and using a wheelchair. She had on more than one occasion placed herself and psychiatric staff in compromising positions through life-threatening behavior, including pulling out her trach tube or putting in items (e.g., craft beads) to block her airway. While I am certain that a more formal, thorough, and respectful presentation of Amara was available, this introduction was lacking any of those qualities. I was worried this emotionally loaded introduction to Amara would adversely impact the treatment team's ability to know her on a more personal and holistic level and work with her in a clinically focused and collaborative manner.

Nursing staff on the psychiatric unit advocated for Amara's transfer to a medical unit, stating that they did not have the appropriate staffing or medical equipment available on the psychiatric unit to care for her properly. While true, this request appeared informed by their explicit bias towards working with such a complex patient, as well as a stigma around presumed difficulty of working with Borderline diagnosed individuals.[1] Additionally, health care professionals frequently feel ill-equipped or poorly supported in providing treatment to complex-care patients, resulting in negative emotional reactions.[2,3]

Amara also held multiple intersecting identities as a multiply disabled, larger-bodied Black woman which subjected her to socio-cultural biases (i.e., ableism, fatphobia, racism, and sexism) known to affect everything from day-to-day interactions to the quality of care provided during hospitalization.[4,5] This was exemplified by some of the nurses' early statements and actions and is an important subtext throughout this case. Equally, these oppressive structures were important for me to acknowledge in understanding Amara's lived experience beyond the session room.

Amara remained in the psychiatric unit for a couple of weeks without incident before being transferred to the medical unit for continued psychiatric care alongside her medical care. While in the psychiatric unit, she occasionally attended group therapies with 1:1 support, appearing to enjoy herself while engaging minimally in group-oriented interactions. However, shortly after her transfer, social workers had reported the medical unit's inability "to handle" Amara, requesting additional services from the inpatient psychiatric unit. The art therapist had been working with her but no longer had availability to do so. Consequently, my supervisor reached out several months later to ask if I would be available to provide Amara individual bedside sessions on a biweekly basis.

Coming out of our initial session, there were aspects of Amara I was surprised had not been previously reported, primarily the need to lipread her speaking due to her having no audible voice, no comprehensive knowledge of sign language, and no current use of augmentative and alternative communication (AAC) devices. Amara was also easily frustrated with being asked to repeat herself, which regularly occurred. Amara appeared mildly receptive to music therapy and expressed a desire to work on bracelet-making, an activity that she had begun with the art therapist. Despite some uncertainty, I followed her lead as it appeared significant for her to be able to complete these projects in the seemingly short timeline we had together. I was often already running recreational art groups in addition to music therapy groups and reasoned that this was not completely out of my scope of practice.

During this early stage of our work, I would show up to Amara's hospital room with a select assortment of beads, scissors, and string. She was typically with a 1:1 staff member due to her complex medical needs, ongoing passive suicidality, and potential for harm to self and others on the unit. Often, however, the 1:1 would step out upon me entering the room, giving us the room for the duration of the 45- to 50-minute session. Amara shared her preferred music through receptive listening to recordings, ranging from 90s R&B and gospel to contemporary country/pop, often mouthing the words along. We simultaneously tackled her beadwork, each starting at opposite ends of the string so she could instruct me, due to continuous tremors that inhibited her fine motor movement. Upon completion, she often asked for assistance in putting these beads over her head or on her wrist, taking a prideful moment to examine our work.

Eventually, I took it upon myself to bring the guitar and a standing tubano drum to our session for the first time. I had slowly become aware that Amara's time on the medical unit would not be so short, and I was questioning the significance of our bead-making, which had begun to feel more like recreation than therapy. I chose to move more definitively into music therapy so our work could become more dynamic and interactive in nature. I brought my guitar and the tubano with consideration of its sturdiness, accessibility, and fullness of range as an instrument.

Amara's eyes immediately widened with excitement, motioning for me to bring the drum closer to her as she immediately began to play. She played with a dynamically loud yet steady rhythm, and as I motioned to close the door, Amara stated: "Leave it open! I want them to hear me." I replied, "You do?!" and invited her to elaborate. However, after some sustained moments of continued loud play, I closed the door, feeling that it was in the best interest of her privacy and allowing us to play at this loud dynamic with consideration for other patients on the unit.

Without knowing the dynamics between Amara and the unit staff, I was unsure of what this meant for her. *Did she desire to be heard in a new context, in this creative and expressive manner? Was it a desire to bother the unit or to genuinely share her music-making experience with others?* Due to her musical engagement, I left these questions unanswered and joined her on the guitar as we explored this new form of communicating with one another. I recall her mouthing "WOW" and laughing, motioning for a high-five after the music concluded.

As we verbally checked in following our improvisation, Amara informed me that she had a "meltdown" the day prior. While I knew of this prior to our session, this was the first time Amara had disclosed to me this type of behavior. She described how she had decided to lower herself out of her wheelchair and onto the floor, putting herself in a situation that demanded staff support for her safety. As she previously reflected upon the struggle of being heard without an audible voice, Amara acknowledged resorting to behavior that "needs to be heard, since no one can actually hear what I need."

We reflected upon the strength and skill with which she approached the drum during this session, and she contrasted her skillful expression and communication in our musical exchange to her more chaotic expression of lowering herself to the floor. Amara often split between staff, and as she regularly placed me on the positive side of that split, I encouraged her to bring this same quality of communication to other staff interactions. Through this new intermusical dynamic, Amara presented with a more integrated sense of self, exploring more challenging emotional content through our play and considering more effective and nuanced interactions.

As our work continued, Amara developed improved relationships with some of the unit staff. Notably, she increasingly invited her 1:1 staff member to remain in the room as either an active play partner or a listener in our musical exchanges. Eventually, the 1:1 staff member became more reliably the same person, adding to an increased depth of safety, rapport, and understanding shared within the therapy space.

However, this process was not without significant hurdles, including fluctuations in Amara's physical and mental health, interpersonal dynamics, and life stressors. There was a lingering sense of uncertainty around Amara's remaining time on the unit, often resulting in a shared ambivalence around the direction of our work. This uncertain timeline resulted from placement difficulties, as Amara had lost whatever housing she'd had upon her admission to the hospital. Due to her complex combination of medical and mental health diagnoses, she was regularly disqualified from varying residences that were meant to focus on either one domain or the other, but not open to serving both sets of needs.

This desperation for placement was reflected in both the dispositions of Amara and the staff, who would often excitedly communicate loose murmurings of "a placement coming through next week," only to be drawn out and eventually not come through. This took a toll on Amara, who often ranged from a depressive affect to frustrated emotional outbursts. I slowly came to a more holistic understanding of Amara during this extended hospitalization; in the rising and falling energy around unmet expectations for discharge and resulting emotional fatigue, we had mutually lost some sense of direction, falling into holding patterns that mirrored the continued lack of progress in treatment beyond the session room.

Challenges Beyond the Session Room

In an attempt to make Amara's time in the hospital more bearable, the treatment team gave permission for Amara to go down to the lobby one to two times per day. One day, upon coming to the medical unit for Amara's session, I was informed by the head nurse that there was an incident with her occurring in the hospital lobby. Proposing that I head downstairs if I could be of any assistance, I was met with a seemingly sarcastic: "You can try."

I was reminded that I had heard such off-color comments from various team members before, alluding back to the initial impressions shared on the psychiatric unit. However, as work with Amara and the treatment teams had developed, I felt more aware that such comments communicated a level of frustration, fatigue, and even burnout from working with Amara, as well as how this might have reflected Amara's own emotional experience. While such comments occur regularly in everyday practice, I have found these moments require a level of thoughtfulness and recentering as a music therapist to avoid playing into such toxic relational dynamics. I wanted to acknowledge and hold space for these comments, while reframing them to deepen empathy for stakeholders and potentially lessen harm and redirect care between professional caregivers and the individuals with whom they work.

I was fearful of how general staff and bystanders might respond to Amara. Despite not knowing exactly what was occurring, I hoped that my presence could somehow help, as Amara had seemed to view me as a positive and supportive role in her care. Personally, I was frustrated by continually engaging on the reparative end of interactions with Amara, following reports of her acting out that ultimately required medical restraint. It was my feeling that perhaps these interactions might resolve differently if I had been present. Simultaneously, I wanted to check myself in this thought pattern. *Was I being grandiose or attempting to be a white savior?*[6] With a sense of uncertainty around the boundaries of my role and the appropriateness of my decision, I decided to head downstairs to the lobby.

Once downstairs, I found Amara's 1:1 standing distanced from her, seemingly unsure of what to do. She explained to me that Amara had brought down cash to the lobby coffee shop to buy herself a cup of coffee but did not have enough money. When they would not allow her to take the coffee, Amara locked the brakes of her wheelchair in front of the register, not only choosing to not leave this spot but complicating ease of exit for other customers. The 1:1 asked if I could approach her, noting our rapport and stating she had been trying with no success thus far.

As I approached Amara, I noted that she had turned herself in towards the coffee shop and did not see me approaching. I announced my presence before walking around to face her. Asking her what was going on, Amara first motioned with a shake of her head that she was not going to speak with me. When explaining that I wanted to hear it from her rather than from someone else, Amara insisted: "You know what's going on. This is what you all do. Nobody wants to help me." Amara explained to me that she was short a dollar and change for a cup of coffee "and *she* won't give it to me," pointing exasperatedly at the woman working the register. Amara commanded a strong and intimidating posture, making it clear that she was not going to be moved.

Shortly after, hospital police arrived followed by the doctor on-call, who prepared an injection of antipsychotic medication as a medical restraint given to lessen patients' "acute agitation." While effective, medical restraints usually have a significantly sedating effect upon the patient and prioritize managing behavioral symptoms over psychiatric symptoms or emotional needs. At times, this approach is necessary when behavior becomes unsafe to the individual or others and they appear less available to verbal or musical interventions. However, in this instance it felt like a threat and an abuse of power, particularly when considering the socio-cultural locations of the individuals in this interaction; the doctor, a white male accompanied by law enforcement and Amara, whose identities reside primarily in the margins. I questioned whether this would have happened if she were white and nondisabled, and the answer I came to is "no." I was mindful of how oppressive this interaction was, how her fight for a cup of coffee had devolved into her struggle to hold on to a sense of humanity in the face of discriminatory violence.

Amara again asserted to me: "You see? This is what they do!" I recall contending: "This may be a choice they are offering you, but you still get to make the choice. We can still head back upstairs together." In my role and socio-cultural identities as a white, nondisabled, cis-presenting male, I wanted to use my words to hold space, recenter her voice, and empower her to have autonomy and freedom in this interaction. I attempted to locate myself in this way to also inform others that Amara would be the one making the choice with the limited options which she was being presented. As the introduction of the doctor had felt like an escalation of the situation, I wanted Amara to feel that the ball was in her court and that she did not need to give them what they were expecting – that is, a reason to involuntarily medicate her.

A few minutes into this discussion, the doctor on-call standing verbalized, "Are we giving her the shot or not?" with a seemingly impatient tone. At this point, I recall experiencing a surge of anger in response to this approach that sought to take the very power away from Amara that I was supporting her to claim for herself. Even as the clinician, it was difficult to not want to give in to this goading. Crouching slightly to eye-level, I asked: "What are we doing?" Amara replied: "We are going upstairs."

The 1:1 and I helped Amara back herself out of the exit, followed by the hospital police and the doctor-on-call, who quickly dismissed himself. The 1:1 joked: "You've got your posse with you." "Yeah, I do," said Amara, who appeared to be both trembling and laughing. Upon returning to the room, I acknowledged her upset about not getting the coffee and more so how the hospital staff responded to her, to which Amara nodded. As a member of the systems that had just harmed her, it was important to name these injustices rather than assume a complacent role in acknowledging them as a given. I wanted to assure her that her feelings of upset were warranted, to help her not feel gaslit by a system not working in her favor. With Amara's consent, I guided a music-assisted deep breathing technique to help her reground and release the stress experienced in her body. She was receptive but remained slightly tremulous as we slowed the breath together. Alongside the music, Amara's ability in that moment to make choices, use humor, explicitly name and call out barriers, and experience allyship with staff was part of a resource-oriented approach that allowed her to experience a sense of empowerment coming out of this scenario. It is important to note that these resources, while effective in helping to immediately stabilize and ground, should not be thought of as reparative to the trauma experienced.

I have witnessed and dealt with other such interactions of unwarranted force and am not always so "successful" in supporting the client and healthcare staff to de-escalate. I have experienced this as an ongoing problem within the medical model of psychiatric care but am hopeful that a broader range of staff is becoming aware of systemic injustices and willing to speak truth to power. This valuing of social justice is necessarily intertwined in my role as a music therapy clinician, particularly when considering the individual's self-advocacy and equitable care as tenets of the therapeutic process.

A similar incident occurred once more for Amara over the course of our work together, this time regarding buying a watch from the gift shop and again being a few dollars short. I recall her crying deeply, as she was seemingly unable to bring herself to leave this scenario. This time, however, the hospital police already stationed in the lobby had joined me in speaking with her. She slowly showed capacity to calm herself down and brought herself back to the unit. In a later session, she processed feeling like a resident in the hospital and wanting to have the liberty to order food and buy items from the gift shop like an independent individual. Staff seemed to empathize with this as well, as Amara received vouchers for coffee from this point on and every now and then would have new items in her possession. While questionable in terms of boundaries, I admit feeling satisfaction that she was being heard and valued in this way by those around her.

As Amara continued to explore ways of making the most of her time in the hospital, she began to invite me to join her on the hospital patio for our sessions. This was an outdoor area, shared by staff and patients for taking breaks and meals outdoors. Yet again stretching my comfort in the spatial boundaries of our work, I agreed to join her for a few sessions outside. Initially, I was worried about her privacy with others sharing the space. I also worried that I was losing grasp on my role as a music therapy clinician. I thought: *As a music therapist, shouldn't I be doing music with her?* However, to join her and her 1:1 outside in the warm weather felt like the most normalized experience we'd had to date, as well as important for her mental health. We chose to engage in dialogue around her everyday interactions, with recorded music serving as background to our interaction. Amara seemed content and at ease during these sessions, eventually leading us more naturally back to active music making.

Final Months: Making Meaning and Closing

Amara remained in the hospital for a little while longer, with no clear prospects for discharge. Upon coming to her session room one day, Amara shared with me that she had come into ownership of a talkpad, an AAC device, that she was eager to put into use. We explored it together, figuring out ways of putting her text into talk. While she was excited about it, she expressed feeling frustrated with the amount of time that it took to put her thoughts into words on the device. She noted that, while some staff had shown a particular inclination for lipreading when she would speak, the talkpad would come in handy with a majority of people who struggled with lipreading.

Previously in our work, Amara had written original poetry with shared attempts to set it to music. However, we always agreed there was a disconnect when I would sing her poetry myself. Amara decided that she would write her poetry on the talkpad and we would integrate it into a musical context. Using a sampler application to record her poem, I recorded aspects of my voice, guitar, and percussion into the app as well. We explored ways of performing this poem back in a remix type format, creating varying beats that accompanied and contextualized the poem.

> In a world full of noise when my lips make no sounds
> Decreasing my level of importance to just above the ground
> Crying to be heard yet many only view your tears
> Alone engulfed in silence wondering if someone truly cares
> Do they understand though silent your emotions still at time are I's
> Silence can be depressed, deadly, and a utter great surprise
> When one is used to talking and sound to them was the key
> Now they sit alone in silence in the land of Lady Liberty

Reflecting on this poem, I noted that Amara had chosen to return to familiar themes of being un/misheard, unacknowledged, and un/misrepresented. It became apparent that, despite our extensive time focused on increasing autonomy, encouraging outlets for self-expression, and empowering skills for managing various arising stressors, her time in the hospital was a microcosm of her daily lived experience and internalized impressions. In fact, it explained many of her "behaviors" during challenging moments throughout her hospitalization. The hospital was only one of the many systems in which Amara experienced this multiplicity of structural oppression. While our work did not explicitly focus on these broader forces beyond the hospital (i.e., white supremacy, capitalism, racism, ableism), I believe doing so could have provided an opportunity to further process her resistance in the face of current and historical trauma.[7] Amara's presence in the hospital had inevitably become political in nature; however, she always remained focused on her own individual care.

Shortly thereafter it appeared that housing had finally come through for Amara. She had gone on a few interviews, accompanied by her 1:1, and been accepted to her own apartment in a complex. She was to be provided with 1:1 support within the apartment and would continue to receive outpatient services through the hospital with transportation provided. As throughout our work, there was an uncertainty of which day would be her last in the hospital, and so we planned together to coordinate our termination of treatment, regardless of whether she left that week or the next.

Showing up for our last scheduled session, I found Amara going through bags of papers that she had laid out across the bed and floor of the room. She appeared anxious but appropriately so, an anxiety that felt more akin to someone moving than being discharged from a hospital. She excitedly showed me a laptop that a friend had gifted to her, explaining that she needed help setting it up. She had hoped to set up her email accounts and things of this nature before leaving the hospital but was unable to log into the laptop. Reading me words off of multiple folded-up sheets of paper, she guessed passwords that her friend might have written down for her. Finally, finding a telephone number on a piece of paper, she asked me, "Can you call her for me?"

Yet again feeling compromised to everything I had planned or expected from our termination, it seemed that even our closure would not process through traditional music therapy practices. Considering her request, it became clear to me that she was utilizing me in the way that she felt was most supportive to her in this critical time. My role had become more in line with that of an advocate for her and I felt that it was appropriate for me to be available to her in this way. I picked up the phone and dialed out. A woman answered and I spoke:

"Yes, hello, is this [friend's name] . . . I am working with Amara here at [hospital name] and am trying to help her out with a few things before she leaves. Would you happen to know the password for this laptop? . . . OK, it works! Thank you so much!"

With eyes widened, Amara motioned a deep exhale, communicating a sense of relief. At her request, I spent the remainder of our time assisting Amara in setting up email accounts and various applications that she expected to need on the computer. We exchanged expressions of gratitude for the time spent working together, said our goodbyes and, after 11 months of working together, Amara was discharged three days following our last session.

Summarizing Ideas and Questions for Discussion

1. As a music therapist, you are continuously challenged to make meaning of the clinical work even when it requires you to step outside of roles as commonly modeled and taught.

    a. In what ways have you been asked by a client or challenged by a circumstance to engage in the work differently than you had been taught?
    b. What are ethical boundaries you feel uncomfortable crossing when assuming a new and unique role? What are ethical boundaries you feel comfortable coming into contact with?

2. As a music therapist may work in various institutions, it is important to develop an awareness of systemic and structural biases that can impact quality of care for clients.

    a. In what ways can we recognize and navigate systemic and structural biases in order to best serve the quality of care for our clients?
    b. How can we locate ourselves as clinicians within these institutions to best inform our practice? What is the significance of self-location?

Notes

1 Sansone, R. A., & Sansone, L. A. (2013). Responses of mental health clinicians to patients with borderline personality disorder. *Innovations in Clinical Neuroscience, 10*(5–6), 39–43. www.ncbi.nlm.nih.gov/pmc/articles/PMC3719460/
2 Manning, E., & Gagnon, M. (2017). The complex patient: A concept clarification. *Nursing & Health Sciences, 19*(1), 13–21. https://doi.org/10.1111/nhs.12320
3 Roskos, S. E., Fitzpatrick, L., Arnetz, B., Arnetz, J., Shrotriya, S., & Hengstebeck, E. (2020). Complex patients' effect on family physicians: High cognitive load and negative emotional impact. *Family Practice, 38*(4), 454–459. https://doi.org/10.1093/fampra/cmaa137
4 Sue, D. W., Capodilupo, C. M., Torino, G. C., Bucceri, J. M., Holder, A., Nadal, K. L., & Esquilin, M. (2007). Racial microaggressions in everyday life: Implications for clinical practice. *American Psychologist, 62*(4), 271–286. https://doi.org/10.1037/0003-066X.62.4.271

5 The language "larger-bodied" is used as a weight-neutral descriptor in place of the BMI categories of "obesity" which are known to perpetuate health falsities, stigma, and harm towards individuals. See https://www.acs.org/about/diversity/inclusivity-style-guide.html for more information on body size.
6 The complex of white saviorism is the problematic enactment through which white individuals in positions of power impress their views and actions upon non-white communities, denying lack of access to agency and relegating these communities and individuals to an "inferior" role.
7 Scrine, E. (2021). The limits of resilience and the need for resistance: Articulating the role of music therapy with young people within a shifting trauma paradigm. *Frontiers in Psychology*, *12*(600245). https://doi.org/10.3389/fpsyg.2021.600245

Chapter 15

I Can Be With What She Brings

Stephenie Sofield

Abstract

Trauma work, which can manifest in any treatment setting, is emergent and unpredictable, relying upon the music therapist to be able and willing to reinvent their practice at any point along the process. Such reinvention can include ways of relating and engaging, both inside and around music encounters, that require balancing vulnerability with safety. Additionally, drawing from other creative mediums (e.g., art, play, and movement) is frequently necessary when working with children.

Tags: Therapeutic Relationship

Content warning: Mention of intimate partner violence and s*xual assault.

Prelude

When I was fresh out of internship in my mid-20s, I accepted a position at a program with the primary aim of providing creative arts therapies to 3- to 17-year-old child witnesses of intimate partner violence. My internship had prepared me for some aspects of the position; I had spent half of my internship at an acute psychiatric facility and the other half in a children's hospital. I understood the basics of delivering music therapy to meet the emotional and physical needs of people stuck in a medical facility where they didn't want to be. The patients I encountered during my internship craved not only music, but also kind and compassionate contact with a care provider. Because of the nature of the facilities I had interned at, the relationships I built with patients did not last long. The

DOI: 10.4324/9781003123798-20

sessions also mostly took on a similar structure: assess the patient's in-the-moment needs, create music to meet those needs, and provide closure.

During my first week as a new professional, I observed an art therapist work with the clients whose cases I would take over. The children and their needs were vastly different from those at my internship sites. They weren't kept in the facility by adults; in fact, they didn't *need* to be at our facility at all. They weren't in crisis. They needed longer-term trauma processing, something that we actively avoided at the acute psychiatric facility at which I had interned. While I was ready to use music to stabilize a client[1] in crisis, I had no idea how to lead six months of weekly sessions that would be full of meaningful musical interactions meant to somehow help a child with their trauma. After these weekly sessions, the children could go home, back to their phones and computers where they could access music and various streaming services. I had grown accustomed to being the "music giver," walking into a space where music was being denied to clients. Now I thought: *What am I? What am I doing? How could I have gone through my degree program and a clinical internship and still have no idea what to do?*

With the acceptance of this position, I had entered a treatment paradigm for which I felt mostly unprepared. Yes, I was board-certified. Yes, I understood psychiatric and pediatric music therapy. Yes, I could connect with children and adolescents. And yet . . . how could I maintain and progress a therapeutic relationship for six months? How would I create 24 different music therapy sessions for each client? How could I support a child witness? How could music therapy actually work to process a child's trauma?

My solution was to dig into the available knowledge bases and resources, to attack the new position as a task that could be overcome with careful rationalization. I didn't let myself feel the anxiety, inadequacy, or over-whelm that threatened to spiral into my body and take over. Instead, I spent the first few weeks at the facility consuming as much information as I could about music therapy approaches with complex trauma, treatment for complexly traumatized children, and the neuroscience of inter-personal trauma. I felt that if I could preemptively understand as much as possible about the children who would walk into my office, I would be a good music therapist for them. *If I read enough, I can do this.*

Because I didn't have the direct clinical experience, my approach took shape through the guidance of literature and my previous university training. Theoretical literature taught me to work with the children in phases: they needed to feel safe before we could approach their trauma narratives.[2] Clinical literature taught me to embrace a simple binary of two typologies of child witness: apathetic/depressed/melancholic/clingy and emotional/anx-ious/distracted/aggressive.[3,4] Neuroscience literature taught me to regulate their nervous systems.[5] My university training taught me that children were appropriate for music therapy if they were motivated by music and pro-gressed towards their goals better with music than with non-music stimuli.

Over the first few months, I developed a formulaic music therapy approach to treating complex trauma in child witnesses. For younger children, I created varying levels of structure: the more violent behaviors a child displayed, as reported by the non-offending parent, the more structure I imposed upon the sessions. I hoped that structure and predictability would create containment and safety for both the children and me. I had been trained in a behavioral approach at my university, yet had started to wonder during my internship if my authentic therapeutic self was actually humanist or feminist. My experiences as a cisgender, heterosexual, chronically ill white woman were something I was exploring through new therapeutic frameworks. Yet, instead of processing my own feelings of anxiety and overwhelm, I returned to a behavioral therapeutic approach, which provided me with the control that felt emotionally safe: *Change the trauma behavior through music. Teach coping skills. Regulate the body. If the children can be appropriate and respectful in the space, we can have more choices. I am structured. I am prepared. I know what the literature says. I've read enough. I can do this.*

Just as I started to feel comfortable with my understanding of music therapy for child witnesses – and, frankly, the formulaic categorization of children based on their behaviors – Violet and her family enrolled in our program. Violet was a 5-year-old African American child who had been repeatedly sexually assaulted by her mother's recent ex-boyfriend. We learned that Violet had protected her younger sister from the abuse and that when she told her grandmother, she was believed and immediately taken to the hospital. The perpetrator had also threatened that if Violet ever told anyone what was happening, he would hurt her mother. Her family sought treatment at our facility because Violet's fear and anxiety was becoming progressively worse after she came forward. She was terrified to leave her mother's side in case something were to happen to her.

I met Violet and her family during an intake session with the art therapist. We introduced ourselves, gave space for the family to ask questions, informally assessed the children's preferences, and collaboratively constructed family goals. When the family walked into the music room for their session, I was struck by how different Violet seemed from her younger sister, Ruby, and mother, Vee. Vee was funny and talkative. She listened attentively to her children and spoke in silly voices to make them laugh. Ruby seemed to take after her mother, bouncing around the music room during our family session, making everyone in the room laugh with her silly songs and dances. Violet smiled at them both, but kept her eyes averted and asked several times when they could go home. During these initial sessions, I typically introduced children to the instruments and explored the space with them. These sessions often resulted in spontaneous musicking, dancing, and playing. However, Violet refused to touch any of the instruments. She would only walk towards the instruments if Ruby was playing them. Violet was far more interested in the basket of stuffed animals that sat on the piano than the actual piano. She spent most of the session ignoring me.

After the family session, I asked my supervisor if music therapy was appropriate for Violet. As per my music therapy training, she was not a match for music therapy. Further, my musical identity, informed by a background of rigorous training in Western music, left me feeling hesitant to enter into any musical space that wasn't overtly musical. Ruby, who had banged away on the piano and sang her heart out, seemed to be a better fit. However, my supervisor insisted that we continue as planned, given the overall severity of Violet's trauma background and my background in acute psychiatric care; thus, she would receive music therapy, and her sister would receive art therapy. Within our treatment team, I had the most directly related clinical training to meet Violet's needs. I had to find a way to make it work.

Movement I: Exploration

This phase of Violet's music therapy experience was marked by my attempt to provide structured sessions. Based on Violet's case file and my initial assessment, I decided that her immediate needs were regulating anxiety, feeling in control, and experiencing predictability from a safe adult. Thus, I structured my sessions with three consistent elements: 1) active music-making experiences; 2) Violet choosing an activity; and 3) singing of a closing lullaby. To my surprise, Violet engaged in the musical interventions that I presented in the first two sessions. She chose instruments, followed movement prompts within songs, and played along during call-and-response drumming. When offered a choice, Violet chose to play with the stuffed animals. I was not invited into this play; Violet turned her back to me and carried out stories amongst the animals. We didn't get to the lullaby in these early sessions. She instead spoke up in the middle of interventions, once while I was singing and once while I was reading a book aloud, to let me know that she needed to check on her mom. We ended those sessions immediately. I thanked her for letting me know that she was done, and we joined Vee in the lobby.

Reflecting on those first two sessions, I wonder if she felt she had to comply with something that an adult was asking her to do. Because I was determined to compensate for my looming feelings of inadequacy and overwhelm with a well-controlled structure, I unconsciously perpetuated the role of the adult authority figure. While I was kind and gentle, I had prioritized my knowledge of music, music therapy, and trauma over both of our lived emotional experiences.

In the third session, Violet completely ignored my invitation into music. She asked instead if she could draw or play with the animals. I felt my control over the treatment plan dissolving. My need to carefully plan sessions reflected not only how I had been trained as a music therapist, but also my fear of losing control of Violet's experience. Her trauma felt so big to me, so consuming; I was as terrified as she was to approach it. My rationalization had been that a carefully constructed environment would protect her from harm and re-traumatization. Maybe what I was protecting us both

Figure 15.1 While Violet plays with stuffed animals, our emotions swirl out of our bodies. I stand behind Violet, using my body to hold back both of our emotions from entering the space.

from was an imperfect and emotional therapist: *What will happen if I can't control our emotions?*

During this first drawing experience, I sat beside her at the table and worried: *Shouldn't Violet be in art therapy if she wanted to draw?* Her drawing didn't last long. Within minutes she was pulling the stuffed animals out of their basket and throwing them around the room. *Should she be in play therapy?* While Violet began to act out anger, sadness, and joy with the animals, I struggled to be fully present in her play. I focused on finding opportunities to insert music. If I tried to repeat back in song something an animal said, Violet turned her back to me or rolled her eyes. My feelings of inadequacy as a music therapist wrapped around me like a bubble – a bubble that stopped me from being able to connect with her. I could hear her, I could see her, but I couldn't understand her.

My inner dialogue starts to spiral:

> *I am a music therapist.*
>> But Violent doesn't want music.
> *Why doesn't Violet want music?*
>> You didn't prepare enough.
> *I read so much.*
>> It wasn't enough. You have to read more.
> *She doesn't like when I sing.*
>> The music isn't good enough. You need to learn more.
> *I can try to be funny.*
>> She's ignoring you.

I'm not funny enough. She doesn't like me. I'm not a good music therapist. I'm not a good musician. I can't do this. I don't know what I'm doing. She doesn't like me. I don't know what to do . . .

And somehow, I catch the spiral and put it away. Because I can try harder.

For a few sessions I was able to hold onto the ritual of singing "You Are My Sunshine" as the closing lullaby, but soon she began walking away from that. Because Vee shared that Violet was struggling with getting to sleep and having nightmares, I worked with her to write a personalized lullaby that let Violet know she was safe and loved. Violet declined to work on the lullaby with us, so I asked Vee to think about some words that she would want incorporated into the music. Vee had brought in a piece of paper with full sentences that explained to Violet how very loved she was. I thought *this* would be the key! *When Violet hears this, she will start to feel safe, and she will like music.*

I was so determined that when Violet chose not to engage with the lullaby in my office, I recorded it and sent it home to her mom instead. Vee promised to sing it at home for Violet, and that was the last I heard of that lullaby for a long time. I had to start to be honest with myself: maybe music wasn't going to work for this child. *Now what?*

By the fifth session, I was at a loss. I had become increasingly anxious and stressed about Violet's sessions. No matter what I planned, it wasn't working. We weren't doing music therapy. *I give up. Violet is having so much fun with the animals – can I have fun with her?* So, in our next session, I followed her around the room with my own stuffed animal, as I usually did, but the room seemed a bit clearer. She kept space between us but told me how I was supposed to play. She said my animal was mad. She said my animal had to talk when she says. We bounced around the room together. We bounced off drums; we fell on the floor, rolling and laughing.

We found a new rhythm. We started by drawing. Violet told me about her day. Then we picked our animals and jumped around the room. I couldn't keep up with her storylines, they were so chaotic and confusing. The animals' roles changed constantly – the rooster is a mom, now it's a police officer. Violet told me what to do and was delighted when I followed her directions – Roll on the ground! Jump on one leg! Throw the animal on the beanbag! We laughed. This felt like cheating. It was so easy. It was so fun. I could breathe and feel, and I could *see* her. She was laughing and singing. She was singing now! Her animals were bursting into song. The songs were short and fleeting, but I didn't interrupt. I felt honored to witness the songs. I wondered if she would let me join soon.

Despite this shift in music therapy, Violet's trauma symptoms worsened. She was withdrawn from school because she couldn't make it through the day without panicking about what was happening to her mom. Vee let us know that her interactions with male family members were becoming inappropriate. Our sessions also began taking a turn. She began to throw drums, scarves, and animals at me. I tried to explain our safety rules to her, how we can't do anything that might hurt someone. She laughed at me. I let her know that I didn't feel safe when she threw things at me. She laughed at me again. I reinstated the original structure of our sessions and still the safety did not return. Our physical contact became unpredictable. Sometimes she tried to crawl all over me and other times I was banned to the opposite side of the room. During a particularly intense session, I realized that I had no idea what was happening: *Did I mess up? Does she feel unsafe with me? Why does she want to hurt me?* A drum flew by my head and – *I am scared. I am confused. I am out of control.*

My stomach hurt. My heart was racing. *I don't know what to do. I can't think clearly because I am scared.* She was laughing and reaching for another drum. And, finally, I noticed: she was in control. *She has power. She is scary. I am small, and she isn't listening, and I can't make it stop. Maybe this is what it feels like to be Violet.*

With this realization, I came back into my body. I could tell her she was scaring me! I cried out, "I'm scared!" and hid under the table. The room became quiet. Violet crawled under the table with me. She told me this was a good place to hide from the storm. We sat together. I asked if she would like to play the storm again. After she nodded, we picked instruments for the storm. This time, when Violet threw them, we both knew that I was going to run under the table. She shrieked with laughter. She asked to switch. I was the storm, she was the storm, but mostly we hid together under the table.

I realized that I had completely missed the music in our play. The animals had bounced on drums, their voices had risen and fallen to express their feelings, the loud storm rose and forced us to hide. While Violet ran around the room, I stomped behind in a steady rhythm. While the animals' voices embodied variations on several themes, my voice held the tonic for them to return to. And now we were sitting together in much-needed musical rest.[6,7,8]

Movement II: Rupture

In Violet's 10th session, while we were playing with scarves, she experienced a dissociative episode. Seemingly out of nowhere, she collapsed to the ground, became rigid, and started whimpering. I tried a few times to speak to her and call her name, but she didn't seem to hear me. I sat on her left side and gently touched her hand. When she didn't pull away, I began to tap her hand against the ground and sang "You Are My Sunshine." Violet's body relaxed throughout the song. She reoriented to the space and gripped my hand for a moment, then did something I had never seen before: she began to babble like an infant. I asked her if she was okay and if she needed anything, but she continued to babble, almost insistently. In this moment I had to decide: *Do I follow her? Or do I tell her that she isn't a baby?*

I was beginning to trust the out-of-control moments, so I welcomed baby Violet. She crawled around the room and pointed at objects. I told her their names and let her hold them. When she progressed to speaking a few words, I couldn't understand them. She babbled and crawled around the room. I looked at the clock. We were running out of time. I stood her up, touched her feet, and said: "You are Violet. This is your body." She babbled back. I asked: "Are you ready to be Violet again?" She stared at me without replying.

Our session time was up. I took her out to the lobby. Before I could tell my supervisor that I needed help, that we needed more time, Vee and her counselor came out and let us know that they needed more time themselves. I tried to guide Violet back towards the music room to ground her, but she refused to return. She chose instead to play with Ruby in the lobby.

The art therapist and I watched Violet become a puppy. Ruby began to take care of her. Ruby filled Violet's water bowl, she brought her food, and then patted her head and threw toys for her to fetch. I watched the clock and grew nervous: *Is this inappropriate? Are we letting Ruby be parentified?*

Vee came back. Violet was not her 5-year-old self yet. Vee gathered their things and told them that it was time to go. Violet barked at her mom in response. Try as we might to tell her to get up, that it was time to go, she would not get off the floor. Finally, and slowly, I sat on the floor with her and asked once more, "Are you ready to be Violet again?" We made eye contact for several moments before she stood up, clasped her hands behind

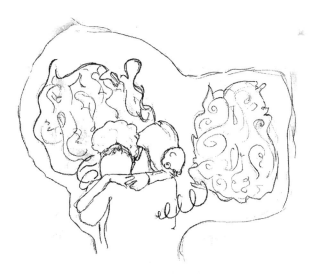

Figure 15.2 Violet and I embrace. Our emotions swirl out of our bodies, but I am able to be with them, as well as Violet.

my neck, and buried her face in my chest. I wrapped my arms around her and held her for what felt like an eternity. We stayed like this. There was peace, and silence, and a knowing. *I can be with whatever she brings.*

Finally, Violet released me, gave me a big smile, and grabbed her mom's hand. She talked to her mom and sister animatedly all the way down to the elevator.

Movement III: Partnering

In a following session, we played a call-and-response improvisation on piano while singing and dancing with scarves. She told me that she wanted to sing our Sunshine Song. I began to sing "You Are My Sunshine." She told me that this wasn't the right song. I asked, "Can you sing it for me?" Violent sang:

The sunshine is mean
It's gonna start rainin
Rainin, rainin, rainin, rainin
The sunshine is goin away
It's goin away, a'cuz it's gonna be rainin!
Okay, I can see the sunshine
The sunshine is goin away
I just love it a'cuz there's sunshine
The rain is goin away
Uh oh! There's gonna be snow!
Snow! The whiteness is comin down, yeah yeah yeah
I can't believe it, I'm gonna go inside
My water, it's melting, oh no!
It's rainin and I am done with school
I'm goin home
I'm so mad, I can't even, I'll scream!
I want my sunshine back!
A'cuz I'm so mad, I just wanna scream
             Stephenie: *Ahhhhhhh!!*
It's rainin and sunshine, can't believe there's tears comin out
I can't believe it a'cuz the sunshine is slippin over
I guess sometimes, the rain's goin away
Uh oh, the leafs is fallin down
Uh oh, I just wanna scream really loud! Ahhhhhh!!!
             Stephenie: *Ahhhhhhh!!*
I can't believe it's sunshine, I want my sunshine back!
I can't believe it, my sunshine is back
It's runnin, the leafs is fallin down

I just wanna scream – this time, I'm gonna scream! (shrieks)
I just wanna leave
Uh oh! I can't believe it is rainin and snowin and fallin
Uh oh! I can't see the sunshine now
I just want to scream a'cuz I know the sunshine
Uh oh! I think I hate the sunshine now
Now I'm sick, I have to go home, to the hospital, goodbye, this is the end!
Bye!

Stephenie: *Bye*

After this session, Violet requested to not play music for several weeks. She chose instead to draw on the whiteboard and play with the stuffed animals. I often sang along while she drew, and she allowed me to sing/narrate her drawings. About a month later, Violet told me that we would be making more music. She played ukulele and directed me in a musical show, complete with narration. This pendulation between no music and music lasted throughout the rest of her time with me. I no longer felt threatened by the sessions in which she requested to not make music. I could find the musicality in our being together, in the clicks of the markers on the whiteboard and the rhythm of our hands hitting the table. I knew that when she wanted to re-enter the music, music as sonic and performative, she would tell me.

I began to think that Violet had processed all that she needed to process. Her play didn't enact interpersonal conflict anymore, and her songs didn't explore protection, anger, or fear. I transitioned my music interventions to address school-readiness. We practiced reading, played musical games to increase Violet's confidence, and I introduced musical challenges to increase her feeling of independence.

Then, in one session near the end of our time together, Violet was writing letters on the whiteboard and we were singing the alphabet song. She abruptly stopped singing, erased the letters, and drew a stickman. "This is the bad man," she proclaimed.

My heartbeat quickened. I watched her body. She stared at the drawing calmly while I asked her: "Is there anything you want me to know about him?"

"He is a bad man. He did bad things to me and Ruby."

"Are you safe now?"

"Yes. He's gone now."

She erased him and returned to the alphabet song. She appeared to be unbothered by the appearance of the stickman. I, though, was not. My heart was still racing. *I should have processed more. I should have asked more questions. I have to tell her that she didn't deserve that. I have to make sure she's okay . . . is she okay . . . how will I know if she's okay . . .*

I took a breath: *I can be with whatever she brings.* I listened for the music. I listened to her body, to her voice, and the space she was taking up: *She is processing in ways I can't and don't need to understand. She has what she needs.*

Coda

Violet is not the only child I have met that didn't seem interested in music. She is one of many who have turned their backs to me, held their hands over my mouth, or screamed at me to stop singing. It was alongside Violet that I reconceptualized music, musical experiences, and the musical relationship. While I had been trained in and felt confident with behavioral techniques, my time with Violet acted as the catalyst necessary to move past my preconceived ideas about supporting traumatized children. When I let go of my carefully planned sessions, Violet was able to explore her trauma story in a way that I could have never planned for. I have grown to expect similar non-linear engagements with music from the children I support. They explore their stories in bursts of creativity and catharsis, then withdraw into protective states before telling me that they want to play music again.

Because of my journey with Violet, I can find the music in the space between myself and a child. I can notice the themes that repeat in and between sessions, I can compose variations to offer for consideration, and I can hold the grounding voice for them to come back to. Before I can offer my music to the children, I must be willing to be with *their* music. I can't approach these relationships as transactional formulas in which I carefully build their trust so that I can force them to engage in what I have been trained to do. I must deeply and humbly experience their music because it is only within the context of their music that *our* music can develop.

Summarizing Ideas and Questions for Discussion

1. Clients, especially those affected by complex trauma, may not initially feel safe to engage in music experiences that we typically consider characteristic of music therapy treatment.

   a. How might you as a music therapist engage with a client who seems uninterested in music processes?
   b. While developing the therapeutic relationship, how might you balance planning music experiences with following a traumatized child's lead?

2. A music therapist's work and expertise go beyond performative sound and includes a musical way of being in relationship with others.

   a. How can you broaden your conceptualization of music and music making beyond traditional musical experiences?
   b. What are characteristics of musical ways of being in relationship?

Notes

1 I note here that the word "client" can imply a specific power dynamic, wherein the therapist holds power over an individual who is required to receive intervention, possibly against their will. Throughout this chapter, however, I will refer to the children that I worked with as "clients" because at the facility where I work, we perceive clients more as community partners, where we work together to identify needs and goals related to the trauma and violence they have endured.

2 Cloitre, M., Koenen, K. C., Cohen, L. R., & Han, H. (2002). Skills training in affective and interpersonal regulation followed by exposure: A phase-based treatment for PTSD related to childhood abuse. *Journal of Consulting and Clinical Psychology, 70*(5), 1067–1074. https://doi.org/10.1037//0022-006x.70.5.1067

3 English, D. J., Marshall, D. B., & Stewart, A. J. (2003). Effects of family violence on child behavior and health during early childhood. *Journal of Family Violence, 18*(1), 43–57. https://doi.org/10.1023/A:1021453431252

4 Spinazzola, J., Ford, J., Zucker, M., van der Kolk, B., Silva, S., Smith, S., & Blaustein, M. (2005). National survey of complex trauma exposure, outcome and intervention for children and adolescents. *Psychiatric Annals, 35*(5), 433–439. https://doi.org/10.3928/00485713-20050501-09

5 Lanius, R. A., Bluhm, R. L., & Frewen, P. A. (2011). How understanding the neurobiology of complex post-traumatic stress disorder can inform clinical practice: A social cognitive and affective neuroscience approach. *Acta Psychiatrica Scandinavica, 124*(5), 331–348. https://doi.org/10.1111/j.1600-0447.2011.01755.x

6 Abrams, B. (2011). Understanding music as a temporal-aesthetic way of being: Implications for a general theory of music therapy. *The Arts in Psychotherapy, 38*(2), 114–119. https://doi.org/10.1016/j.aip.2011.02.001

7 Abrams, B. (2012). A relationship-based theory of music therapy: Understanding processes and goals as being-together-musically. In K. E. Bruscia (Ed.), *Readings on music therapy theory* (pp. 58–76). Barcelona Publishers.

8 Malloch, S., & Trevarthen, C. (Eds.). (2009). *Communicative musicality: Exploring the basis of human companionship*. Oxford University Press.

Chapter 16

Sound, Silence, and Spoken Word
Music as a Holistic Aesthetic of Experience

Noah Potvin

Abstract

Instrumental and vocal sounds are often considered a necessary condition for there to be music, but silence, verbalizations, and gestural language are often just as prevalent, and necessary, in everyday musicing. Music therapy practice stands to broaden and deepen when music is embraced as a holistic aesthetic drawing from multiple mediums of experience that authentically emerge in the clinical encounter.

Tags: Therapeutic Relationship

This is a story about Jacob, an 89-year-old man with congestive heart failure receiving hospice care, and how we radically attuned as collaborative stakeholders to co-construct a holistic music aesthetic that – without reliance on organized sound – helped Jacob move through the loss of his wife and address his pre-bereavement preparations. Of particular focus is a clinical musical encounter between Jacob and me that occurred at the end of our six-month process. It was a sound-based encounter musically informed and shaped by multiple extra-musical encounters (e.g., verbal, cultural, and intrapsychic) that preceded it. "Encounter" is defined here – from a Gestalt perspective – as a point of contact between the self and the field catalyzing a unique, distinctive response.

This story will be told through metissage, a form of storytelling that weaves disparate strands, or plots, into a braid to tell a comprehensive, integral narrative. Strand One is Jacob's plot and provides the story's chapters. Strand Two is my plot, and Strand Three is a description of the music aesthetic co-constructed between Jacob and me as we navigated our relationship in the context of his death. These strands do not exist independent of one another, but rather mutually interact throughout the point of encounter in the therapeutic process.

DOI: 10.4324/9781003123798-21

Jacob the Caregiver

My time with Jacob began at his kitchen table where he sat with his wife, Gerty, who was also receiving hospice services. I had been referred to Jacob and Gerty to address goals related to emotional comfort, social isolation, and pre-bereavement preparation. Gerty's health was clearly more fragile than Jacob's at that point. She struggled to move around the kitchen in a steady manner but persisted with that special quality of resilience that matures as one ages. While she was pleasant and sociable, Jacob hovered with a roiling anxiety that communicated an internal state of "I don't know what's going on, I don't how to fix that, I'm scared."

For Jacob, Gerty had broken an unspoken tenet by declining in health faster than he was; he had anticipated she would be his caregiver, not the other way around. Jacob was part of a generation of men groomed to be care providers rather than caregivers. Care providers focus on concrete outcomes, relying upon acts of service to communicate love and offer comfort. Caregivers, in contrast, turn to compassion, empathy, and patience to provide support in situations with no clear outcomes, establishing a presence that bears witness to pain, growth, and transitions.

Jacob subsequently emotionally and existentially struggled in this space where he could not fix anything. It was a powerlessness I resonated with. As a child, I was emotionally bullied through a death-by-a-thousand-cuts strategy. To compensate for this lack of power, I learned to control every other element of my life and silently rage at that which I had no control over, much like Jacob was at this time.

It was through this resonance that Jacob and I aligned, but not yet in a way that fostered partnership. Our alignment initially overwhelmed me. Bearing witness to his struggle to be in power triggered my own struggle for control, and I fell deeply into that vortex of fear and pain. Jacob unconsciously experienced this alignment and flowed with our reciprocal sharing of energy, becoming more animated with pressured speech, excessive facial affect, and wild hand gesticulations. As this enmeshment deepened, I struggled to manage my emerging intrapsychic material and retain the professional boundaries necessary for providing professional support that, ultimately, was tepid and superficial in that moment. Our alignment was most clearly evidenced in Jacob displacing his anger – a sublimated fear over losing his wife – onto me, trusting me to be a container for this suppressed rage. With great force, he demanded more services to stop Gerty's inevitable decline and, when I was unable to make any such assurances, his anger intensified.

Shortly after that first visit, Gerty broke her hip and moved to a long-term care facility. I met Jacob in the common area of Gerty's rehab and sat with him to provide, if nothing else, social support in a more informal manner. Jacob, however, unleashed a torrent of anger built upon the last session, loudly rejecting any offered support. He challenged the services that had been provided to date and demanded Gerty be taken home due to the perceived poor care she was receiving. I immediately absorbed his vitriol as a personal, harsh indictment of my shortcomings as a treatment team member and regressed to the bullied child; I objectively knew the irrationality of Jacob demanding that I compensate for his powerlessness by stopping Gerty from dying but subjectively experienced the shame of not being able to meet those needs.

Moderating these visceral in-the-moment responses was the threat Jacob was to my privilege as White, cisgender, heterosexual, and nondisabled. While my personal historicity with bullying taught me how to protect myself, the privileged parts of my identity afforded me space to be assertive in clinical encounters with limited fear of retribution. To have my competence and intentions so openly questioned was jarring and disorienting. I was not able to understand how my caring and compassion were not readily recognized, acknowledged, and honored. For seemingly the first time, it was not simply assumed on the basis of my external presentations that I was the "good guy." In hindsight, it is not surprising that it was Jacob, with whom I shared many cultural and ecological similarities, who levied this challenge. Jacob's own privilege was being threatened both by the circumstances of Gerty's decline and the privilege I was unconsciously wielding in that session, thus he responded defensively and with force.

Within a few days, Gerty died. I was told during treatment team the next week that, during Gerty's actively dying phase, Jacob had climbed into her bed, holding her hand while singing softly. I told the nurse case manager I would place a visit to Jacob following Gerty's funeral.

Jacob the Bereaved

One week after Gerty's funeral, I found myself warily approaching Jacob's front door. *Would Gerty's death indeed be seen as a direct result of the hospice's care, as Jacob accused? Was I entering once more into a space where my vulnerabilities would be exposed? Would I be forced into a position by the end of this visit where I would have to determine whether music therapy was contraindicated for Jacob due to the potential for harm?*

Instead, upon entering and finding Jacob in his den, he gave me a slight smile and pointed to a small mahogany box above the television and said, "I keep her right there, right above the TV so when I turn the Yankee game on, she's watching it with me." Jacob proceeded to share details of their relationship, focusing less on specific details (i.e., how they met, where they lived, etc.) and more on what her role in his life was. This was the first time Jacob provided me access to parts of him not rooted in fear or anger. Jacob grew up in a working-class environment and aspired to be a physician but was grievously hurt when told by his father that medical school was beyond their financial means. Using that experience as a motivator, Jacob started a small business with a singular focus to provide his future family with access to professional careers and the upward mobility he had been denied.

Many of Jacob's stories were similarly developed in response to his perceived failures and successes. During my visits, the yarns he would spin were often punctuated by seemingly small moments that, in hindsight, significantly expanded his narrative. For instance, the time he animatedly answered a phone call from a past business associate requesting he make an overseas trip to help mediate a new working partnership and the quick deflation, upon hanging up the phone, when he realized that such trips were behind him. At the heart of these encounters revealing additional layers of his authentic self was a fundamental, existential truth: his self-concept was powered by his perceived ability to impact his surrounding environment. As his health declined that perception faltered, leading to a depleted sense of self-efficacy. Gerty's death had intensified this process; he did not experience her death as the completion of a natural process but rather – as noted earlier – a personal failure to protect.

Over the next several months, I would visit Jacob in his home every other week. I would dutifully bring my usual materials – guitar, music books, small hand percussion, and digital recorder – but they inevitably remained unused. So unused, in fact, that in our seventh session I forgot to unload my gear and bring it into the house. On the surface, these sessions were nothing more than social calls with talk focused on sports, politics, and current events.

It became clear, however, that these verbal interactions were gateways to deeper processes that first required safety and rapport. As a businessman, Jacob was a wordsmith. His interactions were punctuated by a dry wit and self-deprecating humor that kept me invested as he teased the punchline to a joke or the climax of a story. Jacob wanted me to see this authentic dimension of his Self and wanted to see if I could engage authentically in kind. It was an evolution of the alignment we had previously experienced only when Jacob was in states of anger and fear, but now replaced by an interpersonal desire. Simmering underneath these interactions was the pointed question of "Do you give enough of a damn about me to stay engaged?," an offshoot of his drive to leave impact tremors with whomever he engaged with. This drive fueled a transferential desire to mentor a young man in ways he had in the past when healthy.

And I, in turn, accepted that warm male presence with open arms, activating a powerful countertransference I was peripherally becoming aware of. I had grown up in the shadow of a paternal grandfather and uncle dying quickly from heart attacks in their 40s and, subconsciously, I always expected a similar death to await my father. While my father moved through middle age without issue, the fear I would lose my primary male role model at a young age without the opportunity to say goodbye never fully abated. In response to Jacob's own transferential mentorship of me, I distorted our relationship into a fantasized enactment of saying to my father the goodbye I had always assumed would be robbed from me.

Jacob and I enmeshed in a relationship that was mutually beneficial on a personal level due to our shared desires to use the other to address pre-existing needs outside the therapeutic process. Garred draws upon Martin Buber's I/Thou relating to explain such "a novel intersubjective contact" as being unto themselves meaningful and purposeful: "the relation is its own fulfillment, not directed toward bringing about something other than itself."[1] Garred is speaking to a specific type of relating occurring within musical encounters, and yet nary a song had been sung or a guitar string plucked or a drumhead slapped.

How could a mode of relating within music manifest without sound? To be sure, this was not a question I consciously struggled with at the time; it has been in hindsight that I have returned to this paradox, and yet for years it continued to flummox me. It was only upon critical examination of a singular session – and within that singular session a singular encounter – that I became aware of the music that Jacob and I had been co-constructing.

Jacob the Integrated Person

Approximately six months into our work together, Jacob's health declines intensified, and he became largely bedbound. It was difficult to witness Jacob's agile mind be constrained by a physical vessel denying him the opportunities to engage the full breadth of his creative and relational gifts. Over time, this immobility – and the endpoint that it represented – wore on Jacob's emotional and psychological well-being. The volatile mood swings and dour outlook present at the start of our work together began to re-emerge.

After spending a session with Jacob in this condition and watching him vacillate between boredom and anger, I decided the next session would be when I re-introduced music into our shared space. While I was not sure what Jacob would explore within the music encounter, I trusted in the music's intrinsic ability to be a malleable container capable of accommodating his affective intensity and lability. When I entered Jacob's bedroom upon our next session, I brought my guitar, songbook, and recording device and prominently displayed each, establishing music as my co-therapist. This was in stark contrast to previous sessions when I would bring my gear but leave it off to the side. I had wanted to avoid a defensive dismissal or minimizing from Jacob while coaxing a self-initiated engagement with the music. Jacob's faltering physical health, however, infused a time-sensitive urgency into the process, and I had come to trust that our therapeutic relationship could tolerate greater directiveness and challenging from me.

To my surprise, Jacob's face brightened when he saw my guitar, and though he declined to play an active role in song selection, he was open to receptively engaging. As a fellow New York Yankees fan, I knew Jacob would at least be familiar with the tune played after every home game win: "New York, New York" by Frank Sinatra. My initial assumption was that Jacob would be slow to engage, perhaps even internally withdrawing or minimizing his responses to the music, and that the totality of the encounter would last approximately 15 minutes before we would transition into our usual verbal engagement. From there, I figured to use this initial musical encounter as a foundation upon which to introduce new music experiences and expand Jacob's ability to emotionally, spiritually, and socially engage.

And was I ever wrong.

The moment I began to sing, Jacob thrust himself into the song with the same vigor and intensity that I had seen in all his other interactions. With a rich, booming bass, Jacob assumed the lead vocal, and while the initial key was a bit beyond his range, Jacob never faltered as he triumphantly blared the climax with great feeling infused into the rubato.

At the end of the song, after allowing the music to settle around us and for Jacob to regain a sense of grounding in the here-and-now, I invited Jacob to use words to help him organize his experience and also draw upon readily available defenses in case he was feeling too vulnerable following such a catharsis. Here is Jacob's response to an opening prompt about what he was thinking about while singing:

> My wife. You have no idea, Noah . . . as rough as it was, she made . . . well, let's put it this way: 68 years proved it. And now, as we're singing and talking and trying to get me into a different frame of mind, it comes right back again. These feet remind me, "You ain't going nowhere, baby. Your dancing days are over." I used to do a lot of that stuff. I enjoyed socializing – it was really a part of business when you think about it. But here I am now with music giving me, taking me . . . it gives me a lift. And that's a good thing. Laying here, my attitude towards music when I am sick, my attitude when I'm sicker, it gives me a little bit more peace and feeling like I want to partake in something instead of lying around like an old dead man. It's important for you to get out and express yourself, and if you're not able to do that then you're wasting away just by sitting here and waiting for the next one to come in.

Taken at face value, Jacob's experience in the music demonstrates that a powerful memory recall and re-enactment occurred. Such is a common framing of many music experiences with older adults, both within and outside of music therapy. However, looking underneath the surface of both the experience and Jacob's verbal recall reveals a deeper, more comprehensive process in play.

Within the musical encounter Jacob entered a liminal space – what Victor Turner described as the "betwixt and between"[2] – where the individual embodies multiple identities at one time in an exploratory encounter with what is possible. Singing with a youthful vigor and abandon while bedbound, Jacob had discovered an existential balancing point between who he was in his past, who he was in the present, and who he was to become in death. He was one and all of those manifestations of Self, navigating a musical encounter that elicited, nurtured, and held the past, present, and future. Each actualized role was honored as a salient component of his full personhood, a personhood that was soon to reach a point of completion through his death.

An analysis of Jacob's reflections on the music experience reveals a number of embodied roles that originated at various points in his life: husband, healthy adult, entrepreneur, older adult, and dying adult. Here is his response reconceptualized as a script with each of these identities framed as an individual character:

Husband

My wife. You have no idea, Noah . . . as rough as it was, she made . . . well, let's put it this way: 68 years proved it.

Healthy adult

And now, as we're singing and talking and trying to get me into a different frame mind, it comes right back again. These feet remind me, "You ain't going nowhere, baby. Your dancing days are over." I used to do a lot of that stuff.

Entrepreneur

I enjoyed socializing – it was really a part of business when you think about it. But here I am now with music giving me, taking me . . . it gives me a lift. And that's a good thing.

Older adult

Laying here, my attitude towards music when I am sick, my attitude when I'm sicker, it gives me a little bit more peace and feeling like I want to partake in something instead of lying around like an old dead man.

Dying adult

It's important for you to get out and express yourself, and if you're not able to do that then you're wasting away just by sitting here and waiting for the next one to come in.

Jacob fluidly moved through each of these roles central to his whole-person identity. He was at once all and none of these roles, experiencing his past abilities alongside his present limitations in context of his future end-of-life transition.

Sharing in this liminal space with Jacob, I actualized roles that had me cycling from leading/guiding, supporting, and receptively witnessing the music encounter. Movement among these identities was intuitive and in response to Jacob's engagement. At times he would forget which verse he was on so I would provide a cue before quickly backing away when he assumed control; other times he had expended the energy he could, and I jumped back in to form a musical bridge until he was ready to rejoin. Sustaining that level of contact with Jacob and the music was intensely exhausting, and I felt aware that time within the encounter was lengthened in juxtaposition to the objective passing of time on my watch.

Epilogue: Music Beyond Sound as a Part of Everyday Practice

Jacob died soon after this experience, without the opportunity to re-engage in music therapy. It was several weeks before I could return due to the size of my caseload, and by then Jacob's health had declined such that his family had converged and created a firewall between him and non-nursing hospice staff. While objectively I know there was nothing else that could have been done, the lost opportunity to engage with Jacob after a breakthrough session elicited then – and still now – a profound sense of guilt.

That guilt ultimately functioned as a springboard, however, as I held close my time with Jacob. If music therapy is to be understood as a practice founded upon a diverse collection of relationships between the patient, music therapist, and music, then Jacob's burst of music in month six could not have been as random as it appeared. Was it possible that my encounter with Jacob and the music similarly encapsulated aspects of practice fundamental to my practice in end-of-life care?

I started exploring this question by considering Jacob's cathartic and intentional musicking with "New York, New York." Through clinical supervision and a developing philosophy of practice, I identified certain conditions in the therapeutic process that helped Jacob engage with this whole-person transformation in the music: trust, rapport, investment, motivation, and purpose. Yet, if no music had been engaged with prior to, how were these foundational conditions of a therapeutic process met?

I struggled with this question until recognizing I was approaching it from a faulty vantage point. I was assuming that no music had been co-constructed between Jacob and me in any of our previous visits, that it was only when I strummed the guitar chords and Jacob belted his first lyrics that a music encounter had taken place. However, what if Jacob and I had been engaging in musical encounters with each visit? What if the manner of our collaborative musicking was located in mediums other than "just" sound?

Music is frequently framed as a medium of experience in music therapy literature, but with the tacit assumption that the term "music" assumes some manner of sound production. Such an assumption is natural; most music therapists have, for the majority of their lives, been engaged in a variety of traditional musical contexts relying upon sound (e.g., performance ensembles, concerts, etc.). The assumption of music-as-sound is similarly natural; we are surrounded – perhaps even saturated – by pre-recorded commercial jingles, streaming music on mobile platforms, podcasts amplifying storytelling with music tracks, and songs drifting in and out of informal social settings. Consequently, sound is the medium through which we have become acculturated to becoming aware of and engaging with music.

When music manifests through sound production, it relies upon organizations of rhythms and harmonies; variations in timbres and melodies; mixing of instrumentation and dynamics; and modes of production (i.e., live performance, downloaded audio files, and streaming data). Listeners and performers alike engage with and make sense of the resulting sound through filters shaped by culturally transmitted values that dictate, among other things, what qualifies as music; what typology of music the sound in question is (e.g., genre, style, etc.); the social, performative, and spiritual functions of that music; and the meanings that can or should be derived from that music. In such moments, metaphors such as "tension" and "release" are applied to help listeners and performers internally make sense of and externally articulate the sound experience. Additional mediums are also paired with the sound to help amplify the aural qualities (i.e., lights and fog at a concert or coffee at a café open mic). Such is a traditional Western approach to engagement in music, evidenced in no small part by avid live music and "audiophile" sub-cultures.

However, is music reliant upon sound in order for that experience to manifest, or is it possible for the experience to occur irrespective of sound? Daily music therapy practice is rife with musical encounters that exist outside of, or parallel to, sound wherein sound is secondary or complementary. Music therapists have been locating the musical encounter from a spectrum of experience for many years, such as in community,[3] relationship,[4] play,[5] and spirituality.[6] And yet, music that exists outside of sound is typically framed by what is missing (e.g., "nonverbal") instead of by what was present, obscuring the fact that individuals meaningfully engage with music across all manner of experience.

Consider, when playing a drum, the slap of skin against the drumhead in synchrony with the physical sensation of arms moving in concert and the torso responding in kind. Or a moment of mirrored facial affect shared between two people in a moment of attunement as a song reaches a climax. Such encounters happen in context of a sound-based experience, yet do not require sound in order to be experienced physically, emotionally, spiritually, and/or relationally as part of a holistic, multimodal music aesthetic.

Indeed, to remove any of these elements from the experience would compromise the musicality of the experience.

Through this lens, I understood that co-constructing "New York, New York" was not the beginning of our musicking, but rather an evolution of the intersubjective duet that began the moment I first sat at the kitchen table. Our shared sociocultural histories aligned our ecologies in a way that promoted an intuitive understanding of our gestural language. My accommodation of his intense moods through a supportive presence was similar to the musical containers frequently created in music therapy practice to help patients experience the uncomfortable in a safe way. Our time spent in verbal conversations were saturated with cadences, rhythmic patterns, timbres, and hand gestures that were as expressive of our internal worlds as they were responsive to the other's expressions. We developed a foundation of rapport and relating in these verbal, spiritual, and relational engagements that reflected qualities we typically assign to musical engagements.

Critically, our encounter in "New York, New York" did not resonate because it was extraordinary or outside the norm. Rather, it reflected a central feature of everyday music therapy practice: musically engaged through a relationship-based medium rather than a sound-based medium. The challenge to expand beyond sound is a reality for music therapists as many patients – due to cognitive functioning, psychological health, and/ or personal relationships with music – choose to primarily engage outside of traditional sound-based receptive, recreative, improvisational, and compositional experiences. Sometimes this manifests as resistance to music, while other times patients see music fitting into broader patterns of spiritual and/or social relating that are frequent features in music therapy in end-of-life care.

Through this clinical experience and my subsequent experiences as a supervisor and educator, I have found the skills required for this type of engagement to be part of music therapy's entry-level competencies. Instead of framing non-sound-based interventions as extra-musical, thus creating the impression that any non-musical medium of engagement is outside the music therapist's scope, all forms of intersubjective engagement can be framed as part of a holistic and integrative music aesthetic. As musicians, music therapists instinctively hear the interplay of tension and release in music through dissonant harmonies, climactic melodies, and series of cadences; the subtextual themes that exist underneath the surface of lyrics; and the relational aspects of creating and engaging with music with self and other. It is only natural, then, that these well-honed skills in deep, intentional listening and resonant interpersonal engagement would extend beyond "just" sound to encompass diverse intersubjective fields. No verbal interventions were facilitated that an authentic humanistic connection between two individuals is unable to organically replicate with every encounter.

My work with Jacob was transformative, both in the time I spent with him and the individual reflexive work I engaged with after he died. He taught me that music is infused into all forms of human engagement by virtue of that engagement being human, that people can no more avoid being musical than weather can avoid being wet, and that my job as a music therapist had far less to do with making music than it had to with attuning to the music already around me. When I reflect on this growth, it reminds me of how the catalysts for my periods of most significant professional development have involved challenging long-held beliefs or assumptions. That does not mean my ways of practicing prior to were wrong or invalid, but rather that I had matured into another phase of my practice and that such maturation is, by nature, often challenging. May my resilience to weather such change remain steadfast so my practice can continue growing alongside those I am working with.

Summarizing Ideas and Questions for Discussion

1. Music therapy practice involves engagement in diverse mediums of experience (i.e., social, emotional, and psychological).

   a. What mediums can you identify in your practice that contribute to the music in session?
   b. How do the culturally informed values and expectations of both you and your patient(s) shape the nature of your shared engagement within these mediums?

2. Music is a multi-dimensional aesthetic comprised of sound-based and non-sound-based mediums interacting within an encounter.

   a. How do you and your patient(s) engage within these mediums to co-construct the music as stakeholders?
   b. How do the culturally informed values and expectations of both you and your patients shape the nature of this co-constructed musicking?

Notes

1 Garred, R. (2006). *Music as therapy: A dialogical perspective* (pp. 45, 112). Barcelona Publishers.
2 Turner, V. (1979). Dramatic ritual/ritual drama: Performative and reflexive anthropology. *The Kenyong Review*, *1*(3), 80–93. www.jstor.org/stable/4335047

3 Stige, B. (2017). *Where music helps: Community music therapy in action and reflection.* Routledge.

4 Mössler, K., Gold, C., Aßmus, J., Schumacher, K., Calvet, C., Reimer, S., Iversen, G., & Schmid, W. (2019). The therapeutic relationship as predictor of change in music therapy with young children with autism spectrum disorder. *Journal of Autism and Developmental Disorders, 49*(7), 2795–2809. https://doi.org/10.1007/s10803-017-3306-y

5 Carpente, J. A. (2013). *IMCAP-ND: The individual music-centered assessment profile for neurodevelopmental disorders: A clinical manual.* Regina.

6 Potvin, N., & Flynn, C. (2019). Music therapy as a psychospiritual ministry of intercession during imminent death. *Music Therapy Perspectives, 37*(2), 120–132. https://doi.org/10.1093/mtp/miz002

Chapter 17

Reconnecting Musicians With Music at the End of Life

Developing Musical Identity Beyond Performance

Dalita Getzoyan

Abstract

Musicians are commonly referred to music therapy in end-of-life care settings under the assumption that past musical training means they are better attuned and more receptive to the health benefits of music. However, their complex musical identities require a music therapist to approach the case with great care and humility to ensure music experiences do not evoke past traumas, mirror past harms, or create new negative associations.

Tags: Treatment Planning; Therapeutic Relationship

As a classical musician, I am well acquainted with the pressures of Western music's traditions of perfectionism and performance standards. Though musician cultures can promote creativity and connection, Western musical training sometimes implies the need to maintain a comparatively high technical competence to make music.[1] I struggled with the strict rules I had been taught about "good" music and "bad" music, and my subsequent desires to be seen as a "good enough" musician so that I would also be seen, by extension, as a "good enough" person.

In contrast, when I began my music therapy training, I was encouraged to shift from a product-oriented to process-oriented approach to music. Success became about engagement with the music, not about whether the music was "right" or "wrong." I found this new experience to be liberating and healing. At the same time, my music therapy training still focused on the traditional signs of rhythmic, harmonic, and melodic connection as a sign of success within a session.

As I began working with older adults in hospice, I noticed that patients who were trained musicians – especially those with music careers – tended to struggle with those same elements of perfectionism. Older adults often experience identity and skill loss due to declines from illness,[2] and I observed their disappointment and frustration in music experiences when unable to

DOI: 10.4324/9781003123798-22

sing or play a song at their previously high technical standard. Patients can benefit from collaboration with music therapists to cultivate positive new musical experiences rooted in authenticity and self-expression to both connect to and reconstruct their musical identities as they age. However, this requires the music therapist to grapple with the harmful music traditions they may have come from. My work with Bob challenged me to jointly explore with him new personal and musical identities so that therapeutic experiences could be fruitful while also honoring his musical training.

Clinical and Cultural Contexts

Bob was initially admitted to hospice care with diagnoses of idiopathic normal pressure hydrocephalus and Alzheimer's disease with late onset, including symptoms of confusion, short-term and long-term memory loss, feelings of frustration, repetitive speech, difficulty with word retrieval, and excessive sleeping. He received hospice care primarily in a nursing home where I worked with him in monthly music therapy sessions for seven months. While hospice traditionally focuses on a patient's medical declines to continue providing care, I focused on using strengths-based and resource-based approaches to benefit Bob's mental, emotional, physical, and interpersonal wellness through his decline.

I am a cisgender female of Armenian descent and was in my late 20s while working with Bob. I grew up in a middle-class suburb throughout most of my life and had moved to a middle- to upper-middle-class area of a nearby city shortly before working with Bob. Bob was a 77-year-old cisgender, heterosexual, white male raised in upstate NY and married with children. Bob lived with his wife in a middle- to upper-class beach town prior to his admission and was well-educated with a degree in electrical engineering. Bob was from a generation expecting men to be providers, leaders, contributors, and conversationalists. His cognitive and physical declines likely resulted in a frustration of perceived inability to contribute and maintain his independence, more deeply rooted than a sadness about losing his musical ability.

Bob and I shared some cultural similarities, such as being university educated and trained in Western styles of music, which contributed to an immediate connection due to mutual experiences despite our otherwise different locations. Our connection was also established through how Bob reminded me of my grandfather, who had also been a well-educated man with musical talents. I grew up as an only child in a multigenerational household with my great-grandmother, maternal grandparents, and parents. I watched my grandfather decline and had witnessed his personal frustrations with aphasia and his inability to walk. His change occurred rapidly, and my family had struggled to adjust to his new mode of functioning. I therefore understood the possibility of Bob's internal frustrations with himself, just as my grandfather experienced, as well as his family's potential struggle to adjust to his new reality.

The primary cultural differences between us were in age and gender identity. I worked to maintain awareness of the potential for ageism and sexism in our work together. Bob was from a generation when men had significantly more power and privilege than women, especially younger women, and it was possible he was uncomfortable being in a session led by a young female. I similarly recognized my potential to assert my power against age and gender stereotypes. I noticed in reflection that some of my early decisions in my treatment with Bob may have been influenced by a need to have power and control within the session. As seen here, I set a standard for Bob to meet my level and expectations, rather than fully exploring what would be most beneficial for him at the start of treatment. Though I was unaware of it at the time, I may have been unconsciously trying to elevate my own status in our therapeutic relationship as an attempt to gain his respect, based on the bias that he may not have respected me due to my age and gender.

Initial Treatment Approaches

From the beginning of our work together, it was clear that Bob had a strong connection to music. He had CDs in his room of many different jazz musicians. In the first session, actively listening to live music was primarily a distraction for Bob and helped him to experience enjoyment in the moment to mitigate frustrations related to memory loss and difficulty communicating.

When we started working together, I assessed Bob was struggling with an incomplete sense of identity due to his memory loss. He struggled to share facts about his personal history, could not identify personal preferences, struggled to make decisions, and appeared disconnected from himself and others. Our initial music experiences revolved around receptive engagement: listening to music together provided an initial point of connection that did not put pressure on him to engage through sharing facts about himself or playing music.

Towards the end of the first session, a facility staff member showed me Bob's trumpet in a dresser drawer in his room. From that point forward through the third session, I integrated the trumpet into improvisations, believing I was facilitating a way for Bob to remain connected with his identity as a musician. However, Bob often made statements as he began to play that indicated personal disappointment (e.g., "I need to warm up" or "It's been a while since I've played"). He constantly attempted to utilize mutes for his trumpet to improve the sound, forgetting each time that it was unsuccessful and creating more difficulty for his playing. At one point, Bob even removed his dentures, thinking it would improve his playing, though he realized it did not and put them back in.

I offered encouragement by reassuring him to "Just play a few notes" or cheerfully reinforcing: "It does not need to be perfect." What I had not realized at the time is that in reflecting on my desire to be a "good" musician, I was influenced to be a "good" music therapist. I reasoned that by getting him to play with me, it would be a marker of my success because he would be maintaining connection to himself as a musician. There were many personal and professional layers contributing to the deep desire to maintain his traditional musical functioning.

When my family initially struggled to accept my grandfather's decline, they made efforts to keep as much the same for him as possible. My family often tried to maintain normalcy to mitigate his anger and grief about his personal losses, which sometimes resulted in denial about this new reality. I was pulled in as a resource in this process due to my music therapy education, but I was fearful of upsetting family members at different stages of readiness.

This people-pleasing tendency was directly reflected in my work with Bob wherein I was similarly afraid of upsetting or disappointing him and his family if we could not maintain his previous level of functioning. In my family, there was a subtle pressure to respect older adults and modify my own behavior to keep them "happy" in order to be a "good" child. Therefore, if I upset or disappointed these older patients and their families, I may not be a "good" music therapist.

I was also contending with internalized pressure about Bob playing the trumpet. This pressure was a byproduct of Western-influenced music therapy training that taught me success is when a client or patient improvises using a certain tonality or rhythmic structure. Additionally, at my internship the focus had been on maintenance of a previous identity through re-telling personal narratives or singing familiar songs; this reinforced an ageist belief that older adults are unable to formulate new identities, thoughts, feelings, or actions. Had Bob and I not both been Western classically trained musicians, I may not have projected these expectations of identity formation onto him.

Though I did not recognize it in the moment, Bob's struggle to align his self-concept as a musician with his current musical capabilities triggered my fears and frustration about imperfection when struggling to execute music. When grappling with achieving the perfect tone playing the flute, I made statements such as: "I must have a leak in one of the keys." It was easier to place blame on an external source of technical shortcomings, rather than recognize and honor my imperfections as something other than inherently bad. These intense feelings about imperfection manifested as a countertransference wherein I wanted to help Bob – and, by extension, me – hold onto any part of his identity as a musician that could be salvaged. I believed any connection to his former skill was better than none at all.

Therefore, I considered the moments Bob improvised with me to be "perfect." I neglected to consider the option of helping him play pre-composed music because I was so focused on his success in improvisation. Rather than offer Bob options and follow his lead, I felt the need to "pre-scribe" certain musical experiences to give him the exact right structure that would set him up for what I thought would be success. The decision to improvise was based on my own unchecked biases about him being a jazz musician (i.e., believing he would prefer to improvise) and having dementia (i.e., not trusting he could read music or recall how to play pre-composed songs, and would feel undue pressure to perform). This was both ironic and counterproductive, since I was looking for him to improvise with technical skill even though technical pressure was the very thing I was trying to avoid by focusing on improvisation.

I celebrated and offered praise when he produced a sound, improvised in the "correct" key, and aligned rhythmically. However, despite my subjective appraisal of our musicking, Bob appeared to be struggling to feel happy or satisfied in these encounters. His affect was flat, and he would say little and not present with the same excitement and celebration that I tried to encourage. Ultimately, playing together with Bob on the trumpet did not produce a sustainable or meaningful reconnection to his identity as a musician. After a couple of minutes, Bob would stop playing, and immediately fixate on his perceived inability to play. If anything, it appeared that engaging with the trumpet in this way was causing harm.

By the end of the third session, I recognized Bob's internal world was still connected to his identity as a trumpet player, but he was unable to fully actualize that identity. He had greater difficulty providing adequate breath support and control of his embouchure to produce a sound and constantly judged himself, appearing to feel less successful than his younger self had been on trumpet. The statements he made about not having played or practiced in a while appeared to be attempts to make sense of his overall decline. Much as I had done, Bob externalized the reasons he was unable to play when the reality of his decline became too painful (e.g., "That's not my trumpet" and "My children messed with it"). Being able to empathize with Bob from my lived experiences as a Western trained musician helped me move through my countertransference to more deeply understand what was happening for him in those moments. I came to realize how, for Bob, musicking with the trumpet as a performer was not a means for growth, but rather a risk to his mood, self-esteem, and end-of-life identity formation.

It became clear other options needed to be introduced to allow Bob to musick without feeling his sense of identity and ego threatened, but I was at a loss. I had a few ideas, but they required letting go of both my performer expectations and the idea that Bob's musical fulfillment would solely come from playing the trumpet. I needed to redefine what it meant for Bob to be "successful" in music therapy. This also challenged me to come to terms with my grief about the changes to musical skill and identity as we age and recognize how my need to people-please in the therapeutic relationship was impacting the therapeutic process.

New Musical Approaches

Working from a Community Music Therapy[3] perspective, I began supporting Bob to engage in a music activity with the peers and staff he interacted with daily at the facility. I determined that connection with his daily life would be more beneficial to his social and emotional health than working one-on-one with me. Around the same time, I suffered an injury in my hand that rendered me unable to accompany our musical experiences with piano and guitar. My Western music therapy education taught me that my value was defined by my proficiency on guitar and piano. I passed a proficiency exam that told me I was a "good enough" musician from a traditional Western musical standard. *What happens when I am unable to provide music in that traditional sense? Without these instruments, am I still a music therapist?*

When I began letting go of my insecurities and notions about Western dominant music therapy practice, however, Bob became more engaged and connected in music therapy. Bob still loved music and wanted to engage with it, and now it was clear that musicking did not need to be about creating the perfect piece. Instead, Bob benefited from any musical experience that served as a vehicle for social connection. Social connectedness became a reminder of his worthiness and acceptance as a human being amid medical care that was completed daily for his physical needs. In other words, being asked to play the trumpet may have been another "task" for him to complete, rather than an opportunity for socialization.

During this time, I had to be mindful of what music experiences I could provide without using my fingers on an instrument and discovered adjustments that ultimately expanded clinical possibilities. I incorporated karaoke tracks and pre-existing community music activities into music therapy, providing opportunities for Bob to connect with other residents and not solely me. We receptively engaged with familiar music that Bob easily recognized, providing a common ground for us to relate and interact. I also used more percussive, rather than melodic or harmonic, instruments that Bob did not have any previous expectations of a "right" or "wrong" way to play. The power dynamics between our physical capabilities began leveling, allowing for Bob to feel ease instead of pressure when playing.

In the fourth session, Bob's engagement in music shifted. When offered a few instruments to improvise with, he chose jingle bells and verbally commented on pre-recorded music. Here, instead of relying solely on the trumpet with its complex emotional history, Bob connected to his broader identity as a musician. The change was not in utilizing a completely different style of music, as we were still singing and playing along to songs Bob would recognize in Western musical tonalities. Instead, the change occurred in creating a space where music could be for everyone, regardless of how anyone played it or heard it. The newer community-based music experiences had a positive impact on Bob's health. He had a greater sense of belonging to his community, which potentially helped him recognize he was worthy of social and musical connections.

As I became more creative in my clinical decision-making and expanded my notions of what it meant to be a competent music therapist, I also released my people-pleasing tendencies. In a way, I did not have a choice. I temporarily had to reconstruct my own identity as a musician and music therapist since my physical functioning from my injured hand had been altered. When I recognized what I was doing would not be beneficial to Bob, my ethical obligation to reduce harm superseded projection of my own fears and insecurities. I could no longer please the imaginary professors in my head telling me what to play, or the narratives of family members who had not been ready to hear about construction of new identities in the face of change. As I became more comfortable with my new musical identity, it might have provided Bob an unspoken permission to start becoming more comfortable in his. Similarly, as I released a desperation for Bob's technical skill to act as a measure of my success, he no longer needed to feel the pressure to satisfy me so that I, in turn, could be what I thought others wanted to see.

This freed us both to enter a new musical world. He was able to remain connected to his musical identity more playfully and freely. His identity became rooted in the intermusical connections with others rather than his technical skills. He happened to play the trumpet, but his true identity came from connecting with other band members in a group. When provided with an instrument, rather than being distracted by technical challenges that caused excuses and disappointment, Bob musically engaged while smiling and appearing grounded in the moment. He no longer presented with hesitation or self-judging statements. As a music therapist and classical musician, I was reminded of my freedom to facilitate the use of any music experience to connect with others and work toward wellness.

The sixth session was the final session of this hospice admission for Bob, with no opportunity for termination due to an abrupt discharge. The work of previous sessions, including staying in the community area and utilizing percussion instruments, continued into this session. Bob chose to play the tambourine. As our session was taking place in a common area, other residents complimented our music, providing further positive reinforcement for Bob's familiar but reconstructed identity as a musician. He was used to external praise from music making, which contributed to a sense of normalcy in connection through music, despite using a new instrument.

At the end of this session, Bob's wife unexpectedly arrived with their dog. Previously, I may have felt shame or pressure that we were "caught" not trying to use his trumpet in music, and I may have become anxious about not following a fully structured session plan. However, I had become confident in the positive impact of Bob's new ways of engagement in music therapy and looked forward to sharing in this space with his family. Bob's wife encouraged and validated him as he musically engaged with freedom and expression, and the visit created an important opportunity for his wife to witness this new musical identity. She responded with joy, positivity, and acceptance at seeing how he activated within the music.

Final Reflections

In my practice, I have worked with other patients who have a background as a musician, including some who performed professionally. I have seen them face challenges similar to the ones Bob moved through as they tackled the grief of their mortality, life changes, and age-related declines through music. Given the dominance of the Western music tradition in entry-level training of music therapists in the United States, other music therapists may be at risk of feeling pressure to help older adults hold onto their traditional musical identities. However, new musical and creative experiences for former musicians can help them to express, prove, and accept their current reality in a gentle and easy manner, rather than having a constant reminder that they are no longer the same person they were. At the same time, keeping some of their experience within musical connection helps to maintain some of their traditional identity.

As a Western trained music therapist, I needed to release the notion of musical perfection, technical skill, or even simply making sounds in music therapy as a measure of success. I remembered the "creative" in creative arts therapies and learned to be honest with myself in allowing my musical, therapeutic, and personal identities to expand and shift in response to Bob's needs.

By adjusting the nature and type of music experiences in music therapy, Bob was able to develop his identity as a musician in context of this new phase of his life while honoring his past musical experiences and roles. I am grateful for the many opportunities to connect with Bob in music, and I hope he is resting peacefully somewhere reveling in beautiful musical connection with others, whenever and however he wants.

Summarizing Ideas and Questions for Discussion

1. Music therapists may feel pressure to maintain a patient's traditional musical identity, especially for patients who were former musicians. They may also seek a level of technical perfection as a measure of therapeutic success. However, as patients experience declines and changes from illness, the use of former musical experiences may trigger feelings of grief, disappointment, frustration, And identity loss.

    a. How do your past musical experiences and training impact your feelings about the music created during sessions?

    b.   Have you worked with patients who were former musicians? What anxieties, self-judgments, or insecurities did you notice, if any? If these were experienced, in what contexts were they triggered?

2.   Patients can move into expression, processing, and acceptance of the changes occurring as they age by engaging in musical experiences that help to construct new musical identities. Aspects of these new experiences can honor their past history and training while allowing for more freedom and authenticity without the pressure to perform.

    a.   How do you assess the resources, both internal and external, that patients already have available to them? What roles do these resources play during your sessions?

    b.   How might you spontaneously use resources provided by the patient in the context of their community-based setting?

Notes

1 Evans, P., McPherson, G. E., & Davidson, J. W. (2013). The role of psychological needs in ceasing music and music learning activities. *Psychology of Music*, *41*(5), 600–619. http://dx.doi.org/10.1177/0305735612441736

2 Gillies, B., & Johnston, G. (2004). Identity loss and maintenance: Commonality of experience in cancer and dementia. *European Journal of Cancer Care*, *13*(5), 436–442. https://doi.org/10.1111/j.1365-2354.2004.00550.x

3 Pavlicevic, M., & Ansdell, G. (2004). *Community music therapy*. Jessica Kingsley Publishers.

Chapter 18

"Luchando tu Estas"

Interdisciplinary Collaboration in the Pediatric Intensive Care Unit

Gabriela Asch-Ortiz, Suzanne Miller, and Abby Patch

Abstract

Music therapists may be tasked with caring for individuals, families, and communities navigating the toughest of life experiences. Interdisciplinary collaboration enables opportunities for broadening and deepening the level of therapeutic support individuals receive while also extending an intimate degree of emotional and professional support for one another as care providers.

Tags: Professional Development; Therapeutic Relationship; Treatment Planning

Content warning: infant death

The following case took place many years ago and challenged us as clinicians and human beings. We are still grappling with its various complexities and the feelings it elicited within us. The voice used within the case study shifts between the collective "we" and individually named perspectives presented in the third person as a means of conveying collectively shared and individually held experiences and reflections. This case highlights how an interdisciplinary psychosocial team collaborated to provide holistic, culturally reflexive, family-centered care that none of us could have accomplished if we were working alone.

Rosalyn and Family

Rosalyn's story began in utero. The family was told she would be born with Down syndrome, but when she entered this world, she was diagnosed in the neonatal intensive care unit (NICU) with a life-threatening

DOI: 10.4324/9781003123798-23

disease called pyruvate dehydrogenase deficiency. Rosalyn spent the first two months of her life in the NICU before transferring to the pediatric intensive care unit (PICU) and subsequently dying at 6 months old. The medical team struggled to explain this complex and life-limiting illness to the family, though the reasons for the struggle were not clear. Was it a language barrier due to the family primarily speaking Spanish? Religious or cultural differences? A patriarchal "we know best" approach that medical providers too often assume? Perhaps it was an unfortunate combination.

According to the doctors, Rosalyn emerged from the womb "limp and dusky." She was critically ill, requiring breathing support, heart surgery, and frequent draining of liquid in her lungs. Her brain imaging was highly abnormal, but her family saw their precious Rosalyn, whose imperfect life was eagerly awaited and who held on tight to her family members' fingers. They wanted every available medical intervention offered to their daughter in order to take her home. The medical team, however, knew she would not survive.

When the time came to discuss Rosalyn's need for a tracheostomy tube and gastrostomy tube for long-term breathing and feeding support, respectively, more difficult conversations were held. Rosalyn's mother asked, "Will I hear my baby cry with this tube?" while pointing at her throat. There was silence in the room, followed by an uncomfortable chuckle from one of the doctors. Her feelings of hurt, confusion, and mistrust showed on her face.

When the family returned to the NICU from home one morning and found a different child in Rosalyn's room, their hearts fell. Where was she? What happened? Did she die? She was stable but had been transferred to the PICU, and no one told the family.

In the PICU, treatment teams see families with unique and complex narratives. Rosalyn's parents, Guadalupe and Jose, were undocumented Latine immigrants who embarked on the perilous journey to the United States to pursue the "American dream." Their teenage daughters, Xiomara and Yesenia, were American citizens and fluent in English. They often visited the hospital after school, serving as translators for their parents when at the bedside. Guadalupe's mother, Abuela, functioned as the family matriarch and additional parent to Rosalyn and her sisters. Rosalyn's presence held a strong gravitational pull on the family, with Abuela and Guadalupe alternating being at the bedside and her father, sisters, and extended family rotating their visits. *Familismo* is a quality adopted by some Latine families that refers to a strong sense of family cohesion and familial ideals extending beyond the nuclear family to include a broader network of support, such as aunts, uncles, grandparents, and close family friends.[1] This cultural value was a central tenant for Rosalyn's family, as they relied on each other and their strong Catholic faith.

Establishing Therapeutic Relationships

In addition to the medical care provided to every child, our hospital recognizes the psychosocial needs of critically ill children and their families and supports the interdisciplinary collaboration between the social worker, child life specialist, and music therapist. Each child in the PICU is assigned a social worker (in this case, Suzanne) to provide mental health counseling, resource management, and discharge planning. Since the social work role entails following the patient from birth to death, Suzanne was one of a few people who knew Rosalyn and her family from the beginning. Suzanne identifies as a cisgender Caucasian, English- and Hebrew-speaking, Jewish female. Abby, the child life specialist in the PICU, provided emotional support and offered opportunities for play and normalization of the patient's environment. Abby identifies as a Caucasian, English-speaking, cisgender Christian. Gabriela, the music therapist in the PICU, used individualized cultural-relational, music-based interventions to target psychological and emotional distress. This involves shifting into an inner space of curiosity, placing cultural contexts and their associated power dynamics occurring for the music therapist and client as central in the meaning-making, communication, and exchange. Gabriela identifies as a nondisabled, neurotypical, hetero-cisgender, first-generation Salvadoreña with Indigenous roots in Maya-Pipil.

Using the skills inherent in each of our disciplines, we provided emotional support, comfort, and consistency to the family as they navigated Rosalyn's prolonged and unpredictable hospitalization. The family's needs varied by day, week, and month, depending on Rosalyn's medical status and how they were coping. The frequency of our visits varied, with Suzanne and Abby visiting daily and Gabriela three times per week. We also facilitated sessions together, sensing that the support we could provide to the family as a collective was richer when compared to the sum of our individual parts.

During the initial weeks, Suzanne focused on building trust with Rosalyn's family and helping them process the information offered by the NICU medical teams regarding these devastating diseases and the expected impact on Rosalyn's health. In addition, she utilized grief-focused counseling to acknowledge and explore the differences between the reality they anticipated and the one they were living.[2]

Child Life was a new service to Rosalyn's family in the PICU. Upon transfer to the PICU, Abby met and assessed the family's coping and ways to best support them. Due to the complexity of Rosalyn's medical needs, Abby focused on exploring ways to create a comforting environment and foster bonding through play and memory-making opportunities.

Since the family was familiar with music therapy from their time in the NICU, Abby referred Rosalyn to Gabriela in the PICU. This provided comfort to the family during their lengthy hospitalization and a sense of relief for Abby in knowing that support and collaboration from her colleague was available. Having received the referral, Gabriela entered Rosalyn's room and, in Spanish, introduced herself and her function on the unit to Guadalupe, who consented to treatment. As a fluent Spanish speaker and knowing that the family was primarily Spanish-speaking, Gabriela continued to use Spanish throughout her work with Rosalyn's family. Almost every interaction between Suzanne, Abby, and Rosalyn's family involved using a hospital-contracted Spanish interpreter, though there were times when Gabriela was present and assisted with translation. This natural collaboration was both advantageous and tricky, as hospital policy discourages the use of coworkers as translators. This policy is to both ensure optimal communication with the assistance of trained translators and to protect untrained colleagues and patients from being caught in exchanges of complex and sensitive information.

To begin, we conducted initial assessments specific to our disciplines with shared aims to understand the family composition; their socio-cultural identities; cultural understandings related to health, hospitalization, treatment, and music; and available resources. We strove to humanize their hospital experience to promote positive coping and resilience and made efforts to connect with each other about the case to process feelings and discuss our emergent questions. *How could we support this family through their biggest and longest nightmare? How will the language barrier impact Rosalyn's care? What cultural factors would we need to consider in her care? What could we offer to make their time with her more meaningful?*

In the initial music therapy assessment, Gabriela utilized a song of kin intervention[3] involving culturally-based, parent-selected songs to foster bonding and attachment. Guadalupe was eager to play her song of kin, "Mariposita" from the series "Gallina Pintadita." While she played on the ocean disk and D Major Hapi Drum, Gabriela sought to promote a sense of containment, intimacy, and relatedness on the guitar by shifting the music to a 3/4 time signature (approximately 90 bpm) in D Major. Guadalupe became a provider for Rosalyn in music-making, so much so that she requested to play the guitar and serve as the primary music maker despite having no previous knowledge of how to play.

In that moment, Gabriela imagined how so much of Guadalupe's role as mother was taken away in this hospital setting. Most of Rosalyn's care (e.g., diaper changes, bathing, changing clothes, and feeding) was assumed by the nurses, given Rosalyn's fragile state. Gabriela readily offered her guitar to Guadalupe and facilitated music instruction using a simplified G Major chord to a Cadd9, helping her to alternate between both chords in a rubato-like 3/4 time signature. While Guadalupe played, Gabriela began to hum the song "Los Pollitos," helping to accompany her melody and reinforce her role as caregiver. It became apparent that music therapy could assist the family in developing psychotherapeutic ways to provide interactive and stimulating nurturance to Rosalyn and support mother/infant bonding.

Rosalyn was initially expected to pass quickly but when that didn't happen, Suzanne was asked to look into discharging her to a type of pediatric rehab that would be less acute than the hospital but more medically equipped than home. Unfortunately, she wasn't a candidate – she was too sick – so she continued to live in the hospital.

Continuing Bonds

As time went by, Rosalyn's family repeatedly felt disappointed by communication with the teams, as exemplified by the NICU team forgetting to notify them of her transfer between units. As the social worker, Suzanne facilitated weekly family meetings to improve communication between the family and teams, provide medical updates, and discuss next steps. These meetings typically included Guadalupe, Abuela, Jose, the PICU team, various specialty teams (including genetics, neurology, and palliative care), Abby, and an in-person Spanish translator. Suzanne and Abby sat alongside the family during tough conversations with these treatment teams and empowered them to advocate for themselves.

Having established trusting relationships, they sought out connection during these meetings by making eye contact with us when speaking to the medical team or glancing at us for reassurance while mustering the courage to ask tough questions or make requests on Rosalyn's behalf. Gabriela maintained distance from the medical discussions as she felt the room was already overcrowded and that there was adequate representation from the psychosocial team. As such, she often verbally processed the family's experiences with them following their meetings. She also wondered if doing so in their native language allowed them to access psychological processing not possible through a translator.[4]

Rosalyn's transfer to the PICU was an opportunity for the family to start fresh with a new team, but the rupture between family and medical providers was too deep to heal. The doctors could not give the family what they wanted most: to take Rosalyn home and watch her grow and develop throughout her life. Their grief manifested in anger and frustration toward the medical team which, while understandable, was unpleasant. As the psychosocial team, we had it "easier" as we were absolved of that responsibility. In response, we held space for whatever feelings were most present – including sadness, anger, guilt, and love – by utilizing reflective and empathic listening, asking open-ended questions about their feelings, and allowing for long pauses of silence.

Our interventions created a safe space for the family to bring up challenges they faced and ask for help with the resources they needed. Each time Suzanne entered Rosalyn's room, she felt unsure about what the family would want to discuss: Would they focus on her current medical care and their frustrations? Perhaps they would talk about the impact this experience had on their relationships with one another? Suzanne connected them to various resources, including forms to correct the misspelling of Rosalyn's name on her birth certificate, mental health referrals for her sisters, and financial assistance for her funeral.

Rosalyn's room, located at the end of the hallway, had little to no sunlight throughout the day. It felt dark and somber or, as Guadalupe and

Abuela described it, "Es como vivir en una celda" (It's like living in a jail cell). Abby worked with Guadalupe and Abuela to personalize her room with a pink name sign and family photos. Abby found that simple gestures often meant the most to the family, including putting Rosalyn in a new onesie or advocating for them to hold her while she was connected to many machines. Even though Rosalyn's awareness of her surroundings was suspected to be limited, Abby encouraged the family to utilize infant rattles and musical toys to engage in play. Abby felt that these interventions brought the family comfort and hope during unsettling times.

When someone lives in the hospital for six months, there are bound to be mistakes or, at the very least, unfortunate problems without great solutions. One such problem involved skin breakdown around Rosalyn's tracheostomy tube. Due to her Down syndrome, Rosalyn had a short neck and, as such, the tracheostomy tube caused skin irritation. The family expressed anger that the skin breakdown continued despite the involvement of the palliative care nurse practitioner, a wound and skin expert, and a special tube that would cause less skin damage. Another issue that upset the family was that Rosalyn cried a lot and was difficult to console. The family viewed this as discomfort and pain left untreated, but the medical team knew that children with brain damage often exhibit persistent crying and irritability, which they believed was occurring for Rosalyn.

In music therapy, Gabriela noticed that the family attempted to soothe Rosalyn using gentle touch and verbal comforting during these moments. Her work then extended to offer the family additional ways to comfort and bond with Rosalyn, once more using songs of kin.[5] The songs "Piel Canela" by Los Panchos, "Amor Eterno" by Juan Gabriel, "Yo te Esperaba" by Alejandra Guzman, and other Boleros served as the songs that accompanied Rosalyn and her family through the most difficult of times. These songs expressed their fears, desires, and innermost feelings, while offering momentary comfort and joy.

Sometimes Abby and Suzanne were present for Gabriela's music therapy sessions and were welcomed in by Abuela or Guadalupe to join in music-making. During these moments, Rosalyn's family sang while also using a range of Latine percussive instruments, including maracas, guiros, tambourines, and bongos. Gabriela often added vocal harmony to increase the aesthetic richness of the music while allowing the family to sing the song's melody, reinforcing their role as primary caregivers. Abby and Suzanne were given a handheld instrument and a tablet with the lyrics to join in singing. Gabriela visually and musically cued them to join the basic beat on their instruments to take a more supportive and complementary role to the family's music. Following the conclusion of music-making, Gabriela verbally processed with the family their experiences of musicking and relating to Rosalyn in this manner. Themes that arose dealt with grief, fear, sadness, love, and hope that they experienced as relating to Rosalyn. To this day, Abby and Suzanne remember the words to songs used during these sessions.

In addition, Guadalupe and Abuela engaged in life review with Gabriela, considering what their life would have been like if they remained in Mexico. They shared their difficult and dangerous experiences of immigrating to the United States and adapting to American society. Gabriela was often struck by how their experience in the hospital mirrored their immigration experiences; the PICU was another foreign land and they were dealing with uncertainty, much like the stories shared about immigrating.

Abby and Gabriela felt that their work with the family was very intimate. Going into Rosalyn's hospital room often felt like being invited into the family's home; they were welcomed with open arms, trust, and vulnerability. Likewise, Gabriela felt a Latine cultural connection to the family, resulting in a desire to help them navigate the cultural barriers present in the hospital. It was a countertransferential pull, reflective of moments in her childhood when serving as a translator for her mother. For Abby, this feeling of helplessness also manifested when exploring her clinical goals in Rosalyn's case, as she felt a need to give "light" through her interventions during their darkest moments. In some ways, these overextended offerings made us feel better in that we could provide or be present for the family in a way that made their horrible experience a little more bearable.

While Suzanne felt a special connection and closeness with this family, she also felt like she bore the brunt of their anger as they trusted her to share their honest feelings. Rather than creating a sense of intimacy with the family, this fueled emotional exhaustion and readiness for the case to end. However, it did not breed a sense of resentment toward Gabriela and Abby, as she was glad for them to be spared this particular source of burnout.

Legacy and Bereavement

Over time, Rosalyn's heart was getting weaker, and her ability to circulate oxygen throughout her body decreased. The family became experts in understanding her monitors, vital signs, and knowing when her oxygen saturations would dip dangerously low (i.e., a de-sat episode). During one family meeting, exhibiting a sense of acceptance, the family decided that should Rosalyn's heart stop, they did not want her to be resuscitated.

At this time, we shifted our focus on the quality of time Rosalyn's family spent together with her. We racked our brains to consider any way of turning Rosalyn's hospital room into a warm and loving space since she would likely never leave. We switched rooms to one with a calming and peaceful view and moved Rosalyn out of an infant crib and into an adult-sized bed so that her family could lay next to her.

Much like at the beginning of her life, the doctors expected that Rosalyn's time was coming to an end, but to our surprise these de-sat episodes continued and her medical status waxed and waned for months. Eventually, the medical team, feeling restless and struggling with using PICU resources toward this seemingly futile case, asked Suzanne to look into appropriate transfer options again but, this time, in a hospice setting rather than a rehabilitation center. While understandable from the perspective of limited PICU beds and the need to make space for other children, we felt there was an emotional component to the team's request – perhaps they, much like the family, were struggling with the powerlessness evoked as they bore witness to the slow demise of Rosalyn's life.

Despite the rifts and disappointments the family felt toward the hospital staff, they didn't want Rosalyn to be transferred. Instead, they wanted to stay with us, at the hospital where she lived her whole life. In many ways, we had a better understanding of Rosalyn and her family's life – and spent more time with them – over the six months than many of their close friends and community members. We had become their proxy family.

Each day we left work with uncertainty about whether Rosalyn would be in her room come the morning. Watching the suffering of Rosalyn and her family was emotionally draining. Our unstructured sessions in the room were long and mirrored the extended nature of her hospitalization. We had thoughts of wanting Rosalyn to pass away to end what seemed to be an unnecessarily prolonged suffering that she and the family were experiencing, thoughts that likely came from compassion fatigue due to continuously holding space for their grief. This fatigue manifested in physical and emotional exhaustion and was exacerbated by the burden of protecting the family from knowing this. We felt an occasional sense of dread before entering Rosalyn's room. Even though we knew our feelings were normal, we felt pangs of guilt and benefited from being able to talk this through with one another. Entering the room together helped us combat these challenges as well as feelings of emotional isolation. In that way and many others, our collaboration was essential.

During this heightened period of unknown, Abby began to offer memory-making opportunities that highlighted the family's love and commitment to Rosalyn. To celebrate her 3-month birthday, Abby offered the family a chance to have a photo session with a professional photographer in Rosalyn's room. Since Rosalyn was on a ventilator, it took creativity to fit 12 family members into her tiny room. With Rosalyn's name sign as the backdrop, Guadalupe and Abuela gently held Rosalyn while others crowded around. Gabriela joined Abby, helping to translate and serve as support. Suzanne was on vacation and felt remiss at not bearing witness to this special moment.

The family also participated in creating beautiful plaster 3D hand- and footprint molds for the family to take home. A fingerprint charm was also created into a piece of jewelry for Rosalyn's family to wear. The creation of these items served as remembrance of Rosalyn after her death, as well as bonding opportunities and lasting memories for the family.

In another example of here-and-now collaboration, when Abby needed more sets of hands, Suzanne jumped in to help. Gabriela also played music during these moments, improvising on the piano with the clinical intent to develop an overall sense of containment and holding in the sonic environment. She intentionally utilized tonal centering, musically referencing the tonalities of the machines in the room, and carefully considered the harmony, melody, dynamics, and musical structure. In addition, musical references to "Mariposita" and other songs of kin were introduced to offer comfort and predictability in the soundscape.

Given the uncertainty of Rosalyn's prognosis, Gabriela focused on facilitating additional legacy opportunities, including creating an original lullaby and recording.[6] Abuela was the originator of this song, improvising the melody and lyrics in a 4/4 time signature (approximately 54 bpm), as Gabriela musically accompanied her on the guitar:

After the session, Abuela worked on the remainder of the lyrics and shared them at their subsequent session. Her lyrics contained themes of love, hope, and gratitude to God for bringing Rosalyn into their lives. Gabriela and Abuela actively worked on integrating and adapting the lyrics to fit the melodic, chordal, and rhythmic phrasing established in the previous session. Gabriela then introduced the idea of recording Abuela's song to serve not only as a living legacy, but validation of Rosalyn's life and her family's love for her. Given that Abuela did not want to leave Rosalyn's side, the recording took place at the bedside. To record the song, Gabriela plugged her guitar and Abuela's microphone into an interface and provided headphones for them to listen to themselves actively. Beeps from machines and hospital noises were captured in the recording and not removed as Abuela liked it that way. The song, entitled "Luchando tu Estas," became their ritual song for Abuela and any family visitor.

Eventually, the decision was made to pull away as many medical interventions as possible – to "de-medicalize" Rosalyn – and try again to transfer her out of the hospital. Unfortunately, just as the family was warming to this idea and visiting different pediatric centers, Rosalyn died one morning at 2:20, surrounded by her family.

Despite having used anticipatory grief counseling to make all of the necessary referrals and arrangements in advance of her death, Suzanne was told that the family was waiting for her workday to start to see her before

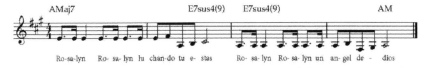

Figure 18.1 Melody and lyrics to Abeula's song. The lyrics translate to "Rosalyn, Rosalyn, fighting you are, Rosalyn, Rosalyn, an angel from god" in English.

they left the hospital. The family had questions about what would happen next, and Suzanne felt them grasping for direction and purpose as their sole focus for six months slipped away. She reviewed the arrangements they had already made and guided them on the immediate next steps. They should go home, be together as a family, and when they felt ready, identify a funeral home, and talk to the director about their wishes for Roslyn's burial.

We all cried and hugged when Gabriela and Abby were called into the room following Rosalyn's passing. It was a moment of shared grief, wherein all of the emotions, hopes, fears, memories, and experiences transcended professional roles, rendering us all humans contained within the space. While crying can be viewed as unprofessional, especially when it shifts the focus away from the family, for us it was a genuine reaction and an acknowledgment of our role as proxy family. Even in retrospect, it did not feel out of place or inappropriate for this empathetic response to occur. The family then requested to sing "Luchando tu Estas" and together, we sang it until we transported her to the morgue.

Summary

There was very little hope and optimism in this case. The fatal prognosis and the sadness of the family's desperation were felt by each of us and, arguably, drove us to extend more of ourselves than we typically would. When Rosalyn passed away, the separation from the family felt agonizingly intense, so we allowed the family to accompany us on her trip to the morgue, which was not common practice in our hospital. When further reflecting on this, we wonder if allowing them to accompany us was a response to our feelings of helplessness in how to support and sit with this family's pain while simultaneously processing our grief. We were relatively young in our careers, particularly in the medical setting, so our sense of boundaries sometimes went unchecked until we critically reflected on our work.

While this case in its entirety is unique, many elements of this case exist regularly in the pediatric hospital milieu. These include the collaborative and interdisciplinary nature of our work; the navigation of systems and structures that exist in the hospital; family-centered care as an approach to working with patients and their families; and becoming a proxy to the family due to medical circumstances. We have found feelings of helplessness and compassion fatigue to commonly arise in our clinical work due to our direct exposure to traumatic events, leaving us vulnerable to the same stressors as the individuals we are caring for. It is important to our practice to name and acknowledge these responses as they arise so we can find ways of working with and through these feelings.

The reality is that grief can be messy, unpredictable, and interwoven. From the moment Rosalyn's family learned of her second diagnosis, they began to grieve, and so too did the staff (whether we recognized it or not). Rosalyn's life in the PICU felt like a rollercoaster, including the emotional ups and downs of the family and staff, the frequent change in discharge planning, and the anticipatory grief felt by all of us as we sat with the knowledge that at some unknown point she would die. We provided emotional support and therapeutic interventions for six months to this family, knowing that it would eventually end in Rosalyn's death.

To get through the emotional hurdles of the case, we leaned on each other, finding comfort in having each other's collaboration. We gave one another a shoulder to lean on, an ear to listen to, and another perspective to understand the meaning of it all. We developed, both personally and professionally, because we trusted one another to openly and honestly reflect on our challenges, countertransferences, and clinical actions. As we developed familial bonds with Rosalyn's family, so too did we develop deep bonds with each other.

To this day, Rosalyn's family continues to attend bereavement events through the hospital and even spoke at a pediatric memorial service, where Guadalupe wrote the speech and Xiomara delivered it. Despite all the challenges and difficult feelings they experienced during Rosalyn's time in the hospital, they continue to return to us for healing and support.

Summarizing Ideas and Questions for Discussion

1. Music therapy practice may involve engagement and collaboration with interdisciplinary professionals.

    a. What are the benefits and challenges of working within an interdisciplinary team?
    b. Explain the relevance of interdisciplinary collaboration to your own career development.

2. In the hospital, providing patient- and family-centered care that addresses the unique psychological, spiritual, social, and cultural orientations and needs is vitally important.

    a. How would you embrace humanity while working with individuals who are dying?
    b. How do culturally informed values and expectations of patients and families at end-of-life influence your work consciously and subconsciously?

Notes

1 Adames, H. Y., Chavez-Dueñas, N. Y., Fuentes, M. A., Salas, S. P., & Perez-Chavez, J. G. (2014). Integration of Latino/a cultural values into palliative health care: A culture centered model. *Palliative & Supportive Care*, *12*(2), 149–157. https://doi.org/10.1017/s147895151300028x

2 Harris, D. L., & Winokuer, H. R. (2019). *Principles and practice of grief counseling.* Springer Publishing Company.

3 Loewy, J. (2015). NICU music therapy: Song of kin as critical lullaby in research and practice. *Annals of the New York Academy of Sciences*, *1337*(1), 178–185. https://doi.org/10.1111/nyas.12648

4 Tannenbaum, M., & Har, E. (2020). Beyond basic communication: The role of the mother tongue in cognitive-behavioral therapy (CBT). *The International Journal of Bilingualism: Cross-Disciplinary, Cross-Linguistic Studies of Language Behavior*, *24*(4), 881–892. https://doi.org/10.1177/1367006920902522

5 Loewy, J. (2015). NICU music therapy: Song of kin as critical lullaby in research and practice. *Annals of the New York Academy of Sciences*, *1337*(1), 178–185. https://doi.org/10.1111/nyas.12648

6 Ghetti, C. (2013). Pediatric intensive care. In J. Bradt (Ed.), *Guidelines for music therapy practice in pediatric care* (pp. 152–204). Barcelona Publishers.

Unit 5

Embracing Loss in Therapeutic Closure

Chapter 19

How It Feels to Be Free

Reflections on the Relationship Between Music and Spirituality at the End of Life

Jasmine Edwards

Abstract

Spiritual journeys with patients reflect both the patients' and music therapists' religious and spiritual historicities. These intersecting ecologies help inform the type(s) of religious and spiritual support patients are asking for and that which music therapists are equipped to provide. These shared spiritual experiences provide opportunity for interdisciplinary collaboration and compassionate movement through grief when that patient dies.

Tags: Therapeutic Closure; Therapeutic Relationship

The definition of therapeutic closure I learned in school lives in an aspirational, but often unrealistic, space. As both an undergraduate and graduate music therapy student, I was given articles and heard lectures on how and when to effectively terminate services. In my time as a professional, I have been called to confront my own ideas about what "good" closure looks like. I have been humbled by the reality that there is an endless number of variables that can impact one's opportunity of closure, or lack thereof. More recently, I have navigated the experience of a therapeutic relationship ending due to a patient's death. In this case, I will share my experience of therapeutic closure after several months of working in a pediatric hematology and oncology unit with a 15-year-old girl named Anna. I worked with Anna over the span of 3 months, and our work together ended when she passed away.

Anna was born and raised in Jamaica with her family. After receiving a cancer diagnosis and undergoing several medical procedures, she and her family came to New York for a chemotherapy treatment that was not available to her at home. I remember hearing her cancer described as "horrific" by one of our attending doctors; her disease had progressed rapidly and aggressively, and she presented with a large mass in her jaw that impacted her ability to speak and eat, causing her discomfort and pain. Before her

DOI: 10.4324/9781003123798-25

arrival in New York, Anna had a gastrostomy tube and a tracheostomy, as both her ability to eat orally and breathe were impacted by the location and size of her tumor. Anna was often accompanied at bedside by her mother and father, and her maternal grandmother and several other family members lived locally in New York City, where the pediatric hospital was located. Anna and her family identified as Christian; Anna shared that she loved attending church, and her family often prayed together at bedside. She loved to make art, read, and was skillful in writing in script and needlepoint.

Situating Myself

Before I tell the story of my time working with Anna, I must first share components of my sociocultural location, lived experience, and clinical training that affected our work and influenced the nature of our therapeutic relationship. I identify as a Black and mixed-race woman, while holding the notion that being mixed-race is a part of the Black experience.

On my father's side, I am a characteristic combination of Oklahoma history, with lineages that include Black, Indigenous, and white.[1,2] On my mother's side, I am Lebanese and Portuguese. When I have worked with Black patients and their families in the past, matters of race often enter the clinical space, be it through the explicit labeling of shared racial identity or a feeling of comfort and easy rapport. I have had patients and families disclose incidents of racism that they experienced in the medical setting, often coupled with nods in my direction along the lines of: "You know what I mean, you've seen it too, or maybe you have experienced it yourself." Some of my sessions have involved discussing certain cultural norms within the Black community, and the specific function and significance of certain kinds of music. And still, as a Black music therapist who has often worked with Black patients, I am obligated to enact my own cultural humility, acknowledging that there is indeed a collective experience of being Black but also immense difference and nuance within the Black cultural identity. An important hallmark of radical, justice-minded, anti-oppressive practice is openness to the individual's unique experience of a specific manifestation of culture.

I was raised in a Catholic household, singing in a church choir for much of my life. As I reflect on the evolution of my identity as a musician, my love of music and singing was born within this religious context. I now identify more broadly as a spiritual person but can deeply understand the function of music in religion as a means of elevating the experience of worship. More tangibly, my musical memory is still filled with hymns and contemporary Christian songs that I sang for many years.

My theoretical orientation is grounded in humanistic psychology, influenced by my initial graduate clinical training as a fieldwork student at the Nordoff-Robbins Center for Music Therapy.[3] I am a trained Austin Vocal Psychotherapist[4] and a primary vocalist, so I believe strongly in the relational capacities of singing and the ability for the voice to illuminate internal experiences. As a music therapist who has worked in a medical setting, I strive to meet my patient's most pressing needs in the moment, be it pain management, sleep support, self-expression, adjustment, socialization, and so on. I hold the reality that much can change within a person's experience of their body, as well as the overall flow of the hospital, within a given day. In my role, I worked to be flexible to the ever-changing tempo of the hospital setting.

I still identify as a new clinician with about six years of experience as a board-certified music therapist, including two years of full-time graduate study. When I met and began working with Anna, I was working as a full-time music therapist in a medical pediatric setting. I started working in this role in March 2020, just as the threat of COVID-19 became very real and everyday life was significantly disrupted. In addition, I was starting this new job in New York City, which at the time was the epicenter in the US of the global pandemic. I was thrust into a state of emergency, attempting to simultaneously cope and continue providing care as fear and uncertainty colored my every move. I have since left this position as I pursue full-time doctoral study, but as I reflect on my time there, I can see how profoundly my experience was impacted by the reality of COVID-19, alongside my own emotional hardships at the hands of the virus. Though I met Anna after a year of working in my position, in the aftermath of that turbulent orientation, I still struggled to feel grounded in the care team and my practice with medically fragile individuals. I felt I was playing catch-up to the realities of providing services in a pediatric medical setting.

Finally, it is germane to acknowledge my understanding of death and dying as I entered a therapeutic relationship with Anna. I am typically avoidant of situations that involve talking or thinking about death. It elicits feelings of fear and uncertainty that I often resolve to ameliorate through avoidance. Because of this, I was almost reluctant toward my initial referral to work with Anna because I knew I would be forced to confront my own discomfort with death and dying. Upon receiving this referral from the floor's child life specialist, I remember thinking: *How could I be in the room and form a relationship with someone who I knew was dying?*

Meeting Anna in Her Music

The first time I met Anna, her mother was moving about the room, changing the sheets while Anna reclined on the pullout chair that her mother typically slept on overnight. I introduced myself, explaining my role within the care team, before asking her if she liked or listened to music. Anna nodded enthusiastically and motioned for me to sit beside her. She pulled out her tablet and began to play a gospel song called "Mercy Said No" by Cece Winans. We sat there, side by side, as I watched her close her eyes and sway subtly to the beat of the music. After the song ended, I offered some reflection around the meaningful nature of the song and expressed gratitude for her sharing it.

Internally, the saliency of the chorus stood out to me, particularly the soothing petition to not be afraid. It called me to wonder about Anna's experience of fear around leaving home and traveling to a new country to receive treatment, along with the realities of hospitalization and her diagnosis. I was beginning to understand that her faith provided an antidote for that uncertainty. I also was struck by the themes of gratitude, thanking Jesus, and acknowledging the protection of Mercy. These lyrics seemed to offer comfort and solace to any listener who grappled with hardship and strife, and it appeared as though Anna connected with that potential meaning.

Anna was able to nod and write to me on her tablet, affirming many of my gentle verbal offerings and questions, as speaking was painful at this point in her medical journey. As this was our first meeting, I was still assessing Anna's relationship to music and was not certain of her understanding of her diagnosis. This held me back from engaging her in song discussion or analysis, despite the meaning the song took on for me given my knowledge of her story. I embodied the role of "witness" in the session, remaining open to and present for whatever Anna wanted to share with me.

Anna continued to play song after song, and it felt as though she was eager for connection, relatedness, and sharing of this part of herself. Her choices – "Carry Your Candle," "Jesus, Take the Wheel," and "Take Me to the King" – communicated a strong connection to her faith, and possibly the use of her Christian identity to make sense of or find meaning within her current hardship. So many of the themes present in these song choices revolved around trusting in and submitting to the will of God. I remember thanking Anna for sharing her music with me and asked if she felt it would be beneficial for us to continue working together in music therapy sessions. She excitedly nodded, "Yes."

After meeting Anna and experiencing her desire for connection and sharing, as well as noting the potential benefits of music therapy in her care, my fear moved aside and in its place emerged a warm feeling of care. I longed to show up for Anna and offer music in a way that was beneficial to her. And still, I recognized that sadness lingered. I was forced to face the ambiguity of my feelings, with multiple emotions existing all at once. I was entering into what felt like uncharted territory by establishing a therapeutic relationship with someone who I knew, from the start, was terminally ill. While I felt energized in music therapy's potential role in her care, my own self-preservation instincts started to kick in. *How could I handle getting to know a person who was dying?*

A few days later, Anna's nurse requested I follow up after she had reported a high pain score. Our second session was grounded in music-assisted relaxation, during which I entrained to her respiratory rate through soft finger picking on the guitar and integrated lyrics and melodic lines from some of her preferred song selections. I noticed that Anna appeared to calm as the session progressed. As her eyes closed and body started to relax, she appeared to resist sleeping while I was in the room. I shared that falling asleep could be a worthy and important goal during our time together, as sleep can be so challenging to obtain in the hospital setting. Anna nodded, I resumed playing, and she gradually fell asleep.

During our third session, our hospital's pediatric chaplain, Stacy, entered the room during a break in the music. Stacy and I were often a part of the same interdisciplinary team meetings and frequently provided care for the same patients. We had collaborated in the past; I offered family-preferred music during several baptisms that happened within the hospital, and it was not uncommon for us to refer patients to one another. I knew that Anna strongly identified with her Christian faith and had been frequently meeting with Stacy for spiritual support, and an easy rapport appeared to exist between them. As Stacy checked in with Anna and me, my intuition inspired me to ask Anna if she would ever be interested in a co-treatment session with Stacy and me. I wondered if this collaboration could make way for additional processing of her selected songs and connect her more deliberately to two of her identifiable resources: music and faith. Both Stacy and Anna were agreeable to this offering, and we soon moved into a new stage in our work together.

The Birth of "Bedside Church"

Stacy and I coordinated the next time we met with Anna to offer a session. Because of our pre-existing working relationship, along with Anna's openness, the co-treatment naturally emerged. I offered improvised guitar music to support our collective transition to a space of prayer and reflection. Stacy read Bible passages Anna had indicated in their previous sessions together, one of which was Psalm 23. After Stacy finished reading, there was a quiet pause and she invited me to play music after the psalm was read to invite meditation on the words. My memory brought me back to my musical experiences in both church and school choir, including learning a choral arrangement that featured the text of this very psalm. Here, I was pulling both from the musical skills and repertoire I acquired during my music therapy training and as a church musician, and from my musical identity that existed long before I knew what music therapy was. I used a C and Fmaj7 chord to create a holding pattern and improvised on the text, alluding to the melody that still lived in my musical memory:

> *The Lord is my shepherd, I shall not want.*
> *He maketh me to lie down in green pastures: He leadeth me beside the*
> *   still waters . . .*
> *Surely goodness and mercy shall follow me all the days of my life: and*
> *   I will dwell in the*
> *house of the Lord forever.*

The selection of this psalm felt significant and illuminating, showing Anna's ability to still have trust in her faith, in tandem with humility and gratitude in the face of profoundly adverse circumstances. Despite my spiritual identity having shifted between the first time I sang this verse in church to this moment of re-creation in music therapy, I felt a connection to the text. I found these two vital but previously distinct aspects of my identity interfacing in this moment of liminality. I felt moved by the gentleness and sanctity of this verse as I sang the words, struck by the sweetness of the notion we are never truly alone, that "goodness" is sure to follow us as we move through the world, and true peace and contentment are attainable. It was striking to me how Anna, who had every reason to be angry with her circumstance, chose to sit in a place of grace and gratitude for her life and her relationship with God.

When the improvisation ended, Anna requested that Stacy offer a prayer. Anna asked her to pray for her family, her nurses, and us, as her care providers. She asked for relief from her pain and that the procedure she was having later that day would go smoothly. Over time, I noticed that Anna almost exclusively prayed for others before herself. As Stacy and Anna closed their eyes, held hands, and entered prayer, I played the guitar softly with a Catholic mass serving as a guiding point of reference. I remembered how music was used in the mass to hold a sacred moment, making it feel even more special and reverent. As the session ended, Anna started to show signs of fatigue, so we quietly transitioned out of the space.

I paused with Stacy outside of the room, my eyes filled with tears. I was overwhelmed by the circumstances. Stacy, who had been a dear and dependable colleague and collaborator, reflected and validated the sadness that followed a session that felt so profound and heavy. I was flooded with different emotions, all existing within me at once: safety in working alongside a coworker, profound sadness for Anna and her family, heartbreak for the fact that her life was ending at such a young age, gratitude to witness and be a part of such a vulnerable moment, and humbled by music's capacity to support and even elevate moments of worship. In a later conversation with Stacy, she shared the following when reflecting on how the sessions functioned and how our modalities interacted with one another:

> In my work, we're always reminded that if someone wants to go to explore the "wilderness of their soul," that you go there with them and stay as long as they want to stay there – but you have to help "bring them back up to the surface," at least a little, before leaving the room. That's the closure for each visit. Otherwise, they're stuck out there by themselves. So, in this case – we followed her brave lead, and explored her suffering and her experience with illness, but we also made sure to "bring her back up" at the end through closing prayer/music. Both parts (the exploration and the soothing) were so important and validating.

Over the next few weeks, Stacy and I continued to offer co-treatment sessions to Anna. We started to playfully and affectionately refer to our time together as "bedside church," as we were indeed doing our best to bring the sanctity of a religious service to the hospital room. Anna's mother was often at bedside, and Anna frequently invited her to select songs or join in prayer. One such song suggestion was "His Eye Is on the Sparrow," which I offered to support a moment of prayer. After the sessions ended, Anna would often ask me to stay in the room after Stacy left and continue providing music to support her relaxation and, sometimes, help her to transition to sleep. Our sessions moving forward, however, were not always marked by supporting rest and relaxation. Other times, they were focused on self-expression, highlighting Anna's religious and cultural identity, and bolstering her sense of self. She continued to share her musical interests with me, specifically several Jamaican gospel songs for which she and her mother would often offer context and history.

In one such session, Anna requested a children's worship song called "God Made Me Special." When I shared that I did not know this song, Anna sang it for me. After weeks of her being unable to use her voice, it was so moving to hear her express herself through singing. Her trach was "capped" or closed at this point in her care, which allowed her to eat and talk more easily. I remember feeling excited about what adding another medium for Anna's emotional expression could mean for our work together. Anna then asked if I could sing the song, so I did my best to emulate the melody line she modeled. When I had first entered the room, she had proudly showed me a poem she had written with her child life specialist in acrostic style, with her name spelled out and a list of attributes that started with each letter. I incorporated these adjectives into the song structure:

> *God made Anna special*
> *Made her **Awesome***
> *And **Nice***
> *Made her **Nurturing***
> *and **Artistic***

A smile crept across Anna's face, and her soft laughter warmed the room. Her mother looked lovingly at her daughter and offered a knowing nod before saying that she did indeed possess all these wonderful attributes, and many more. After the session, I reflected on how, somehow, in the moment, I dispelled my focus on addressing her symptomology and instead centered on highlighting aspects of who she was as a whole person, before and outside of her illness. I hoped that this moment communicated to both Anna and her mom that I both saw and valued the full, dynamic person that Anna was.

In the next few sessions, Anna, Stacy, and myself found a groove in this integration of music and spiritual support. I would work in real time to identify songs that reflected the Bible verses Anna selected. Anna continued to use her voice more and more, now reading the verses herself instead of asking Stacy to do so. I pulled from my own lexicon of Christian music that I developed over years of church choir experience. It was a strange synchronicity that I happened to be Anna's music therapist at this point in time, with my specific lived experiences and knowledge of music aligning with her faith, a major resource of hers playing an essential role during her health journey.

In one of our last sessions together, Anna introduced me to the song "Made a Way" by Travis Greene. I was not familiar with the song but vowed to "do my homework" and learn the song for her. In the next session, Anna was reporting some pain and was agreeable to my offering of music to help her relax and calm. I offered a modified version of "Made a Way," slowing the tempo and entraining Anna's breathing. She closed her eyes and appeared to fall asleep. I quietly packed up my things before I heard Anna say: "That's what I needed today."

While I was profoundly moved by Anna's connection to her faith throughout our work together, I cannot say that my relationship with Christianity necessarily shifted or returned to what it once was. However, I did feel a deepening of my understanding of and respect for how people lean on faith as a source of strength. I witnessed Anna use Bible verses to explore the complicated reality of her own illness. I witnessed her family connect through joining together in collective prayer. I witnessed quiet meditation when worship music entered the space. I was continually awed by Anna's ability to experience peace and garner power in the face of such profound adversity. Despite my own movement away from Christianity, my experiences played an important role in terms of the strength of connection to and affinity for Anna, as witnessing her use her faith as a resource resonated with me deeply.

Anna's Way

In the final month of her hospitalization, palliative care became involved in Anna's care and explored several discharge options with her family. The decision was made that Anna would be discharged home to her extended family's residence while receiving hospice services. Within our Child Life and Creative Arts Therapy Department, we often acknowledge a patient's discharge after a lengthy hospitalization with a song, signs, cards, and other gifts to support the patient's transition back home. Anna was agreeable to the idea of a discharge parade. She often would express gratitude to the team members who cared for her and identified this as an opportunity for her to say goodbye to the folks she had come to know. She requested a song be played but asked that her mother pick it. Her mother, who had been present for our last session, quickly requested "Made a Way," and said, "Because God did make a way. He brought us here, where Anna could get the care that she needed."

On the day of discharge, nurses, doctors, residents, child life specialists, creative arts therapists, and front desk workers gathered to send Anna off with well wishes. I played "Made a Way" as staff members clapped and sang along. Anna's mom became tearful, expressing gratitude for the care that Anna received here. Although I knew that this was likely the last time I would see Anna, I could not bring myself to fully sit with that reality. I felt emotionally frozen by the heavy permanence of loss, and my predisposition to avoid truly engaging with the topic of death kicked in. I focused solely on the here-and-now, which was helpful to remain present in this moment of care and community, but also protected me from having to ponder about what was next.

On Monday of the following week, Stacy texted me early in the morning saying that Anna had been admitted through the emergency department and asked if I wanted to go and see her and her family together. I reminded her that I was not in on Mondays, as I followed a Tuesday through Saturday schedule at the hospital, but I had already begun to make assumptions about what this admission meant. I contemplated my own boundaries. *Should I ask not to be contacted about patient matters when I am off site? But are there exceptions? Surely this would be the exception?* Despite my best efforts, I spent the day wondering about what was going on and resolved that I would be able to see Anna and her family the next day and assess how music could be most helpful to them in that moment.

My boundaries continued to be tested the following morning when I woke up to a few texts that contained "sorry" and other condolences from my coworkers who knew I worked closely with Anna. I was flooded with a number of emotions: confusion about what exactly happened and how her family was coping, overwhelmed that I did not consent to hear this news at this time, profound sadness for Anna, and my grief. As a student, boundaries between the personal and professional had been presented to me as a crucial professional mechanism, yet in this moment, it became abundantly clear that it is not always so easy to "leave work at work."

A part of me wished I had heard this news at the hospital, which had become a physical, external representation of my accustomed compartmentalization of intense emotional material encountered in my role. And still, because many things can exist and be true at the same time, I wished I could have been there for Anna and her family in her last moments. I felt guilt for not being present and struggled to accept the reality of something I did not witness firsthand. I wished that I could have offered music to her and her family if it would have been at all helpful. In this emotional reaction, though, I had to challenge myself and consider: *Is that what the family would have needed or is it what I needed?* My connection to Anna and her story brought my personal values and professional boundaries into direct conflict. It's hard for me to say whether I wished I'd heard this news in a different way, but this grappling did help me to understand my emotional response more deeply and led me to search for self-care measures to help me move through it.

"But . . . How Do You Deal With All the Sadness?"

In the weeks that led up to Anna's passing, I asked my coworkers and supervisor alike: "How do you cope with witnessing sad cases?" I was met with examples of self-care practices and rituals, such as going for a long walk after work, meditating, and treating yourself to a nice meal. In need of space to process this patient loss, I and several members of the team who cared for Anna gathered in the park one afternoon to talk about her, listen to music, and create mandalas. I felt grounded in the process of artmaking and comforted by the community. Our time together showed me that others were experiencing this ambiguous mixture of sadness for the loss alongside gratitude for having known Anna and bearing witness to the person she was.

When I posed to my supervisor the question of how to cope, he shared that there is solace to be found in identifying my function in the patient's care and grounding myself in that. It was comforting to look back on my time working with Anna, and to recognize that we had many meaningful moments together. I watched music bring her rest and respite and elevate her experience of worship. I witnessed a young person express genuine thoughtfulness and care for others, even as she faced immense adversity. I saw her family shower her with love and prayer and constantly highlight her specialness, the gift that she was in their lives. I worked alongside other healthcare workers, whose hearts were stirred by both the tragedy, as well as the resiliency.

I made a commitment to engage in self-care, taking long walks, listening to music, and calling friends. And still, the sadness of Anna's story lingered, and I found myself longing for closure around our time together and the music that existed between us. I started to explore what a ritual for closure could look like for me, pondering how I could move through feelings that came with the witnessing of traumatic circumstances as well as my own grief experience. It struck me that I could forget that music remains available to me as well for my care and healing, so I decided to use my own resource of music to help me reach the closure I sought.

At the end of that week, I sat in my office as I finished the workday and made intentional space to make music. I closed my eyes and checked in with what I was feeling, thinking about what song I felt could encapsulate those feelings. A song came to my mind that I felt contained lyrical content that Anna herself could have sung or felt. The song speaks of freedom, wondering what it would be and feel like, as well as longing for a different life and circumstance. While the singer longs for a freedom she does not possess, she expresses already knowing of its sweetness. I wondered if Anna felt that freedom within the trust she had in her faith, or if she now had freedom from her pain and suffering. I heard myself in these words, a longing to give and do more, feeling at the mercy of things I could not control.

I felt called to play "I Wish I Knew How It Would Feel to Be Free" in the style of Nina Simone at the Montreux Jazz Festival in 1976.[5] I am regularly transfixed by a moment toward the end of the performance where Simone pauses and gazes ahead, before launching into an improvisation. The text she sings here contains hope, resiliency, and imagining. I sang this part, as I felt it encapsulated the way Anna carried herself and the emotions she stirred in others, including myself. I imagined Anna singing or feeling these lyrics that captured an innate knowing, deep trust and safety in her faith, and true freedom. Singing this brought her into the room with me, almost as if it was the first time we met, sitting side by side, and sharing in music.

Summarizing Ideas and Questions for Discussion

1. Opportunities for therapeutic closure may be impacted by several scenarios, depending on the setting that a music therapist works within.

    a. How can you create or co-create a treatment plan that prioritizes the needs of the patient/client in terms of terminating services?

    b. How can you interrogate your own ideas of what "good termination" looks like?

2. Some clinical cases lead us to reflect on thoughts and experiences related to religion and spirituality and how those might impact or enter into the therapeutic space.

    a. What are the religious and spiritual traditions and beliefs you bring with you? What are your relationships with those traditions and beliefs?

    b. How might these traditions and beliefs be a resource in your practice? How might these traditions and beliefs potentially introduce harm into the therapeutic space?

Notes

1 I have made the intentional decision to not capitalize white in adherence with Associated Press' recommendation (Nguyễn & Pendleton, 2020). I agree with their suggestion that capitalizing white is reminiscent of the ways in which whiteness and the agenda of white supremacy has been historically weaponized and enacted. Also, I am using white in reference to my own lineage and identity, and using a lowercase letter, from my vantage point, allows me to address the reality of part of my ancestry that likely exists as a result of profound power imbalance. Nguyễn, A. T., & Pendleton, M. (2020). *Recognizing race in language: Why we capitalize "Black" and "White".* Center for the Study of Social Policy. https://cssp.org/2020/03/recognizing-race-in-language-why-we-capitalize-black-and-white/
2 Daniszewski, J. (2020, July 20). *Why we will lowercase white.* Associated Press, The Definitive Source. https://blog.ap.org/announcements/why-we-will-lowercase-white
3 Nordoff, P., & Robbins, C. (2007). *Creative music therapy: A guide to fostering clinical musicianship* (2nd ed.). Barcelona Publishers.
4 Austin, D. (2008). *The theory and practice of vocal psychotherapy: Songs of the self.* Jessica Kingsley Publishers.
5 TransatlanticMoments (2013, January 16). *Nina Simone – I wish I knew how it would feel to be free* (Montreux 1976). YouTube. Retrieved October 8, 2021, from www.youtube.com/watch?v=-sEP0-8VAow

Chapter 20

Clinical Termination and Emotional Closure

Two Sides of the Same Coin

Anthony Borzi

Abstract

In long-term care with hospitalized children, music therapists are often invited into intimate spaces with families that lead to deep and meaningful connections. Closure with those intimate spaces becomes complicated when death precipitates clinical termination as opposed to more pre-determined clinical processes. Processing closure from such situations requires thoughtful care, self-awareness, and reflexivity to help the music therapist move forward with insight and perspective.

Tags: Therapeutic Closure; Therapeutic Relationship

Content warning: infant death

As a student learning about music therapy, the treatment process appeared simple: receive a referral, conduct an assessment, and design a treatment plan. Ongoing assessment and documentation of a patient's progress toward set goals inform the implementation of the plan, and eventually services are terminated at an appropriate time. Everything seemed clear-cut and well-defined until I started working within the process. It was there I came to understand that the treatment process is not static or linear, but something alive and dynamic. There are intricacies that sometimes cannot be taught and instead must be learned through experience. However, there was one step that often felt elusively ambiguous, and that was termination.

During my pre-internship clinical experiences, termination was always pre-determined because of the time-bound constraints of an academic semester. It was never something that was achieved organically, but instead was a pre-planned task done out of necessity when there was no more time to do the work. As I continued through my internship and into my initial years as a professional,

DOI: 10.4324/9781003123798-26

the nuances of termination became clearer as I gained more diverse clinical experiences. In my current role as a music therapist in the neonatal intensive care unit (NICU), there are four main reasons for termination of services:

(1) A patient discharges or transfers to another hospital
(2) Services are no longer deemed appropriate
(3) The established treatment goals have been achieved
(4) A patient transfers out of the NICU, and I do not have the capacity within my caseload to continue following them.

I have also come to experience death as a means of clinical termination. Working in an intensive care unit, especially in a level IV NICU, patients are often critically ill and require complex medical care. Level IV NICUs are equipped with various levels of respiratory support and have surgical specialists on staff, which allow them to provide the highest level of care to patients and families.[1] Because of their acute, complex medical needs, it is not uncommon for the patients I work with to succumb to their conditions and die.

This case outlines the musical journey I shared with Joshua and his family over the course of multiple admissions, and how Joshua's death became a means of clinical termination. I will also explore how practicing from a family-centered lens allowed me to develop a role within the family unit, and how seeking emotional closure within this role has become a powerful learning experience for me as a clinician.

Theoretical and Cultural Positioning

Within family-centered music therapy, there are three paradigms from which I often practice.[2] In the first paradigm, the patient is the center of the therapeutic process. While members of their family may be present and participate during a session, it is not contingent upon the trajectory of care. Instead, family members may act as a source of information and are often viewed as the "expert" on the patient. In this paradigm, patients and caregivers may be seen separately to focus on individual goals. This is typically where the family-centered care model is situated.

The second paradigm centers dyadic (one caregiver and one child) or triadic (two caregivers and one child) relationships in the therapeutic process. Participation from the family member(s) is imperative in the planning and achieving of goals. The music therapist utilizes their own relationship with each member of the dyad or triad to facilitate or guide change within a session. The entire family unit is the focal point in the third paradigm, and participation from each member of the family is vital to moving through the therapeutic process. The clinical focus in this paradigm is on the family system rather than an individual or singular relationship.

Each of these paradigms were present in my work with Joshua and his family. At times, I worked individually with Joshua, while other times,

I worked individually with his mother, Candace. Sometimes I worked within the dyadic relationships of Joshua and Candace or Joshua and his father, Justin, and other times I worked with the entire family unit. My role within each of these relationships functioned differently at various points throughout Joshua's hospitalizations.

Our diverse cultural intersections played an important role in how the therapeutic process unfolded. Joshua is multiracial, Candace is a woman of color, and Justin is white. During our initial interactions, I worked to be aware as a white male of the power dynamics between Candace and myself, and her views of the healthcare system and her place within it.[3] It was also important to consider how Candace and Justin's lived experiences as an interracial couple may influence the way in which they interact with others. Joshua's parents, although close to me in age, lived and grew up in different regions of the country than me. My experiences, values, and beliefs likely differed from those of Joshua's parents due to our different regional upbringings.[4] As a single, unmarried, and childless gay man, I was in a different place in my life than this married, heteronormative couple navigating what it meant to love and care for their often critically ill child within the context of their own relationship. While I may be able to sympathize with their situation, I can never truly understand the magnitude of loving and losing a child. While not a comprehensive list, these were the most prevalent intersections between me, Joshua, and his parents to reflect upon when preparing this case.

Meeting Joshua and His Parents

Joshua was born at 38 weeks' gestation, and was diagnosed with gastroschisis, a condition that develops in utero where an opening in the fetus's abdominal wall causes the bowel to develop outside of the body.[5] Joshua transferred to the NICU for an intestinal rehabilitation consult after developing short gut syndrome at his birth hospital because of the gastroschisis. Short gut occurs when a large portion of a patient's intestine does not function normally.[6] Over the course of his stay in the NICU, Joshua was diagnosed with liver failure, and it was determined he would need a multi-organ transplant.

Three months into his admission, I received a consult for Joshua from a child life specialist in the NICU to provide developmentally appropriate engagement and family support. Before I had the chance to follow up with the referral, Joshua was transferred to the gastrointestinal floor for further intestinal rehabilitation and preparation for his transplant surgery. It was here that I first met Joshua and Candace. Shortly after an initial rapport-building session with Candace, Joshua was briefly discharged before his second admission, which lasted 247 days. It was during this admission that most of my clinical work with Joshua and his family occurred.

During our first meeting, Candace expressed an interest in music therapy as something to occupy her time while she waited for Joshua's transplant surgery. When I met with Candace at the start of Joshua's second admission, I experienced her infectious optimism, unwavering determination, and devout faith for the first time. She explained to me that she believed "Everything happens on Joshua's time," and prayed that his time on Earth would include a transplant. Throughout our conversation, Candace shared her experience with the hospital system, expressing appreciation for the providers she encountered, and gratitude for the institution giving her hope for the future. She also expressed wanting to find a way to share Joshua's story with others so that he could be a source of inspiration for families experiencing similar medical journeys.

After several discussions and email exchanges about how we could address these goals in music therapy, Candace decided she wanted to rewrite the song "Get Back Up Again" from the movie *Trolls*. The song was from Joshua's favorite movie and encompassed the positivity and optimism she valued, and she already had several lyric ideas. With minimal assistance from me, Candace wrote lyrics imagining Joshua's firsthand account of his hospitalization and her hopes for his upcoming surgery. Once the lyrics were finalized, we met to record her singing along to a backtrack I created with her guidance, including Joshua's heartbeat and the voices of several members of his primary care team:

> *I really know God can do it*
> *'Cause they're all praying for me*
> *I know somewhere a little angel*
> *Will give the best gift that's perfect for me*
> *And bless my body with new organs*
> *How great will life be?*
>
> *Looking up at the ceiling tile, so boring and plain*
> *And there's another "hi"*
> *Well, isn't that a super fantastic sign*
> *It's gonna be a fantastic day*
> *Such marvelousness it's gonna bring*
> *Got a plan full of crazy things I'm gonna wing*
> *And I'm ready to take on everything*
> *Hooray!*
>
> *An OR surgery around the corner*
> *Just waiting on a transplant to make me feel okay*
>
> *Hey!*
> *Today's a lucky day*
> *Soon a transplant will come my way*
> *And if you think, think about it*
> *I get to start my life again*
> *Oh, once the right organs come along*
> *I know I'll come out* [redacted] *strong*

'Cause if you think, think about it, I will pick back up again
Whoa oh oh oh oh, pick back up again, whoa oh oh oh oh

I'm babbling along, I've got confidence
Liver, colon, intestines I think that's most of it
And I haven't been this excited since
I met my last nurse friend!

I'm off on this remarkable adventure
Just sitting in my boppy
What if my life is all at stake?
Is this more than my body can take?
No! I can't think that way
'Cause I know that I'm really gonna be okay

Hey!
Today's a lucky day
Soon a transplant will come my way
And if you think, think about it
I get to start my life again
Oh, once the right organs come along
I know I'll come out [redacted] *strong*
'Cause if you think, think about, I will pick back up again
Whoa oh oh oh oh, pick back up again, whoa oh oh oh oh
'Cause if you think, think about it, think, think about it
I will pick back up again

Candace explained that she chose the phrase "pick back up again" to represent her hope that Joshua's surgery was just a small detour that would not define his life.

Following his transplant surgery, I was able to witness Joshua's personality blossom. Candace frequently teased me that Joshua would "play possum" when I walked into the room, which she attributed to his stubbornness. During our musical play sessions, we explored Joshua's tactile, timbral, and song preferences, which Joshua made very clear over time. There were many instances of trial and error that ended with Joshua throwing an instrument out of his crib that didn't fit his preference. Other times he would refuse to touch an instrument altogether despite multiple cues and constant encouragement from Justin, Candace, or me. However, through these trials, we discovered Joshua had a significant response to music. This was evident in his smiling, laughing, and babbling along to upbeat songs, and his almost immediate relaxation and transition to sleep when the music slowed. These play sessions laid the foundation for trust to build between Joshua's parents and me as we introduced him to music together.

As our mutual understanding of one another grew, I began to notice Candace and I had songs that became staples during our sessions together, such as "Down by the Bay," "How Far I'll Go," and "I Wanna Dance with Somebody (Who Loves Me)." These songs served as anchors in sessions, and we would return to them time and time again because of their clinical versatility: at times they would be upbeat movement songs to ensure Joshua would not fall asleep, and other times they were slowed down into a lullaby style so that Joshua could relax at the conclusion of sessions. Music was something that played a vital role in Candace's and Justin's life, and they were excited to see the joy it brought to Joshua's as well.

As time went on, Joshua began to experience complications related to his surgery. The cells from his transplanted organs began attacking his body's cells, a condition called graft-versus-host disease.[7] He was also diagnosed with autoimmune hemolytic anemia, which occurs when the body's immune system creates antibodies that attack red blood cells, creating a deficiency.[8] I noticed that, as Joshua grew sicker, Candace and Justin increased their requests to hold or pause services. I believe this was not because they were unfamiliar with the benefits of music therapy for pain management or relaxation. Instead, they had grown to value and cherish the joy Joshua displayed during active music therapy sessions. Seeing Joshua interacting with and enjoying the music was seen as a sign of wellness at this point in their journey; during a later admission, Candace referenced Joshua's laughing, babbling, smiling, and playing in music experiences as him "living again."

My Developing Role With the Family

Even though I did not consistently have music therapy sessions with Joshua or his parents, I found it important to still be present and available. I maintained weekly check-ins, during which Candace or Justin would update me on any changes in Joshua's medical status, and I would provide a listening ear when tensions emerged with any staff and treatment team members. Despite the many medical complications and setbacks in care Joshua experienced, Candace maintained her optimism and continued her mantra that "everything happens on Joshua's time." We were all just along for the ride.

Joshua had numerous subsequent admissions that ranged in length from days to months. I had varying levels of interaction with Joshua, Candace, and Justin during these admissions due to many contributing factors. During shorter admissions it was often difficult to catch Joshua due to the size and acuity of my caseload. Additionally, Joshua's medical status often meant that various staff members were trying to see him at the same time, so scheduling and coordinating became difficult. Though we had inconsistent interactions during these shorter admissions, my relationship with Joshua and his parents always felt maintained and unaffected.

One thing that became clear reflecting on this period of our work was that termination was never truly addressed, at least not in the traditional sense. Instead, our relationship and the treatment process were put on hold between admissions. Candace and I often joked upon discharge: "See you once Joshua decides it has been too long since he's seen his friends [at the hospital]." Because of this approach, I found it was easier to pick back up where we had left off at the beginning of each admission. Conversely, this approach made it more difficult to restart services when Joshua constantly came back sicker and less able to musick the way his parents expected and wanted.

Approaching and Moving Through Joshua's Death

Over the next few months, Joshua's medical status continued to worsen. Within four months, Joshua experienced three lengthy hospitalizations and two strokes before being admitted to the hospital for continued decompensations. I made several attempts early in the admission to see Joshua, but because of his medical status he was often sleeping, or his parents opted to hold services so he could rest. Eventually, test results would confirm Joshua's liver had suffered major injury because of his medication requirements. Joshua needed a new liver, but due to his critical status and ongoing complications, he was not a candidate to relist for a liver transplant. Candace and Justin maintained faith in a miracle, opting to pursue aggressive treatment so long as Joshua continued to remain comfortable. It was beginning to become clear that Joshua's death was imminent; it was no longer a matter of if he would die, but when.

To best support Justin and Candace where they were in their journey of recognition and acceptance, I decided to adjust my clinical approach. I transitioned from focusing on developmental support and milestone maintenance to providing opportunities for family support, memory-making, and legacy building. Although we had previously recorded Joshua's heartbeat as part of Candace's songwriting project, I re-introduced heartbeat recordings to Candace and Justin. They agreed and quickly identified a number of songs that were meaningful to them as a family to pair with Joshua's heartbeat. Joshua's grandparents and other extended family members were present at the bedside during the recording process. Candace, Justin, and I shared stories and memories of our previous sessions together, and Joshua's grandma reflected on her own musical journey with her grandson. Joshua's grandmother had been teaching herself the ukulele, and as his interest in music became evident, she wanted to incorporate it as part of their nightly ritual. Daily video calls quickly turned into nightly bedtime routines of grandma singing lullabies while accompanying herself on the ukulele. Music had become an experience Joshua's entire family valued. At the end of my visit, Candace and Justin requested that I come back the next day so that everyone could make music at the bedside for Joshua.

Joshua's health declined overnight and when I returned the next day, there were signs on his door asking to minimize visitors and noise levels to maximize Joshua's ability to rest. Justin met me in the hallway and expressed that the family still wanted me in the room. Upon entering, Joshua was lying in bed with Candace and his grandmother standing nearby with other family members seated around the perimeter of the room. After my initial ask for song requests was met with: "Whatever you want," I began by singing our usual songs, as well as Candace's song. Joshua's grandmother requested hymns and praise songs, including "Jesus Loves Me" and "This Little Light of Mine," and sang consistently while remaining close to Candace to offer proximal support. Candace and Justin sang between frequent interruptions from medical staff.

The family sporadically engaged in memory-sharing. Memories from hospital visits, Joshua's one trip to meet extended family, and other milestone celebrations were shared by all. Candace asked me to share the story of when Joshua threw a maraca out of his crib and it hit me in the face. The room seemed to ebb and flow from somber to jovial, from laughing to crying, and from tense to relaxed. My song choices, as well as the performance of them, often reflected this spectrum of emotions to create a space for the family to experience and recognize the gravity of the moment without having to address it verbally. After an hour of singing, storytelling, laughing, and crying, the session reached a natural ending. Before I left, I told Candace and Justin that I would check in with them after the weekend.

Joshua died early Monday morning, one month shy of his second birthday. I did not have the opportunity to provide a formal termination of services or offer any condolences to Candace and Justin in person, as they had left the hospital by the time I arrived at work. Candace emailed me a week after Joshua's death to finalize the songs she and Justin wanted to pair with Joshua's heartbeat. I communicated with both Candace and Justin over the next few weeks as I completed the heartbeat songs before sending the completed recordings. Hospital policy dictates that communication with bereaved families stop once the extent of our clinical work has been finalized. After that, all communication goes through one of the hospital's bereavement coordinators. Because of this, my email to Justin containing Joshua's heartbeat songs also acted as the termination of services.

Reflection and Conclusion

The morning of Joshua's death, I woke up with an uneasy feeling. Typically, I like to take my time getting ready in the morning, but I rushed through my usual routine to get to the hospital as quickly as possible. I checked my census as soon as I got to the office and saw "dcsd" next to Joshua's name. *Deceased.* Death is a common occurrence given the nature of my job, but this day it caught me off-guard, and *that* was uncommon. Typically, I can set aside the death of a patient until I have a moment to process it, but I could not get Joshua's death off my mind. Joshua and his family consumed my thoughts all day as I realized that I had finally reached the point of termination. Still, our time together felt unfinished. I found myself grappling with newfound grief and started to ask questions. *What does this mean moving forward? How do I just pick myself up and start again?*

Following Joshua's death, I was at a point of divergence, where the treatment process ends and the process of emotional closure begins. The unexpected nature of Joshua's passing coupled with my own misplaced guilt left my emotions reeling. I was having more of an emotional response than was typical for me following the death of a patient. I struggled with this because my rational, clinical brain was at odds with my personal, grieving brain. This was a new experience for me, and I needed to explore why.

I took time to examine the various roles I played with Joshua and his family. I came to realize that my role functioned differently at various points throughout Joshua's hospitalizations, dependent upon the paradigm from which I was working. Where I situated my practice was influenced by Joshua's medical status as well as my own clinical goals. Sometimes I played a supportive role, creating a musical space for Joshua and his parents to be together. Other times, I was more direct in using music to support and motivate Joshua during co-treatment sessions with occupational or physical therapies. I often had to play the role of expert, providing Joshua's parents with education or communicating my observations to the medical team. Other times I was more of an equal, creating music or sharing stories as if I were a member of the family.

As my relationship with Joshua and his parents grew, I think I settled into and maintained the role of equal. My role evolved from "making music for" into "making music with" the family; similarly, I found myself transitioning my music therapist persona into a more authentic and personable presentation during interactions with Justin and Candace. In my experience working with critically ill infants and their families, it is common for them to view staff as their main source of support throughout an admission. This seemed to be exacerbated during the COVID-19 pandemic when visitation was restricted to primary caregivers only. Justin and Candace welcomed me into their "hospital family" early on in our relationship. As I reflect on this shift in mindset, I realize this is what allowed trust to build between Candace and me early on. It is what allowed me to share my most authentic self with the family, and it is also what opened me up to the vulnerability that exists within the duality between clinical termination and emotional closure.

As a student, I always thought that once you reached termination, that was it – your time with your patient was done. In practice, that is far from the truth. Emotions, attachment, ego, and memories are all variables in our everyday lives that are brought into the clinical space, whether consciously or unconsciously, and thus deserve attention and reflection when treatment is over.

Because of this, I have adopted new practices that allow me to hold space for and honor the emotions related to losing a patient. I started making music for myself again. I have a collection of four songs that feel good to play and sing, and through the years they have become a source of comfort during times where I have found myself struggling. I also have a visualization that I learned from a mentor so I do not find myself back on this emotional seesaw: I give myself the space to reflect, emote, and feel, and then imagine folding my emotions, thoughts, and feelings into a boat I send gently downstream. These practices help me to quickly return to a psychological place where I can be my best self for each of my patients and families.

Joshua, Candace, and Justin were a family of firsts. They were the first family I was able to work with for an extended period of time over multiple admissions. They were the first family to invite me into their world – the good, the bad, the wonderful, and the ugly – authentically and without holding back. They were the first family I felt comfortable enough with to expose a bit of my vulnerability and humanity. They were the first, but they will not be and have not been the last. In my everyday practice, I work with diverse, and often complex, patients and their families. I support them as they navigate new diagnoses, treatments, discharges, readmissions, and death. I celebrate their milestones and provide support during their setbacks. Through this work I have come to realize that termination does not always mean that we as clinicians are done working with our patients. While the treatment process may be completed, it is vital to consider how these points of contact may affect us emotionally, especially when working with families during some of the most vulnerable moments of their lives.

This case has been written, edited, and finalized at various points of my own grief journey. When I initially submitted the proposal, Joshua was alive at home, and a month after I found out it was accepted, he died. With each draft I have submitted, I have been pushed more and more to take a critical approach to my processing. All of this to say: it is a process. While I can acknowledge this, it is also important for me to admit that at this time I do not feel as though I have figured it out completely. I still grieve Joshua. Writing this case has given me the opportunity to examine my practice, explore my relationship with Joshua and his parents, and realize that seeking and finding emotional closure is an appropriate and important part of clinical termination.

Summarizing Ideas and Questions for Discussion

1. It is not uncommon for a patient's death to be the reason for the termination of services when working in a medical setting.

   a. How do clinical termination and emotional closure differ, and how do we separate the two when navigating the death of a patient?
   b. What ethical implications does this pose for music therapists?

2. Working closely with patients and families during some of the most vulnerable moments of their lives may sometimes blur boundary lines.

   a. When practicing from a family-centered lens, where does the boundary exist between aligning and enmeshing with patients and families? What might be a cue if that boundary becomes lost?
   b. What might be contexts and/or circumstances in which viewing yourself as a member of the family unit is an ethical practice?

Notes

1 Committee on Fetus and Newborn (2012). Levels of neonatal care. *Pediatrics, 130*(3), 587–597. https://doi.org/10.1542/peds.2012-1999

2 Jacobsen, S. L., & Thompson, G. (2017). Working with families: Emerging characteristics. In S. L. Jacobsen & G. Thompson (Eds.), *Music therapy with families: Therapeutic approaches and theoretical perspectives* (pp. 309–326). Jessica Kingsley Publishers.

3 Reed, K. J., & Brooks, D. (2017). African American perspectives. In A. Whitehead-Pleaux & X. Tan (Eds.), *Cultural intersections in music therapy: Music, health, and the person* (pp. 105–123). Barcelona Publishers.

4 Hahna, N. D. (2017). Reflecting on personal bias. In A. Whitehead-Pleaux & X. Tan (Eds.), *Cultural intersections in music therapy: Music, health, and the person* (pp. 23–34). Barcelona Publishers.

5 Centers for Disease Control and Prevention (2020, December 28). *Facts about gastroschisis.* www.cdc.gov/ncbddd/birthdefects/gastroschisis.html

6 Cleveland Clinic (2019, November 5). *Short bowel syndrome (short gut) in children.* https://my.clevelandclinic.org/health/diseases/14725-short-bowel-sundrome-in-children

7 Zhang, Y., & Ruiz, P. (2010). Solid organ transplant-associated acute graft-versus-host disease. *Archives of Pathology & Laboratory Medicine, 134*(8), 1220–1224. https://doi.org/10.5858/2008-0679-RS.1

8 National Center for Advancing Translational Sciences (2016, March 9). *Autoimmune hemolytic anemia.* https://rarediseases.info.nih.gov/diseases/5870/autoimmune-hemolytic-anemia

Chapter 21

It's Time to Say Goodbye
Stories of Music Therapy Endings in Private Practice

Lindsay Markworth

Abstract

Termination in music therapy can be a complex process with many layers to be considered in the decision. Private practice challenges business owners to be aware of and responsive to many different types of therapeutic closures, some they initiate and others that are initiated for them. Ethical practices when facilitating termination and closure call for a reflective practice that accounts for addressing the multiple stakeholders who are impacting and stand to be impacted by the decision.

Tags: Therapeutic Closure

The music therapy process holds many layers of beginnings and endings. Each session holds opening and closing rituals of music, words, and other modalities, and each music experience itself contains an arc of the first and last notes. Over time, these tones, rhythms, and rituals connect to inform and become the overall course of therapy. Typically, the beginnings are clearly articulated but often the endings feel more ambiguous. Music therapists do not diagnose or prescribe treatment like other health care professions, so how do we know when discharge is appropriate?

My undergraduate education and training in music therapy was primarily through the lens of behavioral theory. Early on, I was taught that the therapist had authority to determine the clinical goal and evaluate when sufficient progress had been made towards this goal to indicate discharge. As a student, the concept of "once the client has improved in the areas of deficit, it is time to discharge" felt concrete.

Then, for my clinical internship, I worked in a residential school setting with a music therapy program grounded in humanistic and music-centered theories. I learned to create music to meet the clients in the moment and build a collaborative therapeutic relationship. Clinical goals were focused

DOI: 10.4324/9781003123798-27

on supporting each student as they discovered and strengthened connections with their existing resources. Nearly all the students received group or individual music therapy and then were discharged upon graduation.

When I started my first job as a music therapist serving individuals with disabilities/disabled individuals, I immediately felt a dissonance between the behavioral frameworks of the agency I worked for and my developing connection to humanistic and music-centered theories. The agency and funding source required goals to be focused on areas of deficit, and clients were to be discharged when the goals were met or when the music therapist determined the client had made sufficient progress. I felt uncomfortable with this concept of improving in areas of deficit and its role in neglecting the client's input on the closure process.

I have spent the past 15 years navigating these polarized lenses, with my theoretical framework informed by each of these experiences. In my current private practice, I continue to navigate the juxtaposition of my personal values as a music therapist, the dominant theoretical framework of the geographical region in which I work, and the requirements of the systems that reimburse my services. I believe in using music to build therapeutic relationships and create opportunities for the client to strengthen their inner resources. At the same time, I am required by the state of Minnesota to write measurable, skills-based goals and document progress through qualitative narrative and quantitative data for continuation of funding for services.

Over the years, I have navigated the requirements from funding sources and how these systems influence and conflict with my theoretical framework and the client's process in therapy. Through my clinical experience, I have learned endings in music therapy are much more complex than simply evaluating goal progress. Many factors inform discharges, including the music therapist's and client's perspectives, and those goodbyes look different for each client, clinical setting, and theoretical context. Sometimes there are shifts in the client's interests, and other times the therapeutic needs shift outside of the music therapist's scope of practice. I have had clients directly tell me they have reached the end of their process, and for others, I have been the one to initiate these conversations when it seems the client is indicating they are at the end of their process. Additionally, in private practice, there may be reasons outside of the clinical process that result in music therapy services ending, including changes in the client's funding and/or finances, changes to the client or therapist's schedules, administrative programming changes, or the client relocating outside of the therapist's service area.

All of my theoretical frameworks inform my decision-making around discharge. Behavioral theory informs the documentation process by using evaluation tools to determine skills-based clinical goals and measurable objectives and to evaluate progress over time. Humanistic and music-centered theories inform the process of therapy and the importance of creating space for clients to indicate, through music or conversations, that they are ready to end therapy.

The stories I am about to share took place in my private practice, where I primarily work with neurodivergent individuals and people with intellectual and developmental disabilities (IDD). The topics of discharge present me with unique ethical challenges as a business owner. When a client discharges from services, this directly impacts the business revenue, presenting a potential conflict when objectively determining a timeline for discharge.

Recently, I have needed to wrestle with this very issue. My practice has received a high volume of referrals due to increased needs for in-person services related to the COVID-19 pandemic. With my team's caseloads full and a waitlist for services, there is added pressure when determining discharge for current clients to make room for new clients. It is essential I be mindful of all these factors when making decisions with clients about ending music therapy services.

As I reflect upon the many goodbyes I have experienced with clients over the years, I feel a tender mix of emotions as I remember these musical humans and our shared processes. I will share the stories of three clients, each of whom highlights the clinical and ethical decision-making process that uniquely informed the end of their therapeutic process.

Need for New Modality

Katie is a 16-year-old autistic girl who enjoys music by Taylor Swift and Katy Perry. She communicates through her facial expressions, assistive technology, and some verbal language. During her first session, her mother mentioned it often took several weeks for Katie to warm up to new people and she hoped music therapy could help her to build confidence and avenues for communication.

In that first session, I introduced a simple, repetitive chord progression (I – vi – IV – V) on guitar and sang the lyrics *It's nice to meet you in music today*. I improvised music within this repeated harmonic form. Katie vocalized on the sound *oh* and I reflected her vocal sounds to communicate validation of her expression and to encourage her to continue singing.[1] Within a few repetitions, Katie's vocalizations became louder and more frequent. She matched pitches, reflected melodic motifs, and then began to imitate sounds and words through her singing. My intention through this improvisation was to begin to build our relationship through the music and celebrate her vocal expression.[1] This vocal improvisation continued for almost 30 minutes and evolved into a playful imitation of words such as *hello, hi, no*, and *yeah*. This marked the beginning of our therapeutic relationship and two-year process in music therapy.

Katie's music therapy sessions were funded by our state Medicaid Waiver program. To meet the state documentation requirements, I completed an assessment, established measurable goals, and tracked her progress through qualitative session notes and quantitative data. Each year, we are required to evaluate progress towards these goals and make recommendations for continuing or discharging from services. While the state documentation requirements were aligned with a behavioral framework of building skills, the therapeutic process I facilitated was guided by the combination of behavioral, humanistic, and music-centered theoretical frameworks I spoke of earlier. I used the Individualized Music-Centered Assessment Profile for Neurodevelopmental Disorders (IMCAP-ND)[2] to guide the initial evaluation and to inform goal-writing for Katie's sessions. This assessment tool provides a lens for gaining insight into the client's developmental strengths and areas for growth while allowing flexibility for the client's individual creative expression through music, movement, and play.

Throughout the first year of music therapy, Katie primarily shared her music within the context of vocal improvisations and songwriting experiences. These collaborative experiences typically began when Katie initiated an idea by vocalizing a word or sound, and I would create a harmonic musical framework to support her vocal expression. Each week, I wrote narrative session notes and reflected upon her process as she began to more freely express through these vocal experiences. I also documented progress on her measurable objective of completing musical phrases with at least one word during songwriting experiences. Towards the end of the first year, she began to explore the keyboard and a variety of small percussion instruments in addition to songwriting experiences.

The annual evaluation process included a review of quantitative documentation, narrative session notes, and a conversation with Katie's mom. Katie strengthened her connection to her voice through a variety of improvised songwriting experiences. She continued to communicate her interest in music therapy each week through her exuberant vocalizations and instrumental exploration. I recommended a continuation of music therapy services with the goal of discovering and building resources for self-expression and communication. We continued to engage through improvised songwriting while also exploring keyboard, drums, shakers, tambourine, and ocean drum through instrumental improvisations and recreations of her favorite songs. At first, Katie played for short durations of 3–4 beats of music at a time. As we musically explored together, she began to play for longer periods of time, and her musical expressions became more interactive through call-and-response and matching tempo and dynamics. Each week, I reflected on the expressive qualities of her instrumental explorations in my session notes, and documented progress on her measurable objective of increasing the duration of instrumental play.

Towards the end of the second year, a significant shift began to occur in how Katie engaged in the music. She began hiding under a blanket when I arrived, and would sing from under the blanket, or playfully pop out briefly to play the keyboard when one of her favorite songs was played. While we had primarily engaged in improvisational and compositional methods thus far, our sessions began shifting towards recreative and receptive methods. Her mom kept me updated with Katie's current favorite songs, and I would sing and play these songs on keyboard or guitar. Sometimes Katie joined in by singing along or playing an instrument, but these experiences became increasingly receptive in nature as she primarily listened with occasional movement to the music. We also explored listening to recordings of these songs together, moving or sometimes just sitting together. Over the next few months, she also began to say *bye bye* or *all done* only a few minutes into the session. There were times when she was able to continue with the session with some visual structures for the amount of time remaining in the session. Ultimately, however, she began walking away from the session area after expressing *all done*. She was clearly communicating that she was ready to be done with music therapy, and perhaps indicating that her overall process was coming to a close.

I began to realize that, throughout the process of evaluation and assessment, I had never checked in with Katie about the overall process of therapy and her interest in continuing. I had reflected in my session notes on Katie's musical expressions as a communication of her resource-building and engagement in the therapeutic process, but now that her engagement had shifted, my initial response was to redirect her back into the music rather than listen to what she was communicating through her words and actions in the sessions. Looking back, it seems so clear that Katie was communicating that she had reached the end of her process in music therapy with me.

At the time, I experienced self-doubt and shame when Katie expressed a desire to be done. *If I were a better, more creative therapist, I would have been able to shift the methods and songs and find a creative way to bring her back into the music.* My theoretical focus also became more behavioral in response to Katie's expression of being done. For the first two years, the therapeutic process had been a collaborative partnership and an exchange of musical ideas, a validation of Katie's expressions through songwriting and improvisations. In my attempt to bring Katie back into music, I had introduced a visual schedule, timer, and other external motivators which were not needed previously in her process and ultimately were not effective in this final phase of therapy.

As I gave voice to my self-doubt through the context of supervision, I was able to accept Katie's communication that she was done with music therapy. I had a conversation about this with her mom, and she agreed with my assessment. She mentioned Katie had shown interest in drawing and painting lately and asked for recommendations for an art therapist. Given that Katie only had enough funding in her waiver budget for one creative arts therapy, it was indicated to discharge her from music therapy so she could explore a different modality.

Katie and I had a final closure session. We improvised a song to say goodbye together, and she joined in singing *bye bye* with a playful confidence that I attempted to match through the music I created, in celebration of her vocal strength and self-expression. We began the therapeutic process with a focus on strengthening her connection to her voice, and now she had used her voice to self-advocate for what she needed: to be done.

Katie was the first client to discharge from my private practice, and I directly felt the connection between a client discharging and the revenue of the company. At the time, my practice was very small – approximately 25 clients between myself and a part-time independent contractor – so when a client was discharged, the change in income was tangible. I wonder, if on some level, I was trying to hold on to this clinical relationship because of the fear of losing revenue, or feelings of shame that my business was not able to provide the service she needed. Moving forward in my career, I have found it especially important to bring these thoughts and fears into awareness so that my decisions around discharge center the client instead of the business.

Needs Emerge Outside of Scope of Practice

Victor is a 13-year-old boy with IDD who loves Disney movie soundtracks and the Beatles and sings phrases from these songs. While he sings song lyrics, he primarily communicates through nonverbal body language and assistive communication technology. He is a sensory seeker and has access to a variety of fidgets to help regulate; however, he occasionally hits himself in the head or bites his hand, seemingly for sensory input. He was referred to music therapy by his waiver case manager to build skills for communication.

In the first session, Victor smiled brightly as I began singing *hello* while playing keyboard. He vocalized along with my singing, reflecting the tonal landscape of the music, and reached out to play the keyboard intermittently. He began to engage in communicative interactions while improvising on xylophone, shakers, and drums while I played piano. He matched the pulse of the music and played music when I created space at the ends of phrases. He communicated choices by singing a short phrase from a favorite song, or by selecting a picture from a visual communication book of instruments and songs. Our sessions primarily included improvisational and recreative methods.[3] As with Katie, Victor's sessions were funded through the Medicaid Waiver program, and I used the IMCAP-ND[2] to complete the assessment and write measurable goals focused on social-emotional areas of development. Each week I wrote a qualitative session note and tracked quantitative progress towards the following objectives focused on strengthening social communication:

1. Victor will vocalize in response to a musical invitation (filling in a pause in the music) twice during the session.
2. Victor will engage in a call-and-response interaction with three back-and-forth exchanges (therapist-client-therapist-client) at least twice per session.

Victor met me at the door each week, and eagerly helped to set up the keyboard and instruments for the session. He was making progress towards his goals and growing in his ability to communicate within the music through exuberant singing and instrumental improvisations.

About six months into the sessions, his mother began to report that outside of the music therapy sessions, Victor would repeatedly hit his head on the floor at seemingly random points throughout the day. While at home his mom could support Victor to meet his sensory needs, the support staff at school were not always able to keep him safe. As this behavior progressed, there was a growing concern for his physical safety. Victor's family navigated options to support his sensory needs as they explored possible explanations for what he was communicating through this behavior.

I joined in these conversations and explored options for how to use the music to meet sensory needs and provide an outlet for self-expression in addition to our communication goals. Victor engaged in loud hand drumming, and I created music to reflect his energetic expressions through minor key accompaniments on the keyboard and guitar.[1] After a few weeks, this behavior began to occur during our music therapy sessions, and it became difficult for him to engage in the music.

It was increasingly clear that Victor's self-injurious behavior was communicating an important unmet need, perhaps physiological or medical. While music had played an important role in Victor's process to that point, it was necessary for him to seek out more specialized evaluation and support for his self-injurious behaviors, which were beyond my scope of practice as a music therapist. We decided to put music therapy services on hold, and Victor was referred to a residential program where he would receive evaluations from a team of therapy professionals and receive 24-hour care to ensure his safety. My heart felt heavy for Victor and his family, seeing what they were going through and knowing I was not able to help. At the same time, it was clear that Victor needed this intensive support to ensure his safety while a team of therapy professionals worked to understand what he was communicating through this behavior.

Music is powerful, and yet sometimes, music is not enough. I have encountered this truth throughout my years in private practice, and coming to this conclusion has always felt complex and challenging. However, it remains my ethical obligation as a music therapist to recognize when the client presents needs outside of the clinician's scope of practice and make referrals and recommendations so the client can receive the support they need. This is especially important in the private practice setting because, often, the practice only involves music therapists. While my practice often receives written permission to communicate with the client's outside teachers and therapists, it is rare for us to collaborate in-person with these professionals, unlike those working in an inpatient or residential treatment setting where music therapists are part of a team of allied health professionals.

When Music Therapy is a Longer Journey

Joshua is a young man with profound IDD and cerebral palsy with whom I am still working at the time of writing this chapter. He loves music and engages through vocalizations, dancing, and instrumental improvisation. During our first session, I began by playing calming music on the keyboard while he explored a rain stick. My intention was to meet him in the music by creating a musical texture reflecting his relaxed energy. Then, I accidentally knocked a tambourine off the table, causing a big crash. Joshua sat up straight in his wheelchair, smiled brightly and vocalized, seemingly with excitement.

In that moment I learned about his preference for loud, rhythmic music that included some dissonance. We have explored a variety of genres, but he continues to communicate a preference for blues and modal music. In music therapy, his preferred instrument is the keyboard, and he seems to especially enjoy playing glissandi and exploring dissonance through minor 2nd patterns. He has been able to communicate these preferences through yes/no head movements, vocalizations, and his interactive engagement in the music.

For Joshua, music is the language where he can share in the beauty, communication, and range of emotional expression as an equal partner in a way that he cannot do with spoken words. We have worked together for seven years, and he continues to benefit from music therapy for relaxation, pain management, improving mood and self-expression. He smiles, dances, vocalizes, and communicates through the music, all while his body visibly relaxes.

Each week, I document Joshua's skill-based goals and measurable objectives, including these examples of communication, expression, and increased relaxation, in a qualitative session note and as quantitative data. While I have tracked progress through quantitative measurements each session, the qualitative session notes provide a more meaningful, richer reflection of Joshua's process in therapy. These notes allow for better illustration of a non-linear therapeutic process and therapeutic progress and hold space and value for progress other than what is skills-based.

However, I did experience dissonance with the Medicaid Waiver requirements for quantitative data tracking skills-based goals. Some public funding sources and private insurance may require discharge when a certain amount of quantifiable progress is not being made. In contrast, I believe there are individuals who could benefit from music therapy throughout their life because it brings them joy, release, partnership, stimulation, and relaxation, in addition to an avenue for creativity they would not otherwise have access to. Many individuals would not financially have access to music therapy services without these public or private funding options, though, so it is essential to meet the documentation requirements using the language required by these programs to ensure continued access to services.

A few years ago, I was able to attend a meeting with Joshua's team to plan goals and support services for him as he graduated from high school and prepared to transition into a new stage of his life. Joshua was not able to verbally express what he wanted his adult years to look like, but he was clear about his preferences using expressive affect and yes/no head gestures. During this meeting, Joshua's mom and case manager centered him in the process of outlining programming that included the therapies and programs that he had expressed preferences for and that enhanced his quality of life. Music therapy was included as a service that was important to him and provided him with opportunities to express himself and meaningfully communicate. One week, Joshua assertively shook his head to communicate *no* when I introduced a new chord progression on guitar, but then smiled and began tapping the keyboard when I shifted to a familiar blues structure. Perhaps someday he will communicate that he no longer wants or needs music therapy services. Until then, we will continue to create music together each week, one glissando at a time.

Reflecting upon Joshua's journey in music therapy, I found myself confronting many questions about my rationale for his continued process in music therapy. *Did his consistency over the years financially benefit my business, and did this play a role in my decision-making to continue to approve services? Am I correctly interpreting Joshua's communication about his motivation and interest in continuing music therapy? How have the documentation requirements from Joshua's funding source influenced my perception of "valuable" progress in therapy and, in turn, influenced how I structure the sessions each week? How have I navigated the dissonance between my clinical philosophy and the value Joshua's funding source placed on skills-based progress?*

As my practice has grown over the years, I no longer feel the direct connection with client discharge and financial impact in the way I did early on. I often record short videos of Joshua's sessions to share with his mom and receive feedback that supports my interpretations of his expressions of joy and expressive engagement in music therapy sessions. It has been helpful to collaborate with his family and support staff regarding the interpretation of his communicative engagement and expression during sessions, so my documentation is not based only on my own observations. Honoring Joshua's qualitative process in music therapy while documenting through a behavioral lens will continue to require the integration of my behavioral and humanistic training and will continue to be a dissonant experience to sort through during supervision and reflective practice. While I have landed on answers for some of these questions, I will continue to engage with these questions throughout Joshua's process in music therapy to ensure I am aware of how these answers continue to evolve.

Final Reflections

A theme in each story I shared is that the client communicated what they needed, and I was tasked with listening and responding to those needs. Katie communicated that she was done with music therapy through her verbalizations saying *bye-bye*, and nonverbal communication of hiding and leaving the session area. Victor communicated that he had emerging needs that required support outside of my scope of practice. Joshua communicated his desire to continue music therapy through his bright affect. In each of these cases, the needs and preferences of the client directly informed the decision to end or continue music therapy services. Of all the methods of determining discharge, the most important is honoring the client's voice and perspective. I am actively learning how to let go of the authority I was taught I had as the music therapist, and instead prioritize a collaborative therapeutic relationship where the clients are stakeholders in the therapeutic process from assessment to discharge.

Another theme is maintaining ongoing quantitative and qualitative documentation of session progress throughout the therapeutic process. Each of these clients received funding for services through the Medicaid Waiver program, requiring skills-based, quantitative documentation that provided the rationale required by the state to continue services. At the same time, qualitative notes documented the stories of each client, holding space for their verbal and nonverbal communication and the subjective and reflective nature of the music therapy process. Both forms of documentation played important roles in reporting on and processing decisions to continue or discontinue services.

A final theme was the importance of engaging in reflective work outside of each session to acknowledge and work through my responses to each ending. Goodbyes are difficult and can bring up complex emotions for the music therapist. I have found supervision and personal therapy to be essential supports. With Katie, I had to work through my feelings of inadequacy as she began to communicate that she was done with music therapy. With Victor, I had to honor my complex feelings associated with not being able to help him through his new challenges, acknowledging that he needed support beyond my scope. For Joshua, I find myself continuously confronting the dissonance between my behavioral and humanistic lenses as I provide justification for continuing services.

Ultimately, each client's process will come to an end, for myriad reasons and in a variety of ways. With each ending, I feel myself confronting and letting go of what I first learned about discharge in music therapy, particularly the behavioral value that places authority with the therapist. Through these experiences, I have come to understand that I do not hold the authority to determine when another human's music therapy process has come to an end. In a collaborative power-sharing process rooted in musically supporting someone to discover and strengthen connection with their existing resources, I must trust the client's ability to indicate when their process in therapy has come to an end and position myself to honor that ability.

I approach each session with great reverence, as an opportunity to meet the client where they are and accompany them to where they will be at the end of the session. Over time, these moments of music build into phases of therapy, and these phases of therapy become the client's process. Just as my clients know the exact version of the song they need in a particular moment, they also know when their process in music therapy has come to an end. My role is to be present, reflective, witnessing, and honoring of each phase of the journey from beginning to end.

Summarizing Ideas and Questions for Discussion

1) At times, a client's needs may extend beyond the therapist's scope of practice and a referral to another provider may be indicated.

   a) What do you consider to be your current music therapy scope? Identify areas of clinical practice with which you feel confident, and any clinical settings you feel are not compatible with your areas of interest and/or training.

   b) What are some ethical considerations when determining a need for discharge connected to clinical scope of practice?

2) It is essential to maintain ongoing documentation of session progress throughout the process of therapy to provide insight when determining the timeline for discharge.

   a) What informs your process of selecting an assessment, determining goals, and re-evaluating a client's progress in your clinical work?

   b) How might integrating qualitative and quantitative documentation be important in providing comprehensive insight about your client's process?

Notes

1 Bruscia, K. E. (1987). *Improvisational models of music therapy.* Charles C. Thomas.
2 Carpente, J. (2013). *Individual music-centered assessment profile for neurodevelopmental disorders: A clinical manual.* Regina.
3 Bruscia, K. E. (2014). *Defining music therapy* (3rd ed.). Barcelona Publishers.

Chapter 22

Integrating Loss Into Life

Termination in Bereavement Counseling and Music Therapy

Molly G. Hicks

Abstract

In music therapy, loss happens for both the music therapist and client, often as shared and/or parallel experiences. The therapeutic process stands to be substantively enriched when the music therapist is able to move through the loss alongside their client, tending to themselves at the same time they are supporting others.

Tags: Therapeutic Closure; Therapeutic Relationship

Getting in the car, I remove my mask, sanitize my hands, and start the ignition. As I drive to my next client, checking the time on my phone against the GPS estimate, wondering about traffic this afternoon, I press record on my voice memo app and repeat these words that my client has just uttered: "I was rapping and singing to God, but he's the only one who will ever hear that song. Freestyle is like a flow or a wave, I don't know when the words are going to come to me."

I use first person, trying to stay with him in his experience a bit longer. I wish I could go right home, take out the creative case notes journal I sporadically keep, and write more about just these two sentences. I wish I could make some music or art to explore the impact of these words, not later, but now. But something shifts in my mind. The practical is suddenly front and center. Some themes have emerged, and I've got to get them down before I forget.

We talked about the beat being a way to organize time. It's been harder for him to structure his time and his schedule since she passed . . . there's some theme about time, the organization of time, and kind of figuring out how he can do that for himself.

I realize I'm interested in themes as a method of linking our sessions together, capturing what my clinical documentation might not. With my large caseload, I can only see this client about once a month, maybe every three weeks if I can figure out a way to be more efficient. I can eat lunch in the car.

DOI: 10.4324/9781003123798-28

Time. I'm still trying to figure out how to structure mine, too. All these years into this job. A constant juggling act. Sounds like a description of grief. Another client recently said, "Grief is like jumping from lily pad to lily pad." Speaking of time, when am I going to fit in documentation tonight? Let me just make a few more voice notes about today's session so I can prep for the next client. Okay, Molly, breathe. Time to think about what happened last session with this next client.

I dust off my sometimes-mantra (is that an oxymoron?) while I circle the block, looking for ever-elusive parking.

May I be peaceful, purposeful, and present.

My music therapy education offered ample time to plan sessions, engage in role-plays, receive frequent supervision and feedback, and make connections between my burgeoning clinical practice and examples from the literature. The reality as a practicing music therapist is that these opportunities now feel like luxuries.

One of the reasons I wrote this case study is because I have longed to process my work with Dex in more detail. Previously, I discussed these sessions in both individual and peer supervision, and even with these support opportunities I have found it challenging to fully synthesize this clinical process, which was not easy for me to acknowledge. I have always had high expectations for myself, along with a critical internal voice. My belief that years of experience plus work ethic equals mastery often blocks self-compassion, a barrier at which I am perpetually chipping away. The missing elements in this equation were time to breathe and space to think. I wanted to give myself these gifts toward the goal of going deeper, so I took on the challenge of writing. After submitting the first draft of this chapter, the editors encouraged me to incorporate more about my own process into the story. Initially, I felt like I had already gone as deep as I could, given the realities of my daily work life. I sought more supervision, shed some tears, procrastinated, and stared at the computer screen. Finally, I felt ready to begin writing again.

I have learned the stories of everyday practice exist in the nebulous, messy, liminal space of music therapy sessions. My music therapy stories also reside between the ideal music therapy career I hoped for (whatever that is) and the job that I have, where I am expected to do the work of more than one person while somehow avoiding burnout. The longer I work, the longer I feel this tension between my career ideal and my career reality. Ironically, my career reality makes it difficult to explore the depth of this professional grief. The overlay of the COVID-19 pandemic intensified this, and I am still adjusting to how the pandemic upended my professional and personal lives. While my grief is quite different from Dex's, the parallels are helping me to understand both of our experiences more completely.

Theoretical Framework

The Dual Process Model of Coping with Bereavement depicts the grief process as an oscillation between loss-oriented and restoration-oriented coping.[1] Examples of loss-oriented experiences include the work of understanding and processing emotions and coping with the intrusion of grief into one's everyday life. Restoration-oriented experiences could be taking time off from the grief through distraction and exploring new identities, interests, and relationships. A bereaved person may bounce between loss-oriented and restoration-oriented coping many times a day, creating a disorienting effect or a feeling of being in survival mode. And yet, that oscillation represents a typical and adaptive grieving process: sole concentration on the loss may come at the expense of functioning and continuing to live, while focusing only on restoration may not make room for the myriad emotions that emerge during bereavement.

During the time Dex and I worked together, I was focused on his movement between the dual processes, but my awareness of my own grief process was centered on my restoration-oriented coping. I had to keep working. There were so many people to support. Under the surface, I was conscious of the frenetic oscillation of survival mode. One layer deeper was my own experience of loss.

Situating Dex and Myself

Beginning a therapeutic relationship with a grieving person, especially a short-term one, is fraught with challenges for client and music therapist. This is a story of how Dex moved through his grief in a non-linear way, navigating back and forth between processing the pain of the loss and finding ways to reinvest in his life, all while continuing to evolve and grow.[1] This is also a story about me, an experienced music therapist and perpetual beginner grappling with personal and professional grief. Finally, it is a story of how Dex and I addressed the loss of our relationship through termination.[2]

Dex is a 54-year-old Black cis man enrolled in the bereavement program at the hospice agency where I work. His wife, Kandy, had died at home from heart failure. Dex resides in an urban area in the Mid-Atlantic region of the US. He is a DJ and rapper, a music lover, and an avid video game player. Dex is a veteran and has a history of traumatic brain injury, post-traumatic stress disorder, depression, and anxiety. He receives medical and mental health care from the Veterans Association and receives Social Security Disability. Dex was a foster child and has a history of childhood trauma and abuse.

I refer to Dex as a *client* as it is the terminology used at my agency. Bereaved family members are referred to as *clients*, while those under hospice care are *patients*. Regardless of this terminology, I approach my work considering the client as a collaborator and strive to dismantle power dynamics that arise as a function of the client-therapist relationship. This requires constant reflexivity and cultural humility, in that I carry a great deal of privilege as a white, cis, nondisabled, middle-class, educated woman. My aspiration is to partner with clients to access internal and external resources, including music and other forms of creativity. I operate from an authentic musical place that reflects my cultural locations while also centering the music culture of my clients. Although I strive for the collaboration and empowerment inherent in resource-oriented music therapy, I understand that my immersion in dominant culture leads to bias about which resources are valued.[3]

I understand grief as a constellation of responses to loss that occur across emotional, physical, cognitive, spiritual, and social domains.[4] I regularly examine how my ideas about grief may be different from those I serve, and how these perceived norms influence my own biases. I recognize that the language I use to think and speak about grief may be quite different than that used by my clients.[5] I do not view grief as pathological, although there are moderating factors that can prolong the intensity of grief responses and interfere with overall wellbeing. These include histories of mental illness or substance use disorder, high dependency on the deceased, limited support system, and present risk of harming self or others. In almost every clinical setting, music therapists will encounter grieving individuals coping with these additional factors.

At the time of our work together, Dex was coping with multiple complicating factors, which prompted the hospice team to refer him for pre-bereavement support. We worked together for about six weeks prior to Kandy's death. Pre-bereavement support refers to counseling or other forms of emotional and spiritual care offered to family members or friends of someone with a life-limiting illness. In the hospice setting, all members of the clinical team may help address the grief that occurs during the dying process, also called anticipatory grief. The bereavement counselor may be brought in to assist when this anticipatory grief is complex in nature or when adaptive coping would be enhanced by building therapeutic rapport before the death occurs. The team hoped Dex would connect with me through music therapy, as music was already one of his resources.

From Pre-Bereavement to Bereavement

Our pre-bereavement work focused on building rapport, assessing his resilience, and affirming his anticipatory grief. Dex shared his original music recordings with me during the second session, which consisted of him freestyle rapping over original beats. The power of his music showed me a different side of the quiet man with whom I found myself working. Dex's beats were multi-layered, attention-grabbing soundscapes anchored by driving drum patterns and bass lines. His lyrics were direct, assertive, and clever. I was excited, as it felt like we had a lot of musical material with which to work, though I remained cautious about not pushing him beyond where he was ready to go.

Dex and I had two in-person visits in February 2020. I was on vacation immediately before the pandemic lockdown in the US and did not get to visit Dex in those early days of March. Kandy died 10 days after the beginning of the lockdown, so our sessions transitioned to a phone format. While Dex described himself as "a loner" in one of our first sessions, it was challenging for him not to have the option of in-person support at the beginning of his grief process. In these early days of the pandemic, my work life was chaotic and constantly changing, even more so than is typical for hospice care. Several of the music therapists who serve as bereavement coordinators were asked to help staff the hospice inpatient units, providing music therapy for patients who could initially have no visitors, and then could only have one. We facilitated virtual goodbyes between family members, holding tablets in front of clients that served as the tangible link between them and their loved ones. I felt supported by my colleagues, but the amount of processing we were able to do was limited; each of us was experiencing ambiguous loss and concern for our health and safety and that of our loved ones.

I conducted several phone sessions with Dex while sitting in my car outside of one of the hospice units. During one, he played me the remix he made of my original song, "Music of My Soul." I had emailed him this song recording to validate his continuing bonds with Kandy.[6] Dex's decision to remix this song felt like evidence that he was open to musical collaboration. Yet, I noticed that the beat didn't quite line up, and there were times when the musical experience sounded disjointed. Looking back, I felt disjointed too. Life as I knew it had been turned upside down. I was tired, and underneath that fatigue was deep sadness, anxiety, and uncertainty.

About four months after Kandy's death, I resumed in-person home visits. Dex revealed challenges with adhering to his medication schedule because Kandy was not there to remind him, and his sleep cycle was disrupted. He also shared that he was coping with nighttime loneliness exclusively by playing video games. I would often arrive at his apartment while he was playing a video game; he would be so engrossed I wondered if he even noticed me. His depression interfered with his hygiene, appetite, and appointments with his psychiatrist and therapist. Dex was not as forthcoming in our sessions, and I had to work harder to engage him.

I left several sessions feeling tired, a physical countertransference of Dex's depression. And, expecting that we would be engaging in music together, I was frustrated – I wanted to make music with clients, with anyone. I also felt frustrated that our sessions during this period, by necessity, focused so much on Dex's basic needs. When working with clients in their homes, it can feel more like case management, which I readily admit is not my preferred role. Reflecting more on my countertransference, I wonder how Kandy felt about her roles in Dex's life. Were there times she felt unable to reach him? How did she feel about providing the rhythm for his daily routines? Was he now freestyling his life without her? I felt caught between wanting Dex to let me in emotionally and not wanting him to become dependent on me. Yet, taking on some of Kandy's role was necessary to provide a supportive container in which Dex could begin to access the pain of the loss.

I began to recognize additional aspects of their roles when Dex reminisced about the house parties they threw. He curated the music, and she provided the food and drink. These were both creative roles requiring the establishment of a stable rhythm and foundation. Looking at their roles through a more dynamic lens led me to believe that Dex and I could co-create a space for him to explore the parts of his identity he wanted to retain in bereavement.[1,6]

In our tenth session, Dex picked up the dusty rhythm composer on the floor, connected it to a small speaker, and began to recreate some of the rhythms that would get the crowd moving at his and Kandy's parties. I saw facility and precision in Dex's movements, along with an energy I had not recently witnessed. I hoped that the rhythm of Dex's musical resources could potentially provide a type of structure to create and explore what his life might look like moving forward.

At this point in the process, I faced a decision. In hospice bereavement work there are parameters to the therapeutic process, none more so than temporal constraints.[7] After the death, I have 13 months to work with a client; this length of time allows me to support them through the one-year anniversary of the death. As such, I must work with the reality of termination from the earliest sessions and continue deliberate and thorough review of the therapeutic process as sessions wind down.[7] Early on, this means clearly discussing the limitations of the program and the scope of the services as part of informed consent. The frequency of sessions and the 13-month limit can be flexible based on client need.

In Dex's case, I knew at this point in the process for certain by month nine after Kandy's death that we would need to extend the counseling process by at least one to two months. The COVID-19 pandemic meant that our first four months of sessions were conducted over the phone, which was not optimal for relationship building or music therapy. Fortunately, I had the clinical autonomy to extend the therapeutic process and facilitate a supportive closure. Although music therapists in a bereavement counselor role focus on loss and are not primary therapists, the nature of grief work is deep. Termination of support services may be perceived as another loss.[2,6] Dex's loss of Kandy and his trauma history made it especially crucial that our termination process be a planned ending so he could prepare.[7]

It felt like there was a new focus in our work: so much groundwork had been laid and yet, in some ways, we were just getting started. I assessed that Dex, who expressed wanting to feel more connected with music and more effectively coping with his grief, wanted to reclaim his creative identity and use it as a bridge between loss-oriented tasks (i.e., tolerating, exploring, and coping with his grief emotions) and the restoration-oriented tasks (i.e., taking time off from grief, developing new roles and relationships, and reinvesting in life).[1] Dex and I discussed how the process would still need to be time-limited, but that we could extend the sessions by a few months. We agreed to check in about this again as the 13-month mark approached. Although we were extending the sessions, I was able to envision termination through the new clarity I had about the inherent structure, form, and freedom within Dex's musical resources and how he could harness these to both process his grief and reinvest in life.

In session 12, our therapeutic connection blossomed into musical collaboration. Dex was also establishing rhythm with his health care. He proudly showed me a new series of medication reminder alarms on his phone. He jumped right into the music, experimenting with his rhythm composer while asking me what the tempo should be. I encouraged Dex to find the tempo that felt right to him; after establishing it, he said he could hear a bassline in his head and lamented that his electric bass was not in working condition. I encouraged Dex to sing the bassline, and, to Dex's delight, I began playing it on my guitar.

Dex began increasing his ability to tolerate and express painful grief emotions and memories, and he was also letting me in both musically and emotionally. During the winter holidays, Dex expressed feeling isolated and "sick with grief," a grief related to early abandonment which erected an emotional wall that even Kandy could not fully break down. He focused on playing recordings of older original songs, which seemed to help him regulate as he took emotional risks. He also started working on a few new tracks between sessions.

For the first time in our therapeutic process, Dex described how he used one of the new beats to help himself when he experienced intense feelings of loneliness and abandonment related to his grief. I saw this as a milestone of awareness, connection, and empowerment that assured me that an adaptive conclusion to our therapeutic process was in sight.[3,7] Dex was now able to access his music resources independently and purposefully as a way to cope with grief responses. I felt more confident that he would also be able to do this after our sessions were complete.

As spring approached, so too did Kandy's birthday and the one-year anniversary of her death. Dex planned to spend both significant dates having a meal and watching movies with his neighbors, acknowledging that he wanted to connect with others. This felt momentous as it represented Dex's development of other relationships in his life, which I hoped was a generalization of our therapeutic process. We continued collaborating on new beats, with Dex developing a variety of tracks and asking me to add acoustic guitar riffs, which he began to refer to as "the missing piece." Dex's musical landscapes were textural and rich, and I remember thinking: *There's nothing missing here at all.*

Recently, I have been reflecting more deeply on this response. At face value, I was offering an internal compliment to Dex, recognizing the seemingly complete sound of his tracks and his solid musical resources. I was also discounting my own ability to contribute, as creating electronic music is not my forte. Additionally, I was recalling my original song that Dex remixed early on in our process when the rhythm did not quite line up. *Did the disjointed rhythm mean that what I had to offer as a therapist did not quite fit or was not useful? Or did it represent the rocky path of developing new relationships amidst the grief process?* My denial that there was anything missing in Dex's tracks may also have been an unintentional denial of how deeply Kandy's death had rocked his world. I wanted him to be okay. Although there is nothing linear about the grief process, the parameters of my role and the time-limited nature of hospice bereavement counseling can introduce a painfully linear element that leads to a dissonance between personal values and system-based constraints. Perhaps I was afraid to acknowledge this.

My denial that there was anything missing in Dex's music also connected directly with my anxieties surrounding termination in context of his trauma history with abandonment and rejection. I worried about perceived abandonment as we prepared to terminate our sessions. I did not want Dex to see me as just another person in his life who left him. I wanted Dex to feel his music was complete just like I wanted him to feel our process was complete. This would help alleviate my guilt that we had to end our time together. If I did not get too involved in his music, maybe there would be less risk of being perceived as someone who was abandoning him.

By denying some aspects of Dex's loss-oriented process, I similarly denied aspects of my sense of loss. How might our work have been different if the pandemic had not happened? If we had gotten to the musical collaboration sooner? If I felt less stymied by the limitations of my role?

Ongoing supervision helped me shift my focus to how significant it was that Dex trusted me enough to continue inviting me into co-creation. He was exploring who and what was missing in his life, and how he could adapt. Dex began reflecting on new beats where one track did not fit with the rhythmic foundation he created. I drew a comparison between these parts that did not "fit" and difficult emotions, suggesting that rather than being "deleted" or pushed away that they could be integrated into the music. I needed this reminder for myself, too.

Sessions 20–24

During session 20, Dex told me an old friend of his, Bella, got in touch to tell him that she needed a place to stay temporarily. He expressed he would enjoy having this kind of company. Over the course of the remaining sessions, Dex shared that he was helping Bella recover from an abusive relationship, and that they were developing a romantic connection but were "taking things slow." I had concerns about Dex jumping into a relationship that would require caregiving when he was simultaneously discovering how to care for himself. When discussing his connection with Bella during these final sessions, Dex acknowledged his grief for Kandy and stated it feels meaningful that he can help Bella with her health and wellbeing in some similar ways as he cared for Kandy. His insight into the reclamation of a prior role as a romantic partner showed his ability to be adaptive in his new relationship and helped put my mind at ease about his readiness for establishing new intimate connections.

As we discussed termination, Dex expressed that he perceives most endings as abandonment but will use self-talk to remind himself that this ending is not personal and would listen to our past music collaborations. Dex played two original beats and said with a smile and a laugh that each was "missing" a guitar part. I smiled too. What had become a familiar expression was simultaneously an acknowledgment of loss and connection. It was the musical door through which Dex allowed me into his life. It would be one of the ways we remembered each other.

During a discussion on the theme of support and lack thereof during our process, Dex cited a meaningful song, "The Greatest Love of All." I asked if I could play and sing this song for him, and he accepted. Dex had tears in his eyes while I played. After the music, he expressed a wish that his foster families had seen his potential and that he could have depended on them to fulfill his needs as a child. He stated he must now be his "own biggest fan" and reflected on how mistakes made during his life have merely been "a drop in the bucket" and do not define him: "I found the greatest love of all inside of me." This was a pivotal moment in our termination process. Love for self and others was part of Dex's internal rhythm, and he could access it. I planned to record the song for Dex.

In the next session, I asked Dex in an open-ended way to speak about the impact of our bereavement sessions. Dex acknowledged he felt "lost" after Kandy died and that it was difficult to disclose details about his grief, depression, and trauma. As our sessions wound down, Dex played several new tracks, commenting that he was inspired by combining experiences mixing records as a DJ with the newer technology of his tablet computer. I asked if this combination of the past and present has any implications for Dex's future. Dex stated he sees this blend as an "elevation" and an opportunity for new possibilities. I heard themes of hope and investment in the future, and I felt a new faith that Dex would see our termination as a part of his transformation.[2]

During the ongoing musical review of our process, Dex pulled up our first song collaboration. He wanted to rework the song, so that each component entered in layers. Dex reflected, "There is always more to do." I verbally connected this with Dex's ongoing grief work, noting there is always additional material for emotional exploration. I saw this exchange as an acknowledgment of the limitations of bereavement support services and a reframing of the ending of our time together as a launch into a future of creative and relational possibilities.[2,7] Dex's wisdom also spoke to my ongoing processing of professional grief, offering me reassurance that we had done our best together. We ended the session by listening to my recording of "The Greatest Love of All." Before the session ended, Dex verbalized wanting to collaborate on one more piece of music during our final session. He said a working title would be "Farewell but Not Forgotten."

We had arrived at the final session. It was a momentous day. I felt sadness and a sense of loss, feeling that the time had gone too quickly. I also was proud of Dex for taking the risk to engage in this sustained process. Dex stated he has been "trying not to think about" the end of our sessions and has been focused on making music instead. Trying to evoke a description of Dex's inspiration for a particular track he played me, I noted, "It sounds like this beat is saying something." Dex laughed, saying, "It says it needs a guitar part." As we had done in many sessions, I played options for creating a guitar loop, and Dex selected one. It proved difficult to line up the recording of the guitar part exactly with the beat, but we did multiple takes. Dex then problem-solved by utilizing multiple takes of the guitar part in a live mix. He also incorporated takes made in error. We both laughed as he looped a clip of me asking, "What?"

As I drove away from his apartment for the final time, I chuckled again at the blooper being incorporated into the song. It was fitting, a humorous acknowledgment of things not lining up, and the oscillation-induced disorientation between loss and restoration. Dex and I were both creating new music, forging new paths through loss, and learning how to say goodbye. There are no perfect endings, and grief has no timeline. But for now, this was enough.

Summarizing Ideas and Questions for Discussion

1. In time-limited therapy, termination planning begins at the start of care, requiring sustained reflection by the music therapist and collaboration with the client at each phase of treatment.

   a. Can you identify specific examples of how and when you have engaged in this type of reflection as a therapist, and how you have involved the client in this process?

    b.   What were some musical and verbal milestones in your client's therapeutic process that demonstrated supportive and adaptive termination was within reach?

2.   The Dual Process Model suggests that both loss-oriented and restoration-oriented forms of coping are necessary for long-term integration.

    a.   What music therapy experiences might you use to help a client engage directly with their feelings of grief?

    b.   What experiences might you use to help a client take time off from the pain of their grief?

Notes

1 Stroebe, M., & Schut, H. (1999). The dual process model of coping with bereavement: Rationale and description. *Death Studies, 23*(3), 197–224. https://doi.org/10.1080/074811899201046

2 Quintana, S. M. (1993). Toward an expanded and updated conceptualization of termination: Implications for short-term, individual psychotherapy. *Professional Psychology: Research and Practice, 24*(4), 426–432. https://doi.org/10.1037/0735-7028.24.4.426

3 Rolvsjord, R. (2006). Therapy as empowerment: Clinical and political implications of empowerment philosophy in mental health practises of music therapy. *Voices: A World Forum for Music Therapy, 6*(3). https://doi.org/10.15845/voices.v6i3.283

4 Corr, C. A., Corr, D. M., & Bordere, T. C. (2013). *Death & dying, life & living*. Wadsworth, Cengage Learning.

5 Corless, I. B., Limbo, R., Bousso, R. S., Wrenn, R. L., Head, D., Lickiss, N., & Wass, H. (2014). Languages of grief: A model for understanding the expressions of the bereaved. *Health Psychology and Behavioral Medicine, 2*(1), 132–143. https://doi.org/10.1080/21642850.2013.879041

6 O'Callaghan, C. C., McDermott, F., Hudson, P., & Zalcberg, J. R. (2013). Sound continuing bonds with the deceased: The relevance of music, including preloss music therapy, for eight bereaved caregivers. *Death Studies, 37*(2), 101–125. https://doi.org/10.1080/07481187.2011.617488

7 McGuire, M. G., & Smeltekop, R. A. (1994). The termination process in music therapy: Part I – theory and clinical implications. *Music Therapy Perspectives, 12*(1), 20–27. https://doi.org/10.1093/mtp/12.1.20

Index

advocacy: advocating for client 60, 162, 164, 206; uncertainty or inexperience in advocacy 27

assistive communication technology 241, 244

boundaries: boundaries as self-care, protection, or growth 62, 63; client-set boundaries for therapist 34; ethical boundaries 41, 165, 241; questioning, stretching, or struggling to set boundaries 92, 105, 162, 163, 182, 210; supervisor/supervisee boundaries 11, 84; therapist-set boundaries for client 28, 62, 63, 105; work-life balance 89, 92, 93, 141, 223, 224

client age: adolescent (13–18 years) 24, 59, 217, 241; adult (24–64 years) 70, 89, 159, 253; child (6–12 years) 59; infant (birth - 12 months) 12, 34, 37, 126, 202, 231; older adult (65 and older) 72, 80, 136, 170, 182, 194; toddler (1–5 years) 47, 50, 101, 171; young adult (19–24 years) 147

clinical documentation 118, 243, 242, 244, 251

clinical limitations 69, 78, 79, 83–86, 258

clinical settings: community-based health center or agency 146, 170, 251; hospice/end-of-life care 18, 78, 80, 136, 182, 194, 251; hospital, adult 89; hospital, pediatric 34, 217; neonatal intensive care unit (NICU) 125, 203, 229; pediatric intensive care unit (PICU) 12, 204; private practice 47, 101, 240; psychiatric care (acute, long-term, residential) 24, 59, 69, 159; school 51, 114; skilled nursing facility 80

clinical supervision: supervisee 11, 27, 31, 35, 50, 59, 61, 69, 71, 78, 105, 106, 186, 189, 244, 248, 252, 258; supervision to mitigate harm 18, 19, 20, 39, 84; supervisor 12, 34; supervisor as supervisee 19, 45; supervisor/supervisee boundaries 19; theories, models, and philosophies of supervision 12, 59, 64, 69, 79

compassion fatigue 108, 210

co-therapists 37, 38, 116, 220, 221, 222

countertransference: experiencing/identifying 11–19, 21, 27–28, 31, 66, 89, 107, 151, 182–185, 197, 220, 254; integrating/applying 22, 103, 119, 198; processing 12, 15, 29, 61, 67, 74–75, 197, 198, 254

COVID-19 pandemic 37, 40, 47, 94, 101, 105, 108, 130, 219, 237, 242, 252, 256

diagnosis, condition or community served: Alzheimer's disease 194; anxiety 89, 147; attention deficit disorder 24, 47; autism spectrum disorder 47, 116, 241; cerebral palsy 245; chronic obstructive pulmonary disease (copd) 89, 137; congenital heart defects 34; congestive heart failure 170; depression 89, 147; disruptive mood dysregulation disorder 24; Down syndrome 116, 203; extreme prematurity 125; gastroschisis 231; hearing impairment 116; hospice/end-of-life care 78, 80, 136, 194; intellectual and developmental disabilities 245; LGBTQIA2+ 59; limited mobility 102; liver failure

231; medically fragile infants 37; moderate learning disability 102; multiple chronic illnesses 89; multiple disabilities 116, 159; nonspeaking 116; obesity 159; obsessive compulsive disorder (OCD) 72; oppositional defiant disorder 24; pancreatic cancer 80; post-traumatic stress disorder 24; pyruvate dehydrogenase deficiency 203; risk of preterm labor 125; schizoaffective disorder 72; self-injurious behavior 245; visual impairments 116

harm: examining potential for clinical harm 28, 183; experiences of clinical harm 83, 197, 198; institutional/ systemic harm 163; see also clinical supervision, supervision to mitigate harm

interdisciplinary collaboration: Chaplain 220; child life specialist 204; social worker 204
intersubjectivity 79, 82, 191

job burnout 70, 71, 79, 89, 94, 208, 252

music therapy approach, theory, or framework: behavioral 94, 137, 128, 146, 171, 240; cognitive-behavioral 136, 146, 150; community music therapy 140, 143, 198; critical theory 146; cultural-relational 126; dual process model of coping with bereavement 252; existentialism 78; family-centered 13, 34, 125, 205, 230; feminism 78, 146, 171; humanistic/person-centered 59, 61, 69, 74, 94, 101, 115, 118, 126, 137, 138, 143, 146, 150, 171, 218, 240; infant-centered 34; justice-oriented 59, 252; music-centered 115, 140, 240; nordoff-robbins 115, 218; process-oriented 194; product-oriented 69, 194; psychodynamic 78, 101, 147; resource-oriented 126, 146, 159, 195, 252; socioculturally located 159, 163; strengths-based approach 195; trauma-informed 59
music therapy method: improvisation 116, 118, 128, 147, 161, 198, 242

(improvisational songwriting 131; Nordoff-Robbins 115, 218; singing 234; vocal psychotherapy 218); receptive 128, 185, 195, 198, 209, 243 (client-preferred music 82, 90, 148; environmental music therapy (EMT) 130; heartbeat recording 234; lyric discussion 148; music assisted relaxation 220; pre-recorded music 90; recreational 198; verbal discussion 90); recreative 50,256 (active music making 172, 207; activities-based 69; live music 90; memory sharing 235; music and movement 48, 233; music lessons 138; music listening 90; song of kin 128, 129, 205, 107); songwriting 14, 131, 148, 150, 163, 209, 231, 242 (freestyle rapping 253; legacy-making songwriting 13–14; life review 207; poetry 163; songwriting journal 14)

navigating systems: funding and reimbursement 241; institutional systems (medical, psychiatric) 73, 159, 163, 164, 210; oppressive societal systems 62, 159

personal therapy 11, 59, 72, 83, 119, 247
professional development 24, 69, 146, 203

self-disclosure 13, 15–17, 63–65, 82
session type: family 12, 40, 101, 106, 126, 203, 229; group 24, 51, 59, 70; individual 13, 36, 38, 48, 78, 89, 101, 114, 126, 136, 148, 159, 172, 182, 194, 203, 217, 229, 240, 251
sociocultural reflexivity: age 19, 73, 82, 182, 195, 196; cultural upbringing 24, 25, 89, 93, 102, 230; culture shock 25; disability 183; family make-up/ context 49, 83, 230; gender 82, 162, 183, 195, 230; institutionalization 73; interrogating appropriateness of music 26, 61; musical background 137, 172, 194; parenthood 118; race/ ethnicity 74, 126, 147, 162, 218, 230; religion/spirituality 127, 219, 220; self-awareness 120, 136, 137; sexual orientation 60, 62, 65, 119, 183, 230; shared/similar cultural identities 59, 207; socioeconomic background 70

telehealth/teletherapy 47, 48, 50–55, 105, 107

therapeutic closure 49, 217, 229, 248, 240, 252

therapeutic goals and objectives: accepting other people's lead 106; access inner resources 129; address stress 130; autonomy 164; behavioral goals 136; being present 148; bereavement support 252; build community on campus 60; communication and social skills 24, 50, 241; create opportunities for each person to choose 105; developing language skills 47; developmental play/ stimulation 36; educate individuals on LGBTQ+ topics 61; emotional comfort 182; experiencing predictability from a safe adult 172; facilitate good experiences in online interactions 105; grounding 148; holding emotions 74; increase auditory tolerance 37; increase engagement and develop relationships 26; mood management 148; opportunity to witness healthy reflections 105; physical comfort 128; positive environmental stimulation 35; pre-bereavement support 182, 253; promote meaningful mother/son interaction 129; provide a space on campus to talk about sexuality openly 61; provide sleep support 37; reduce anxiety/agitation 35, 37, 172; reduce pain 35; relate/connect with other group members 74; relaxation 35, 39, 148; self-agency 103; self-expression 103, 164; sense of belonging in community 198; sense of control 103, 172; shared enjoyment 106; share experiences as queer individuals 61; skills for managing stressors 164; social interactions 103, 170; strengthen inner resources 240; support musical relationship 130; sustain therapeutic relationship 130; therapeutic performance 137; vulnerability 36, 38; witnessing healthy reflection from adults 106

therapeutic relationship/alliance 11, 12, 34, 47, 52, 62, 63, 78, 89, 101, 105, 114, 125, 136, 146, 163, 159, 170, 182, 194, 203, 217, 229, 252

therapists's internal experiences: authenticity 41, 54, 236; clinical identity 63, 80, 95, 146, 155; grief 198, 212, 213, 225, 226, 237, 253; guilt 75, 83, 95, 186, 211, 225, 237, 258; insecurity/self-doubt 35, 40, 49, 50, 136, 138, 170, 173, 198, 224, 244; intuition 53, 220; self-concept 69, 236; vulnerability 20, 34–35, 40, 237–238

transference 65, 185

treatment planning 89, 101, 114, 125, 137, 159, 194, 203